JOSSEY-BASS/PFEIFFER
A Wiley Imprint
www.pfeiffer.com

Strategic Planning for Success

Strategic Planning for Success

Aligning People, Performance, and Payoffs

Roger Kaufman
Hugh Oakley-Browne
Ryan Watkins
Doug Leigh

JOSSEY-BASS/PFEIFFER
A Wiley Imprint
www.pfeiffer.com

Published by Jossey-Bass/Pfeiffer
A Wiley Imprint
989 Market Street, San Francisco, CA 94103-1741   www.pfeiffer.com

ISBN: 0-7879-6503-0

Library of Congress Cataloging-in-Publication Data
Strategic planning for success: aligning people, performance, and
   payoffs/Roger Kaufman .. [et al.].
      p. cm.
   Includes bibliographical references and index.
   ISBN 0-7879-6503-0 (alk. paper)
   1. Strategic planning. I. Kaufman, Roger A.
   HD30.28 .S73964 2003
   658.4'012—dc21
   2002014802

Acquiring Editor: Matthew Davis
Director of Development: Kathleen Dolan Davies
Developmental Editor: Susan Rachmeler
Editor: Rebecca Taff
Senior Production Editor: Dawn Kilgore
Manufacturing Supervisor: Becky Carreño
Cover Design: Michael Cook

Printing   10   9   8   7   6   5

CONTENTS

vii

LIST OF TABLES AND FIGURES

PREFACE

T his book has several potential flaws, so beware.

The first is that it flies in the face of much conventional wisdom about how to go about performance improvement. Thus, some readers will feel uncomfortable about concepts and practical tools that are different from those that gave us the "greatness" of Enron, Global Crossing, Andersen, WorldCom, ImClone, airport security prior to September 11, 2001, government agencies that did not talk with each other and thus never gave anyone the chance to "connect the dots," and single-minded executives and managers who focused narrowly on their patch and forgot the whole. There have been many organizations worldwide that did what was widely expected of them: forget about external clients and society and go for the quick (but not sustainable) profits. Performance improvement that stops at the quarterly profit-and-loss sheet or the next year's budget is still popular but dangerous. This book shows why this is true, and how not to be one of the bodies heaped on others that followed the crowd and conventional advice and did what was acceptable and wrong.

The next potential flaw is that it is written by people who have both researched the bases for what is presented as well as practiced it. It is usual for researchers to be dismissed by the operational types, and for the operational types to be discounted by the academics doing research. All four of us authors have played both sides of the street. And learned from it. We attempt to bring you the integration of research and practice here, perhaps satisfying no one.

A third potential flaw is that we provide lots of hands-on exercises and practical tools. And we have worked hard (and had many reviews) to try to make what we have written clear. Some people like scholarly looking texts with lots of philosophy, and others just want checklists and step-by-step guides. Rather (and perhaps to the satisfaction of no one), we take the time to provide the underlying concepts and the rationale for what we suggest, and only then we go to the trouble of giving you guides to define and deliver high impact results.

Finally, one more potential flaw of which to make you possibly be wary. We define words—common-sounding words such as "need," "requirement," "Outcome," "Outputs," "Product," "evaluation," "assessment"—in very precise and very limited ways. Rather than being like Alice in Wonderland, where words meant anything the user wanted them to mean, we take the time (perhaps too much time every once in a while) to define what we mean and why we make the distinctions. Tools that are not used properly, not used in the right context, and not used consistently will not build useful things. Rather than deal in "semantic quibbling," we spend a lot of time to help you become rigorous—and successful—by not only doing things right (the conventional passion for process) but by doing the right things, by defining and delivering high impact results. Learning and applying what is here will not be easy or popular, but it will be useful.

In writing this book, we did not act alone, although the inevitable criticisms will find us to be intellectual orphans. We are ready to take the blame for everything here, while giving credit (and indemnity) to many people who have encouraged us, read and reviewed our work, given us feedback (often that we did not want to hear, but that we had to hear and consider), and who have directly and indirectly guided and cajoled us. Among those are:

- Ingrid Guerra of the University of Michigan–Dearborn, who provided thought, feedback, and research as she moved from graduate student to research project manager to assistant professor;

- Mariano Bernardez who, as a management consultant and e-learning guru, had the courage to apply these concepts and tools—and provide us with valuable performance data—to many organizations in Latin America, Europe, and the United States;

- Don Triner, Commander, U.S. Coast Guard, who studied and applied this in the operational world, where decisions have to be both immediate and right;

- Ben Wiant, performance consultant, who labored to make sure this would communicate to people who would buy and use this work;

- Bill Swart, Provost and Academic Vice Chancellor at East Carolina University, who worked with the authors of this book to make sure that it was practical and useful for engineers, businesses, and even universities;

- Several Australian public sector executives who used the basics of this, and provided performance data for its continuous improvement, including Peter Sharp, Peter Kennedy, Maj. General Roger Powell, Don Watts, Doug Hinchliffe, and a host of professionals who applied and learned with us;

- Clifton Chadwick, who has used this evolving model and tools almost worldwide, for his reviews and guidance;

- Ronald Forbes, tectonic plate physicist-turned-management consultant, who has thought through these concepts and tools, applied them, and helped us evolve what is here;

- Jane McCann and Carolyn Lane, who brought to us (along with co-author Hugh Oakley-Browne) the New Zealand reality based on their consulting; and

- Peter Drucker, who has been a guide and inspiration to those who would seek measurably useful results.

In addition, there are other contributors: Larry Lipsitz, publisher of *Educational Technology,* has encouraged (and critiqued) many of the concepts and tools here; the editors and publishers of other books leading up to this work (appropriately referenced) who have encouraged this development; Roger Addison, Roger Chevalier, Dale Brethower, and many International Society for Performance Improvement (ISPI) senior contributors who have encouraged this work and what is in this volume; Matt Davis, who first encouraged this book when he was still with ISPI; and the long line of long-suffering graduate students who not only learned this material but who have gone out to apply it.

This list is both incomplete and inadequate. There are many others who early and later connected with the power, pragmatism, and humanism of Mega Planning and these concepts for defining and delivering high impact results, including those in business, industry, government, and the military. We both apologize to those whom we admire and thank them; we are not allowed the luxury of the space to personally name each deserving one of them.

Finally, our thanks to you who are reading and who will apply what is in this book. We know it will work if it is used correctly and consistently. We thank you for your confidence and your professional determination to do both what is right as well as what is responsible.

Roger Kaufman
Tallahassee, Florida

Hugh Oakley-Browne
Devonport, New Zealand, and
Woolengong, Australia

Ryan Watkins
Washington, D.C.

Doug Leigh
Long Beach, California
October 2002

Strategic Planning for Success

Introduction

Welcome to *Strategic Planning for Success: Aligning People, Performance, and Payoffs.*

This is a practical and pragmatic book with cases-in-point, guides, job aids, and exercises. It is not overly theoretical, and yet it is based on firm research and successful applications worldwide.

It is a practical and proven guide for defining the concepts and tools of strategic thinking and planning that in turn provides you with the tools for defining the design and delivery of results that make a difference: high payoff[1] results. It provides some new realities for defining and delivering success to better ensure that disasters such as those at Enron, Global Crossing, Adelphia, HIH, Imclone, Tyco, and even Andersen will not afflict you and your organization. We don't preach, but rather provide the concepts and tools that allow you to say to any internal or external client, "We can deliver success . . . and prove it." Adding value to external clients, and proving it, is ethical and results in useful payoffs. As well as very, very practical. It will allow you to align people, performance, and high payoff results.

Are these concepts different from the standard strategic thinking and planning? You bet. Are they proven and practical? Yes again.

What we provide here is how to align your thinking and planning with high impact payoffs—results that will measurably add value to you, your organization, your external clients, and society. Yes, society. Society is where we all live and to whom we are ultimately responsible. And to which we have to be responsive. As a guide, the 4-Way Test of Rotary International is useful:

- Is it the truth?
- Is it fair to all concerned?
- Will it build goodwill and better friendships?
- Will it be beneficial to all concerned?

These are good guides for business, government, and life. Especially the fourth one: Will it be beneficial to all concerned?

Because this book focuses on "front end alignment," we don't get into the tools and techniques for detailed performance subsystem design, development, implementation, and evaluation but simply give the requirements for the front end—to align what we do with what will be valuable to all stakeholders. There are ample sources for the design and development, many of which are published by Jossey-Bass and Jossey-Bass/Pfeiffer. We list some of them in the book. We recommend turning to these sources after, and only after, you define and align yourself and your organization with external value added.

A hallmark of this approach—and what makes it different—is that internal results must add value to external clients and society. High payoff results are those that will add value for an "entire results (and value added) chain" that flows from individual performance accomplishment to organizational and external/societal contributions.

High payoff/high impact[2] perspectives on success must also include significantly wider definitions of clients than are usually used today: society must be included and be top priority.

Society as primary client is both sensible and practical. Every day we all depend on other organizations, public and private, to put our safety, survival, and quality of life first on their agenda. We depend on all organizations with which we deal each and every day, such as airlines, public transport, cars, supermarkets, food processors, drug manufacturers, and energy suppliers, to assure that our safety and well-being will be first and foremost on their agenda. It is on ours. We take up that challenge, and encourage you to do the same by using what is in this book.

If you want to make a difference, in and for your organization as well as the society in which we all live, this book is written for you. Increasingly, organizations are both being asked and even asking themselves, "What value do we add?" This book is a guide for determining the answer, both in terms of how you define success and of how you measure it. The concepts and tools will work in your professional life as well as in your personal life. It is about success in both the short term and long term, and thus it is the safest approach and most practical approach there is.

This book, then, is different from what is already on your shelf or in the latest "flavor of the month" promotions. There are many names for various conventional (and outmoded) planning approaches in use today, including: "strategic planning" (conventional), "strategic management," "business planning," "corporate planning," "tactical planning," and "operational planning." We provide a framework for defining and linking what any organization uses, does, produces, and delivers to add value for all stakeholders. We help you define success and then prove it. We have used it and improved it in applications almost worldwide. It is based on what has worked in just about every kind of organization that exists.

BUT FIRST A WORD ON SEMANTICS

Let us give you a "heads-up" in advance.

We are going to make some seemingly, at least at first, "fine" distinctions among words and concepts, such as differences between a *system* and a *systems* approach, and differences between *products, outputs,* and *outcomes.* We are not trying to be difficult or annoying in an attempt to find trivial differences to distinguish ourselves from others. (See Appendix B for a glossary and classification of terms and tools.)

Rather, we are defining concepts and tools that will help you be successful because much damage and many false starts happen from popular-but-fuzzy thinking and nebulous definitions. We go past the conventional and nonfunctional vocabulary plaguing management and performance improvement today . . . the popular vocabulary is convenient but will not serve you well. We take the time to define each word and concept so that you are not "flying" on conventional wisdom and old paradigm understandings.

We make these distinctions to help you be successful. Confusing words, terms, and concepts can be a terminal affliction. Please be patient, and please put aside your current definitions and understandings of these terms. New, precise, rigorous, and robust definitions will definitely serve you well.

OK? Let's go.

Notes

1. Payoffs are consequences. They can be both positive and aversive.
2. We actually use "impact" and "payoffs" interchangeably.

CHAPTER ONE

Busting Old Paradigms and Using New Ones

Defining and Shaping Our Future

CHAPTER GOALS

By working though this chapter, you will be able to answer the following questions:

- ❑ What is a paradigm? Why and when is it useful?
- ❑ What are the limitations of a paradigm?
- ❑ What are frames?
- ❑ What are mental models?
- ❑ What are paradigm shifts?
- ❑ What are the frequent fads?
- ❑ What are the causes of fadaholism?
- ❑ What are some of the new realities (new paradigms and "ground rules") impacting organizations?
- ❑ What is a Strategic Thinking and Planning paradigm that works?
- ❑ Why can't we continue on the way we are?
- ❑ Who should care about creating a better shared future?

❏ What are the implications of ignoring the new realities?

❏ How can we assess whether change is strategic?

TODAY'S PARADIGMS

How do we define and deliver success? First we must get rid of the useless baggage of the past. Let's take a look at the future and why we can't rely on old models, methods, and models to define and achieve success . . . to deliver high payoff results. If we are to really think strategically and practically, regardless of where we are or have been, we must create the future rather than be victims of it. It is important to know "what's in our heads" in terms of our understandings, concepts, and biases so that we can decide whether it makes sense to change or not. If we are to change—to do practical strategic planning and deliver high payoff results—we must select the appropriate mental model, or frame of reference, for thinking, planning, doing, and delivering. For our journey to measurable success we must align people, performance, and payoffs. Interested? Let's take a closer look.

If you have skipped the Preface and Introduction, please go back and take a few minutes to read them. They provide an orientation to the whats and whys of the material you are about to read.

There is no denying that the world is rapidly changing. And in that reality, standing still is no different from falling behind. As a result, all fields of human and organizational performance are racing to keep up with the production of knowledge that has accelerated beyond all our dreams—and nightmares. The role of the "futurists" has emerged in this time of change. This influential group of scholars attempt to forecast, inform, and analyze the trends of the chaotic, evolving world we live in (see Table 1.1). The challenge for many of us is to identify, from the knowledge generated by these adept professionals, what can be used to define, justify, and then create a better world through our organizations today.

Table 1.1. Early Futurists and Their Landmark Works.

• Alvin Toffler: *Future Shock* (1970)
• John Naisbitt: *Megatrends* (1982)
• Ian Morrison: *Future Tense* (1984)
• Faith Popcorn: *The Popcorn Report* (1991)
• Ira Matathia & Marion Salzman: *Next* (1999)

Meanwhile, the world of business, government, and management races to keep pace with the ever-changing world around us. The results of frantic efforts are a bewildering profusion of management theories, fads, and fashions that often replace each other before their worth has been tested. Everyone is being competitive, yet few are creating a new future. Many are reactive, but few are proactive in creating the future we want for tomorrow's child.

However, it's possible to distinguish trends in the development of management and leadership paradigms so that those chosen measurably improve performance. Peter Drucker, the acclaimed writer of management wisdom over the last fifty years, popularized the term "the New Realities" to define these new paradigms that are influencing us, our businesses, and our world—even if we don't recognize them.

Paradigms[1]

"Paradigms are the boundaries and ground rules we use to filter and understand reality . . . they allow us to comprehend our world and to successfully deal with it."
—Roger Kaufman, based on Joel Barker, 1989

The concept of "paradigm" is both ancient and modern. Historically, it meant model, framework, pattern, or example, a meaning that survives today. It was the historian of science, Thomas Kuhn (1970), who initiated the idea of evolving and changing paradigms in his book *The Structure of Scientific Revolutions*. For Kuhn, science was characterized by the dominance of succeeding paradigms as models for thinking. Paradigms explain the world to us and influence our actions. A paradigm is one way we see the world—not in the physical sense, but in terms of perceiving, understanding, and interpreting. The futurist Joel Barker has helped our understanding of paradigm shifts in recent years. His definition is applicable to the social sciences, business, and academia alike.

A paradigm is a set of rules and regulations that:

1. Defines boundaries;

2. Tells you what to do to be successful within those boundaries[2]; and

3. Is used to "filter reality." We use paradigms to understand data and information . . . to order, relate, and control our reality.

If we use an outmoded or inaccurate paradigm, useful ways of understanding and then dealing with reality might be filtered from our consideration.

A paradigm shift is a change to a new game, a new set of rules, and a new set of realities. In leadership and management there are a number of competing paradigms available. Paradigms allow us to see things in a certain way, but they also make it difficult to see other things that do not "belong" within the paradigm being used. We usually cling to our paradigms—to stay in our comfort zones—and see only what they enable us to see, even when their assumptions are not clearly or rigorously stated. At its worst, a wrong or incomplete paradigm can result in conceptual imprisonment. Resistance to change is not so much a resistance to new paradigms as it is a fear of abandoning the security of old, familiar ones—even if we know them to be unsuitable.

Eventually, every paradigm encounters new problems, new realities, and changing situations that it is unable to adapt to. Just as critical to adopting new paradigms, then, is recognizing when old paradigms will no longer lead to future success . . . and abandoning them despite opposition of "the mainstream," often without sufficient data to support the new paradigm. Skills of a change leader, then, include "unlearning" the old paradigm in addition to embracing the new.[3]

Frames of Reference

In practical terms, paradigms are expressed through communication with others. Leaders have the greatest potential to change paradigms through the meanings they create. Effective leaders present images, metaphors, and stories that can grab our interest and attention. The use of language is especially influential in either supporting the status quo and existing paradigms or in challenging the status quo and institutionalizing a new paradigm.

Frames of reference are an essential tool for managing meaning. And when you can manage meaning you can get agreement on common destinations and how each person may uniquely contribute to the accomplishment of that shared destination: to determine the meaning of a subject, event, or new reality is to make sense of it; to control this frame of an event or trend is to choose one particular meaning (or set of meanings) over another. When we share our perceptions and mental models with others, we manage meaning. We assert that our interpretations should be taken as a better alternative to other possible interpretations.

There are three key parts to the skill of framing[4]:

1. Language (the most obvious component of the skill);
2. The internal framing we must do before we can frame for others; and
3. Forethought, which prepares us for on-the-spot framing.

Mental Models

"Mental models are simply the pictures we have in our mind
about the way things are and ought to be."
—Nirenberg, 1997

In order to frame for others we must first frame for ourselves. To frame internally we draw on our mental models. In his book *The Fifth Discipline,* Peter

Senge defines mental models as "deeply held internal images of how the world really works" (1990, p. 174). These images, which can range from simple generalizations to complex theories, have a powerful impact on our framing behavior because they affect what we guide others to see. A mental model is an essential resource: it identifies the dimensions along which our experiences will be judged and subsequently communicated to others. It is important to bring our mental models to the conscious level. Unless we do so, our mental models may be limiting, and incorrect assumptions about the world might escape our notice. Therefore, whenever possible we must think through our mental models in advance of our requirement to help frame them for others. Mental models have the following characteristics.

1. They are natural. Everyone has and uses them—whether they are consciously aware of them or not.

2. They are prized and personal but can often be shared (for example, the world is flat, pigs fly, the earth revolves around the sun).

3. They can be changed (some more easily than others). When we lose or drop them they usually go but must be replaced with others.

4. They guide our action and behaviors.

5. We seek reinforcing feedback to confirm and reconfirm them (for example, the "I told you so" scenario).

6. They give meaning to events and help us interpret them.

7. They are not facts, although we sometimes take them to be so.

8. They are deep rooted and sometimes unconscious, yet they predispose us to act in a certain way.

9. We use them to distinguish and decide between what is important and what is not.

10. They can influence us to mistake our view or perspective for reality (for example, we mistake the map for the ground it represents).

11. Mental models are like filters to our senses—they can distort and reinterpret reality. We use them as frames to understand and filter reality.

12. We can learn to challenge our mental models.

In summary, paradigms are interpretations of how things—such as an organization, our world, and our relationships—work, define what is important, and guide our actions to be consistent with that thinking. Mental models are individual paradigms for how our world works. Frames are the ways in which we communicate our interpretations of the meaning of events, situations, and incidents. As we will see, all of these are best related to the new realities and how we frame them in order to positively influence performance at all levels.

Putting Paradigms, Mental Models, and Frames of Reference to Work

In any system of interrelated parts, changing any part of a system influences the whole system. When change produces sufficient momentum because the old ways and means do not really work very well anymore, we can speak of a "paradigm shift." When the rules of what works change, everything that operates within that system changes. When we have such a paradigm shift, a change in all the significant rules, then uncertainty and ambiguity are likely to occur as our mental models transition from the old to the new. Many people become uncertain about how to proceed. Such discontinuities change the rules of operation. It makes little sense to deal with the new situations by applying the old rules, even if we can make them cheaper or faster.

Instead, we must challenge old assumptions and mental models and start thinking strategically. We create new objectives, measurably defining the desired future before selecting the new methods and means to get there. As will be discussed in later chapters, high payoff results are those that will add value to both internal and external stakeholders—from individuals and teams to entire organizations, to external clients, including society (Kaufman, 1998, 2000; Kaufman, Watkins, & Leigh, 2001).

We urge that we all concentrate on a newer paradigm for thinking, planning, doing, and delivering high payoff results. This paradigm begins with a focus on the value to be added for external clients *and* for society.

Why society? Isn't *business* the business of business? That is the conventional paradigm, the old paradigm in which *business* defined *business*. In today's competitive global markets, the business of business now includes adding value for all stakeholders, including society. This is a new reality (a new paradigm).

The old paradigm would explain why an international tire company would push hard for quarterly profits through higher tire production only to find out that in many cases the tires failed under some road conditions. Without an initial focus on the safety and well-being of all stakeholders, including vehicle owners, the short-term results of increased production and profits produces negative consequences for all, including the tire company that will have to spend a very long time recovering the few dollars they saved in production because of resulting societal liabilities.

Such a paradigm of business and management also rewarded executives for collecting golden parachutes and secretly selling stock options while their decisions led the company down a path of destruction. This old paradigm of business management allowed some to temporarily fool themselves into misreporting corporate financial health, publishing incorrect data, and shifting liabilities in shell games for public consumption. It resulted in leaving other stockholders, consumers, and the entire community with worthless retirement accounts, failed investments, imploding stock values, and a disparaging perception of the business world.

Another shift in the conventional wisdom of organizations is about taking big risks. Audacious risks. If one doesn't make big bets, huge-but-rational-risks, you are a fixed target and at significant risk. Another shift from conventional wisdom is about change agents. The usual position is that any organization must have change agents. A new imperative is that the organization itself must be a change agent (Drucker, 2001).

High Payoff Results are the results (ends and consequences) of individual and organizational performance that yield positive contributions for external clients and society. These Results depend on aligning and adding value at all three levels of results—individual, organizational, and societal.

Discontinuities arise from paradigm shifts that invalidate the old paradigms, including those that may have been the basis of a firm's earlier success, strategy, tactics, and culture. Organizational factors that were key success indicators suddenly become liabilities and barriers to future success. Some sources of discontinuity in recent years appear below in Table 1.2.

There are several potential responses to discontinuity:

1. Ignore the new reality.
2. Increase the effort within the status quo to move the organization up a steeper change curve (more of the same), that is, work harder and harder doing the same things in hopes that it will yield different results.[5]

Table 1.2. Why Paradigms Shift.

- Terrorism
- Technology breakthroughs
- Medical and physiological breakthroughs
- Breakdown of governments
- Asian meltdown and rebirth
- European Union
- The World Wide Web
- Long-term diseases/afflictions
- Weather/environmental shifts
- September 11, 2001
- Enron

3. Try to get ahead of the change curve by benchmarking others' methods in hopes that it will change what the organization produces and delivers (play leapfrog by chasing fads).

If these approaches seem insufficient, in this book we explain a fourth alternative.

4. Create a desired future by strategically creating a new paradigm of success, then selecting the appropriate methods and means to get there, that is, defining and delivering high payoff results.

Paradigm Mismatches and Poor Performance

Mismatches between paradigms occur when old paradigms are retained even after a breakthrough has triggered a paradigm shift. Those operating from such an approach keep working from the old paradigm, although a new one has taken its place. For example, many organizations used new information technology simply to speed up their existing processes, rather than rethinking their business practices in order to capitalize on what new technology makes possible in terms of achieving internally and delivering externally.

Obsessed with Newness

"Not surprisingly, ideas acquired with ease are discarded with ease. Fads ebb, flow and even change by 180 degrees."
—Pascale, 1990

The pace of economic and technological change has accelerated almost beyond belief. Computers now perform complex operations in a fraction of the time they took only a few years earlier. In order to merely keep up, continual multi-learning and lifelong learning are essential. Continuous innovation has become fundamental to survival. Measurably demonstrating results to internal and external stakeholders is essential for success . . . and for survival.

The sense of urgency about stimulating and developing the management, organizational skills, and knowledge necessary to deal with accelerating paradigm shifts has triggered a profusion of management gurus, fads, books, and new methods.[6] An obsession with newness, to become *"The Best," "Leading Edge," "World Class,"* or *"High Performing"* can be a distraction from the practical, sensible, and pragmatic. Obsessed with the new, we often consume the "hot" fads year to year—the equivalent of self-medicating without an informed diagnosis of the problem. Organizational self-medication may alleviate symptoms for a short time, but seldom is there evidence of measurable and sustainable contributions to internal and external customers. And sometimes things can get worse.

EXERCISE—ASSESS YOUR EXPERIENCE WITH FADS

Take this opportunity to assess your personal experience with a selected number of the fads and management theories that have ebbed and flowed since the end of the Second World War.[7] This exercise asks you to reflect on your experience and knowledge of each fad and to judge whether you have any evidence that the method improved performance in a measurable way. You may wish to share your assessment with a colleague; you're likely to find that you're not alone.

The list in Table 1.3 is a sample of some of the methods, tools, and models that have been offered as "quick fixes" to improve organizational performance. Assess each one by ticking one or more of the columns.

We are not implying that none of these tools or fads work—only that the evidence on their effectiveness shows that as typically applied they are often small compared to the benefits alleged.

Define the Results before Selecting the Means and Resources

The intent of the previous exercise is to underscore the fact that if you don't know what results you are creating (and why you are creating them), no tool, fad, or method can or will help. The key to obtaining high payoff results for all stakeholders is to begin organizational thinking, planning, and doing with a rigorous assessment of gaps in results based first on value added for external client and society. Needs Assessment can be used to identify the performance gaps and opportunities in measurable results-focused terms. A Needs Assessment identifies gaps between current results and desired (or required) ones and places then in priority order for resolution based on the cost to meet the need as compared to the cost of ignoring it (Kaufman, 2000). And subsequently, needs are best defined only in terms of gaps between current and desired results.

A useful Needs Assessment (covered in Chapter Five) provides the data for the selection of solutions, tools, and interventions that have the greatest probability of accomplishing high payoff results.

Two vital components are usually missing from conventional needs assessments:

1. Linking to all aspects of the internal and external environments (including societal value added).

2. Commitment and follow-through. Clark and Estes (2000, 2002) suggest that less than 40 percent of all change initiatives are ever continued. This might be an optimistic figure.[8]

Table 1.3. Fads Checklist.

	Fad	Don't Know What It Is	Know, but No Experience	Experience	No Evidence It Worked	Evidence It Worked
1	Decision Trees					
2	Managerial Grid					
3	Satisfiers/Dissatisfiers					
4	Maslow's Hierarchy of Needs					
5	Theory X-Theory Y					
6	Brainstorming					
7	T-Group Training					
8	Theory Z					
9	Management by Objectives (MBO)					
10	Strategic Business Units (SBU)					
11	Zero-Based Budgeting					
12	Value Chains					
13	Decentralization					
14	Wellness					
15	Quality Circles					
16	Excellence					

(Continued)

Table 1.3. Fads Checklist. (*Continued*)

	Fad	Don't Know What It Is	Know, but No Experience	Experience	No Evidence It Worked	Evidence It Worked
17	Restructuring					
18	Portfolio Management					
19	Management by Walking Around					
20	Kaizen/Kanban					
21	Hoshin Planning					
22	TQM					
23	Intrapreneuring					
24	Corporate Culture					
25	Reengineering					
26	Economic Value Added (EVA)					
27	Neurolinguistic Programming					
28	One-Minute Managing and Situational Leadership					
29	The Learning Organization					
30	Transformational Leadership					
31	The Network Organization					

32	The Intelligent Organization								
33	The Fifth Discipline								
34	New Science/Chaos Theory								
35	Empowerment								
36	Workplace Community								
37	Self-Managing Work Teams								
38	Servant Leadership								
39	The Seven Habits of Effective Executives								
40	Systems Thinking								
41	Spirituality								
42	Attila the Hun								
43	Zen and the Art of Motorcycle Maintenance								
44	Self-Managing Teams								
45	Sustainability								
46	Third Bottom Line								

Fads Are Usually Means-Related

The fads in the exercise in Table 1.3 are examples of the many methods and means that are available "off the shelf" for use in organizations today. Unfortunately, they are often solutions in search of a problem to solve. And all too often they are chosen before a clear definition of the problem has been derived.

The premature choice of means and methods often leads to the practice of "fadaholism," the consequences of which are failed projects, wasted resources, and low performance. This book emphasizes that proactive strategic thinking—defining and delivering practical useful results—starts with agreement on the required results at three levels (Kaufman, 1992, 1998, 2000; Kaufman, Watkins, & Leigh, 2001):

1. *Mega Results.* Results whose primary client and beneficiary is society.
2. *Macro Results.* Results whose primary client and beneficiary is the organization itself.
3. *Micro Results.* Results whose primary client and beneficiary are the individuals and/or teams within the organization.

This approach to strategic thinking (planning for and achieving results at the Mega, Macro, and Micro levels) overcomes the practice of fadaholism while designing and creating a better world in which the means chosen follow from planning the desired high payoff results.

THE NEW REALITIES

This applications-oriented book and companion CD makes a distinction between strategic thinking and strategic planning. *Strategic thinking* is the mind-set, frame of reference, or paradigm that takes an initial focus on Mega results (that is, positive societal impact) and defines the future we want to help create for our future and for the future of our children and grandchildren. Using it allows for the continuous adjustment and adaptation to the changing realities, thus creating the future instead of simply reacting to it. This requires a new and more effective paradigm.

Strategic planning is the formal process of defining and documenting the desired future and ways to get there. Useful strategic planning builds on and from Mega: it begins with societal value added. Strategic thinking and strategic planning are related, and together they can lead to accomplishment of high payoff results—results with positive contributions at the Mega level.

Why Mega? Because everything we use, do, produce, and deliver must contribute to our shared world. It must result in the health and safety of all. It must contribute to our partners (including external clients) being self-sufficient, self-reliant, and having a positive quality of life. If you are not adding value at the Mega level, chances are you may be subtracting it.[9] You expect all organizations you deal with to focus first on *your* health, safety, and well-being. Should you not do the same? ⤷ their

Strategic thinking can be done every day and is not limited to an annual ritual. Conventionally, however, strategic planning tends to be formalized into annual and multi-year events. Both are essential, but strategic thinking is a mindset—a way in which we live our lives and do our business. It is more flexible to the reality of accelerated rates of change, while at the same time being responsive to the new and evolving paradigms. Strategic planning provides the directions and requirements for delivering high payoff results; it is a formal, yet responsive, process that defines and delivers useful results.

If Your Organization Is the Solution, What's the Problem?

Ends and means. Problems and solutions. Organizations—yours and ours—are all means to societal ends. They are held responsible for adding value to internal and external clients as well as to our shared society. Answering the question "If your organization is the solution, what's the problem?" requires an honest examination of determining what value, if any, we add to external clients and our shared society. Asking and answering this question requires that we start thinking of the required alignment between what we use, do, produce, and deliver and the impact we have externally.

What difference does it make if we align what we do and deliver with external impact? Plenty. Social service agencies (such as welfare or unemployment) have to measurably demonstrate clients' movement toward the accomplishment of self-sufficiency and improved quality of life. Makers of tires have to assure the safety of stakeholders both internally (such as dealers and resellers) and externally (consumers). Consulting companies must successfully align what they deliver to their clients with adding value to their clients' clients and our shared world. No shortcuts. No deals.

This kind of alignment is not only practical (Would we want to be part of a business that doesn't add value to external clients?), but it is ethical.

The New Realities

Listed below are some of the New Realities that are influencing our lives, the teams to which we belong, the organizations within which we work, and the communities in which we live:

1. Tomorrow is not a linear projection of yesterday.
2. You can't solve today's problems with the same paradigms that created them.
3. There are two "bottom lines" for any organization: Conventional and societal (Kaufman, 2000).

4. Change creation and change management are the "twins" of organizational survival and thriving (Kaufman, 2000).

5. Doing good is no longer a corporate option. It is a must (Popcorn, 1991).

6. If you can't predict the future, create it (Drucker, 1993).

7. It is easier to kill an organization than it is to change it (Peters, 1997).

8. Reality is not divided into policies, laws, rules, regulations, sections, departments, or agencies.

9. After September 11, 2001, we realize that a simple and exclusive focus on individual performance improvement or even organizational performance alone will deliver failure.

These are examples of new realities. There are many things that we used to believe that don't apply any more. Aubrey Daniels (1989), in his book *Performance Management,* stated it clearly:

"It ain't what we don't know that is the problem, it is what we know that ain't so."

IGNORING THE NEW REALITIES

What does it cost to ignore the new realities? In this section we select a number of new realities and identify some of the implications of ignoring them. They are shown in Table 1.4.

It would be easy if we could simply and passively observe the passage of time and paradigms. We could be spectators to the disasters and successes of others but avoid the turmoil, chaos, and disruption of accelerated and profound change. But life is not like that. Or if it is, you will be missing out on the excitement of (and responsibility for) making a valuable and valued contribution. We are influenced and affected by many of the new realities, even if we don't recognize the extent to which high payoff results affect us or others. What follows are some of the potential consequences of ignoring the new realities.

Consequences

The consequences and implications of ignoring the new paradigms will be felt more or less immediately, depending on your role. Here are some potential implications for leaders and managers:

- You are hit by a huge litigation case because you are shown to have done serious damage to people's health (think of the tobacco industry, a manager of a tire manufacturing company, an accountancy firm).

- You lose market share to your competitor who adjusted quicker and better or who came out with something new that you did not think of, and profits plummet.

Table 1.4. Implications of Ignoring the New Realities.

Code	New Realities	Implications of Ignoring
1	Tomorrow is not a linear projection of yesterday.	What worked yesterday will not necessarily work today or tomorrow. The world changes suddenly. Those changes or discontinuities are often large, profound, and unexpected. The Swiss watch manufacturers believed their market share would continue to grow on past successes. They rejected the electronic quartz technology and between 1979 and 1981 fifty thousand Swiss watchmakers lost their jobs. Meanwhile SEIKO increased market share from 1 percent to more than 30 percent. The Swiss failed to detect the paradigm shift and failed to think strategically (see Barker, 1989).
2	You can't solve today's problems with the same paradigm that created them.	We get cut off from a better future by the hidden tenacity of our old solutions. Wrong solutions. Wrong, because they are not working. When we are habitually involved in selecting solutions that don't work, our "solutions" have become our problem. New solutions require us to "bust the paradigm" that created the problem. We have to challenge our beliefs, assumptions, and habits and not do what we have been doing. Step out of our comfort zones. The implications of ignoring this new reality could be: • Critical problems remain unsolved. • Money gets wasted on wrong solutions. • Resources are wasted for no added value. • Client satisfaction levels drop. • You lose market share to more successful competitors. • Client safety drops. • Social and political situations get worse.
3	There are two "bottom lines" for any organization: conventional and societal.	Traditional capitalism was obsessed with the quarterly profit and loss statement. Meeting budgets is still *the* priority for many organizations. The conventional bottom line is still the quarterly profit and loss sheet. Peter Drucker (1993) noted the new paradigm when he popularized the notion that knowledge and information is the new capital—not just money and things.

(*Continued*)

Table 1.4. Implications of Ignoring the New Realities. (*Continued*)

Code	New Realities	Implications of Ignoring
		The new economy talks of "intellectual capital" and we now have "knowledge companies." Some inventory has been substituted with information. Profit alone is insufficient to measure these new values. Profit as a prime purpose ignores society as a client. Profit focuses on the short term and ignores social impact in the long term.
		Times have changed and Charles Handy in his book *The Hungry Spirit* states it well: "Unless organizations have both a soul and a conscience they will not deserve their place in modern society and will not long survive" (1997, p. 157).
4	Change creation and change management are the "twins" of organizational survival and thriving (Kaufman, 2000).	Change management is reactive. We attempt to control change that washes upon us. Stress and concern rule the day as people react to new conditions. This is required, for "change happens." A twin of change is creating the change that is responsive . . . instead of being the victims of change, be the masters of it. The "train" industry went flat and declined because it did not see itself as a player in the next generation of requirements—not just supplying trains, seats, and cargo but also getting people and things to where they had to go on time and at cost. If they had seen "change creation" in their perspectives, they would have also run the airlines, and perhaps the forthcoming space travel.
5	Doing good is no longer a corporate option. It is a must (Popcorn, 1991).	The implications of ignoring this paradigm include: • We may have no future if we don't add value to external clients and society. • Competitors who add value to society will pick up your market share. • Most people would like to make a positive difference to society, even in a small way. And if they feel the organization makes no worthwhile impact, then they will look elsewhere for organizations that allow them to define meaning in life—they want to add value to society. • Those organizations that harm society will be challenged and possibly put out of business (for example, the continuing fate of the tobacco industry).

Table 1.4. (*Continued*)

Code	New Realities	Implications of Ignoring
6	If you can't predict the future, create it (Drucker, 1993).	Instead of being reactive to the moves of one's competitors and other changes in society, we should be encouraged to define the future, then take charge and create it. The implications of ignoring this New Reality could likely include: • We become the victims of change. • We are the last to market and are continually playing catch-up with our competitors. • We allow chance, hope, and fate to take control of our lives. • We put the "locus of control" and responsibility for positive outcomes—societal value added—in the hands of others. • We sacrifice doing better, being better, and performance improvement for the status quo. • Leaders are assessed and shown to be irresponsible through trial and error and fad management. It is a sure sign of managerial incompetence when one new technique is introduced before the last has been proven to improve performance.
7	It is easier to kill an organization than it is to change it (Peters, 1997).	Change is usually painful for most people. Tom Peters, and indeed increasing numbers of others, observe that some people are so afraid of change that they will continue with dysfunctional behavior. They will even do so in the face of the organization failing. Peter Drucker said that "we are getting better and better at doing that which should not be done at all." We, when scared, focus on means and resources instead of results and consequences. Failures of organizations to change often lead to their demise. Banks have been struggling to go from "banking" to financial management, and those who could not make the transition have either failed or have been absorbed by those who could. We have often heard, "I am not going to change. I only have three years until I retire." Armies have lost battles for refusing to change—the British refusing to deviate from the "red square" alignment, even after experiencing being slaughtered by hostiles who did not play by the same rules as the British. Airlines continue to cut back on services to save money while alienating customers . . . they look only to the quarterly profit-and-loss sheet and not to the future. Resistance to change, resistance to valid and important change, is a sure way to get killed.

(Continued)

Table 1.4. Implications of Ignoring the New Realities. (*Continued*)

Code	New Realities	Implications of Ignoring
8	Reality is not divided into policies, laws, rules, regulations, sections, departments, or agencies.	In every public operation, governmental or local, organizations are typically focused on one issue, such as health, education, or welfare. Any person wanting services or seeking assistance must turn to each agency for help. However, someone might have interest in the intersections among agencies, such as health (my child has to have shots to enter school), education (you can't enroll without health certification), and welfare (I have to have approvals to get free medical assistance). Yet governments, and most other organizations, operate as if it makes sense to split operations up into entities and not look at the whole. That is why people and cases "fall through the cracks" between agencies, organizations, and jurisdiction. Laws, rules, regulations are passed without looking at whole people and whole communities. Convenient, but a convenient fiction all the same.
9	After 9/11 we realize that a simple and exclusive focus on individual performance improvement or even organizational performance alone will deliver failure.	Airport security in the United States was based on a driver of "get the people to the airplane on time" and only superficially on safety. On September 11, 2001, it was legal to carry a box cutter on an airplane. But the focus of security screeners was on taking away knives, scissors, and explosives, not on a "unifying" driver of "arrive alive." Why did not security screeners, while box cutters were legal, not ask why five unrelated passengers on flights were all carrying box cutters? The training was on immediate tasks, and so they performed. There was no formal concern for "arrive alive." Just focusing on individual jobs and tasks or even organizational outputs alone will not serve us well. What about tire companies that met production and delivery schedules and perhaps overlooked safety? Energy companies that simply looked after the welfare of some executives and not after the buying public or shareholders in general? How about accounting firms that put billable hours before integrity of reporting true financial condition?

- You lose your job because your board of directors perceives you as unable to adjust to change and to deliver continued success.

- You lose the support of constituents because you show no long-term concern for clients and communities.

- You have a revenue crisis because the products and services you sold in the past are no longer meeting your customers' requirements; sales are down, and worse, you still have no alternatives to offer.

- You spend large amounts of money on the latest fads but continue to lose market share and profits—all the while not serving your clients.

- You leave the future to chance, fate, and unplanned reactions, thus condemning tomorrow's child to clean up the catastrophe that you failed to prevent.

- Other disconcerting statistics mount:

  - Products are produced and delivered that put client safety at risk.

  - Violence in parts of cities rises.

  - Tribal wars increase worldwide.

  - Profit is reduced due to growing legal fees and governmental penalties.

  - Water pollution and consequential deaths increase.

  - Crime and corruption increase.

  - Levels of poverty and starvation increase.

  - Cancer as well as stress-related conditions increase, causing loss of life and livelihood.

  - Drug-use deaths and disabilities increase.

In simple terms, the world becomes a dimmer place to live and work for you and others.

EXERCISE—IGNORING THE NEW REALITIES

The following exercise provides you the opportunity to assess the implications of ignoring the new realities related to high payoff results within your organization and community. Choose at least five of the new realities from the list on previous pages.[10]

Write the new realities in the second column on Table 1.5 below and comment on the implications of ignoring each one you choose. Share your perspectives with a colleague.

Table 1.5. Implications of Ignoring the New Realities in Your Organization.

	New Reality	*Potential Implications of Ignoring Within Your Organization*
1		
2		
3		
4		
5		
N		

The New Realities

Given the range of new realities, people and organizations are influenced by them even if they don't consciously recognize their impact on internal and external clients. The proliferation of management fads is often an attempt to adjust to these changing realities.

Causes of Fadaholism

There are several causes for "fadaholism":

1. It is a popular thing to do—as segregation, smoking, and authoritarian leadership once were.

2. Memes: A meme is the psychosocial equivalent of a gene. They are the ways that culture is transmitted. Memes replicate themselves, like a virus or fad.[11]

3. The fad is then promoted by skilful salespeople and gurus to uninformed buyers—convincing them that they "need"[12] it when they really just "want" it.

4. The fad appeals to common sense and appears simple as presented by the salesperson. It takes the complex and makes it appear simple (also known as the KISS lie: Keep It Simple Stupid).

5. The fad worked for someone else (hearsay evidence that often goes unchallenged by the buyers).

6. The fad takes the immediate pressure off getting and using the rigorous research necessary to define our true requirements (data from a needs assessment).

7. The fad will make organizational decision makers look good in the short term.

8. You can espouse flexibility and "leading edge" responsiveness, but you don't have to practice it. Attending lectures on the fad is easier than stepping out of one's comfort zone.

9. You don't have the evidence (data) or skills to know any better. It seemed like common sense, and you didn't know any better.

10. You don't believe in evidence (research) based performance improvement.

11. The fad is sold by the largest multinational consultancy so it must be good for us.

PARADIGMS THAT WORK

Most organizations today are faced with the challenge of change. It is vital to assure that any change is useful, not simply faddish or change for change's sake. The new realities, and new paradigms, present both opportunities and threats to which we must respond. There is a requirement to discriminate between the paradigms that will yield high payoff results at all three levels of results (Mega, Macro, and Micro) and those fads that add no value (and often subtract value). This section presents you with the skills and knowledge to detect the fads.

Fads are usually means-focused. They suggest hot new ideas for "fixing" things, such as empowered working groups, group problem solving, high tech computers, Outward Bound programs, web-based training and the like. They are nothing more (although often less) than potential means, potential solutions. It follows, then, that means should not be chosen until the desired results (ends) are defined and aligned with desired and required high payoff results. When the desired results are agreed on, then the various means can be evaluated and compared and the right one(s) selected.

Appendix A provides a detailed example of how paradigms have shifted for individuals and organizations focused on performance improvement.

New Paradigms Provide New Approaches to and for High Payoff Strategic Planning and Doing

This book provides you with new tools and techniques—to be covered in the subsequent chapters—for the following key organizational activities:

- Thinking strategically to improve organizational performance by making useful contributions.

- Assessing needs—gaps in results, not gaps in resources or methods—to define problems worth fixing.

- Identifying the relationship between various organizational elements (system thinking).

- Developing *Smarter*[13] objectives to design the impossible.

- Creating and managing strategic change to break old paradigms.

- Defining problems and selecting solutions that work.

- Quantifying SWOTs (strengths, weaknesses, opportunities, and threats) and stakeholder demands.

- Analyzing business/organizational logic to develop tactics.

- Conducting a cultural screen to manage culture change.

- Selecting paradigms that improve organizational performance in a measurable way.

- Creating and designing the future and thinking proactively.

- Selecting cost-effective methods and tactics to achieve results.

- Evaluating the effectiveness of your strategic thinking and planning processes and continuously improving.

A PREVIEW OF COMING INFORMATION

We have an interesting challenge. We are trying to help you build a concept of a holistic approach to defining and achieving high payoff results. In order to do this, we may introduce terms—such as *Smarter* objectives—before we can discuss them in detail, as we do for this one in Chapter Seven. Given this, a brief definition of a *Smarter* objective is:

S = Specific performance area
M = Measurable in ratio or interval terms
A = Audacious
R = Results focused
T = Time bound
E = Encompassing
R = Reviewed frequently

This is a deviation from many conventional definitions of an objective (in the literature often referred to as "SMART" objectives). Suggesting that any objective must be "achievable" does not provide a practical framework for defining and delivering high payoff results. Instead, the *A* in *Smarter* objectives signifies that they are to be "audacious" . . . that they encourage us to move out of our old paradigms and comfort zones, that they stretch our imagination (and innovation) and hearten us to take some sensible risks.

We also add another concept to the definition of the attributes of a useful objective: that it be *Encompassing*. While we encourage audacious objectives, we also want whatever we do and deliver to be practical; and being practical involves adding value to the communities in which we work and live, and in which our products are delivered. Objectives must be more "encompassing" than the usual focus on individual performance. Objectives must encompass results and consequences for not just individuals, but also teams, the entire organization, and external clients and our shared society.

CREATE A BETTER FUTURE

Luck or Proactive Thinking and Planning

Teilhard De Chardin, the Jesuit philosopher, believed that humans are the only animals on the planet that could both observe and influence their own evolution. We can say with some certainty that the ability to consciously adjust to changing circumstances is an indicator of healthy individuals, healthy organizations, and healthy communities. The challenge today is to adjust faster because the world around us is changing at speeds that create dysfunction or "future shock" (see Toffler, 1990) and high levels of "information anxiety."

Luck and the Open Market Scenario

"There are two Bottom Lines: Conventional—*short-term profit, short-term continued funding; and* Societal—*measurable societal value added over time."*
—Kaufman, 1992, 2000; Kaufman, Watkins, & Leigh, 2001

One of the most difficult paradigm shifts to make in business is to realize that the objectives of profit and growth are no longer sustainable as the sole objectives of enterprise. Societal value added has become the central business imperative. Why?

The unrestricted open market and poor planning have resulted in the following negative consequences (these may be considered "high impact damage"):

- Increased rate of species extinction.
- Increased rate of habitat depletion.
- Rate of increase in technology application and resulting scientific disaster.
- Desertification.
- Deforestation.
- Acid rain.
- Depletion of nonrenewable resources.
- Industrial pollution.
- Birth defects.
- Industrial accidents, including poisoning.
- Depletion of fishing stocks.
- Erosion of soil.
- Reduction of water resources.
- Decay of trust in public and private organizations.

- High rates of poverty and starvation.
- High rate of usage of nonrenewable resources.
- Workplace violence.
- Social violence.
- Crime.
- Terrorism.
- Jail terms for cheating executives.

In the traditional management paradigm, priorities were limited to short-term profit, growth, and immediate shareholder returns. In addition, positive, long-term contributions were assumed, since the planning was limited to the short term. This book describes a strategic approach to high payoff results that focuses on integrating the three levels of planning and results.

Mega. Defining and planning and creating the desired world for tomorrow's child and tomorrow's citizens. This level of planning begins with an Ideal Vision—the kind of world we want to, together, achieve—and is focused on adding value to society.

Macro. Planning focused on results for your organization to deliver to immediate clients and contributing to the Ideal Vision at the Mega level.

Micro. Planning for results focused on the individuals and teams within the organization. These results are derived from the Mega and Macro results requirements in order to align what we produce and deliver with useful external contributions.

This new paradigm for strategic thinking is proactive and includes the concept of sustainability—closing current gaps in results without compromising the ability of future generations to do the same. It does not ignore profit, but makes sustainability and societal value added the first priority.

Thomas and Clegg (1998) in *Changing Paradigms* give evidence of the new paradigm:[14]

> "Companies are adopting more creative business paradigms, in which they
> regard a deep respect for the environment and a genuine concern for their
> stakeholders as a fundamental strength, not just of their value system, but
> in their business practice." (p. 430)

Any "scorekeeping" on organizational responsibilities and contributions must now include Mega, that is, societal value added. Such is the "stuff" of high payoff results and consequences.

Increasingly, people have in recent years emphasized the new reality of adding value to society (see Kaufman, 1992, 1998, 2000; Maynard & Mehrtens, 1993; Popcorn, 1990). Mega is larger than simply adding the natural environment to one's set of concerns. All of Mega must be included, not just the environment. We must include the environment as well as the health, safety, and welfare of all stakeholders.

A Better Paradigm than Luck

What have we accomplished? What are we doing right? What could we do better? What sort of world do we want to design? What better paradigms, tools, techniques, methods, and means will get us there?

Certainly, we can't carry on as we are. The dominant organizational paradigm in the western world has resulted in widespread problems and has reduced the ability of individuals and organizations to become and remain self-sufficient and self-reliant. Many organizations are clinging to an outdated world view that is no longer able to deal with an under-resourced, overpopulated, and globally interconnected planet. This actually harms future clients and will result in their decreased ability to "do business" with us. See Table 1.6.

Table 1.6. Traditional Planning vs. the High Payoff Results-Oriented Paradigm.

Traditional Planning	The High Payoff Results-Oriented Paradigm
1. Improve the present model— more of the same. Incremental changes to the present way of doing things. Stick to same old rules but do it better.	1. Strategic thinking is by definition "paradigm busting" and involves the design and creation of a new paradigm. It involves new concepts, realistic new rules, new techniques, and new skills to be successful. It often requires leaving the comfortable behind.
2. Short-term profit or funding. Objectives project five years at the most.	2. Long-term objectives that design a better world for both today's and tomorrow's citizens. Sustainability* (and continuous improvement) and profit objectives are five to one hundred years plus.
3. Dwells on tactics and activities unconnected to measurable results. Wants are often confused with needs.	3. Focuses on designing future results in measurable terms before selecting relevant strategies and tactics. Results are long term and set and linked at three levels Mega, Macro, Micro.
4. Objectives define financial results only. Internal clients and future citizens are ignored. Positive societal impact is left to chance.	4. Objectives are designed for a balanced range of stakeholders 4.1. Future citizens 4.2. Today's clients 4.3. Internal clients A balanced range of performance indicators is chosen to evaluate success.

(Continued)

Table 1.6. Traditional Planning vs. the High Payoff Results-Oriented Paradigm. (*Continued*)

Traditional Planning	The High Payoff Results-Oriented Paradigm
5. Sustainability is not an issue in planning.	5. Societal value added and sustainability are the priority issues in planning.
6. "Needs" are defined as gaps in resources methods and means (We "need" more buildings, we want more computers).	6. Needs are defined as gaps in results between current and desired results. Requirement for more resources are quasi-needs.
7. Level of planning focuses on immediate clients and major shareholders. Society and internal clients are not formally or rigorously considered.	7. Planning includes the integration and linking of three groups of clients. 7.1. Society now and in the future 7.2. Immediate external clients 7.3. Internal clients
8. Goals are more often general, vague, and exclude measurable elements.	8. Objectives are SMARTER. They are written for results at three levels, and include a measurable element.
9. Visions are more often short term. Organizational missions are "fuzzy" and sound good but don't include the next generation of citizens. Societal value added is not an issue for the organization.	9. An Ideal Vision states in measurable terms the kind of world we want to design for our grandchildren. The organizational vision defines the contribution the organization will make to the ideal vision in measurable terms. Visions are about societal value added—now and in the future—not about what an organization alone wants to accomplish.
10. No shared meaning of what an organization is or must deliver—usually treated as collection of unrelated parts.	10. Shared meaning on the elements common to all organizations, systemic mental models emphasize relationship between the parts.

*While "sustainability" is a frequently touted word and concept, we suggest that it might, unfortunately, imply that we just want to keep things, including the environment, the same way it is now—no further deterioration. We suggest that we seek to find ways to not just sustain or maintain, but to improve—improve constantly toward perfect natural balance.

EXERCISE—WHO CARES?

In this exercise you are given the opportunity to reflect on the old paradigms that have influenced your life and to compare them to the sort of world you would like for yourself and tomorrow's citizens.

Of organizations that you personally do business with, which do you expect to place high priority on:

- Caring about your survival (health, safety, and well-being), self-sufficiency, and quality of life?
- Caring about your and others' survival (health, safety, and well being)?
- Caring about the sustainability of our planet for the next generation?

Check the YES column in Table 1.7 if you expect them to care. If you have evidence they don't care, check the NO column.

Do Organizations Have to Have Their Focus on Mega?

High payoff results flow directly from a Mega orientation: adding value for all external partners. When first considering using Mega, some who are initially timid or skeptical are concerned that:

- "It's not practical, not real-world."
- "It's not acceptable to my client/associates/boss."
- "This is not part of my role."
- "It's not under my control so is something I cannot/should not deal with or for which I should be responsible."
- "I am having enough trouble booking work and keeping my job. None of my clients would go for it."

Such arguments are self-defeating. Starting the 21st Century were a set of organizational failures, collapses, and implosions that many would now attribute to not taking and maintaining a Mega focus on useful results. For example, evidence indicates that the U.S. energy giant Enron did not, while espousing "the good of shareholders and communities," have a high impact focus. Indeed, some of the organization's executives seemed to be maintaining a focus on their own wealth and well-being, not that of all stakeholders. Another bankruptcy was an international broadband supplier who, at the end of the day, appeared to be catering to the good of a few insiders and not to the stockholders.

"Dot.coms" came crashing down by the hundreds, sending shock waves through international markets as it was increasingly noticed that the stocks were inflated through personal ambitions rather than value they would deliver to shareholders and external clients. A major then-big-six accounting firm was accused of overlooking or ignoring "creative" bookkeeping and business practices for several of their clients. This was being done while maintaining a million dollars a week cash flow from one client that went bankrupt when such practices led to its demise. Both the accounting firm and the client suffered

Table 1.7. Checking Whether Organizations Care.

Organizations You Do Business with	Care About Your Survival (Health, Safety, and Well-Being), Self-Sufficiency, and Quality of Life?		Care About Sustainability for the Next Generations?	
	Yes	*No*	*Yes*	*No*
• Airlines				
• Food manufacturers				
• Car repair shops				
• Furniture makers				
• Entertainment parks				
• Shopping malls				
• Physicians				
• Dentists				
• Nurses				
• Local councils				
• Primary schools				
• Technical institutes				
• Schools and universities				
• Police				
• Fire departments				
• Power and utilities				
• Household appliance manufacturers				
• Pharmaceutical companies				
• Building materials manufacturers				

greatly. The accounting firm seemed to have a number of different clients who faced ruin, while their audit reports showed approval of all financial matters and conditions. The U.S. Justice Department's formal concerns caused public and corporate alarm, as well as a sinking of public trust.

While such disasters mounted, there were those within many of these same flawed and soon-to-fail organizations who either said they were already "serving the good of society" or that such a focus was not "real world" or possible.

When asked to demonstrate "doing good for society," the usual responses were about corporate giving or volunteer work, or vague references to customer satisfaction. There was no formal consideration of measurable high payoff results for external clients and our shared society. When asked why a Mega focus was not real world or practical, many shared their concern that others "would not buy it," or "they are not ready for such yet." The prevailing comfort zone was for a focus on Macro organizational good—and not a solid linkage to what organizations used, did, produced, and delivered with external value added.

When organizations respond that Mega is not part of their role, it is interesting to ask them whether they don't own what they do and its impact on the whole contribution. If people do not "own" the role and contribution to the larger contribution, then they are denying *both* the negative *and* positive consequences of what they use, do, and produce on the larger impacts.

Does it take financial collapse (and some possible jail time) to get people over their impractical and non-justifiable fears? What could be more practical and real world than helping one's organization to survive and thrive? Fear of something new and different is a powerful paralysis source. Success can be fear's alternative.

No longer can the old paradigm of "business is the business of business" be sensibly evoked with confidence or evidence. This outmoded approach doesn't point to a new reality of defining and achieving high payoff results—combining profits and organizational success with societal value added. This new reality is no longer an option but vital for organizational survival. A short-term focus on shareholder value alone does not serve anyone well. The single bottom line concept is now dead. We must use a two-level bottom line with a primary focus on societal value added.[15]

Informed Consent?

What else to do about Mega when you know it is right and your client doesn't? Answer: informed consent.

We often hear from those who understand Mega and believe it is extremely important to all parties "but my client isn't interested." Or "I know it is important, but my client will not be interested." We have even heard from some professionals at remaining large international consulting firms who say, "Yes, but there is no market for it yet."

What might be done when you must attempt to make a contribution and there is resistance to Mega internally or externally? Don't shrug off the requirement, for if things fail (and they usually will if Mega is ignored), you will likely be held responsible (just ask some of the previously respected companies in the early 2000s that faltered for not acting on Mega). We suggest taking a page from medical practice (which has become quite the target for lawsuits and blame) and provide and obtain informed consent.

Informed consent simply notifies a client that there are risks for moving ahead, and the risks are considerably higher if one does not link everything that is used, done, produced, and delivered to external and societal impact and consequences. Client is not interested? No perceived market for Mega? Concerned that the client won't understand and you will still be expecting to go ahead? Simply let clients—internal or external—know that there should be links with Mega. If they say "no," then the burden of proof of negative consequences shifts from you to them.

We note that the interest in, and commitment to, Mega is increasing. Your providing the professional and technical know-how will become increasingly valued. And safe.

SUMMARY

Paradigm Busting Guidelines

This chapter can be summarized in the following guidelines for obtaining high payoff results:

1. The world is changing fast and the implications for people's survival and quality of life are profound. Identify the practical implications for you and your organization. You can choose to be the masters of change or the victims of it.

2. The rules and procedures for living and working effectively are changing or have already changed. Countless old paradigms no longer work, but many will still cling to them despite their failure to solve today's problems. Challenge your mental models, beliefs, and values. Get out of your comfort zones.

3. Paradigms are powerful and difficult to change because they lock us in to rules and screen out new data that conflict with the "conventional wisdom" of the existing paradigm. When locked into the existing paradigm, you are often unable to perceive new data, even when it is right in front of you. Strategic thinking involves challenging existing paradigms: learn to think strategically using societal value added as the guide for all decisions.

4. Shifting paradigms can bring problems and opportunities that cannot be addressed by existing rules, methods, and reward systems. This discovery initiates the development or search for new paradigms that

fix the new problems. Look for new paradigms but evaluate their value. Define results before selecting methods.

5. New tools, techniques, and concepts are not always better (or appropriate) for solving present and future problems. Rushing to a new fad without adequate diagnosis of the problem is called "fadaholism." This rush to action can be just as bad as sticking with the existing paradigm—neither solve the problems. Some paradigms are worth hanging on to; fads are not.

6. Those who are most successful at present "common wisdom" are the most resistant to new "common wisdom." So it is the outsiders who create the new paradigms. Select leaders who challenge conventional wisdom.

7. Sometimes you have to "bust" the old paradigms, and sometimes you have to challenge and "bust" the new fads that might have been incorrectly called "new paradigms." Paradigms can provide insights in order to create and find solutions to new problems. But before a solution is selected, the desired results must be defined: build change on a sound Needs Assessment.

8. Strategic planning and thinking that is focused on societal and then internal results is the proven paradigm for creating and designing a better future for present and future generations. Conventional strategic planning—the old wisdom—has not been successful and has failed because it got bogged down in rituals about methods and means, and tactics (see Kaufman, 1998, 2000; Kaufman, Watkins, & Leigh, 2001). Use a proactive planning model; commit to adding society to conventional planning paradigms.

9. The paradigm for strategic thinking and planning best aligned with high payoff results is one that is responsive to the new realities in a proactive way. It is proactive because it involves all the partners, both from within as well as from outside the organizational walls, in creating systemic linkages among three levels of results in order to deliver high payoff results which contribute to

   - *Mega Results.* What sort of world do we want to create for the future? This is stated and defined as an Ideal Vision, a measurable statement of the kind of world we want to help create for tomorrow's child (see Chapter Four). This is the creation of miracles, designing the impossible, and evolving new paradigms of success that our shared futures depend on. It is "practical dreaming."

- *Macro Results.* What sort of outputs do we want to deliver to our immediate external clients? Will those deliverables contribute to the Ideal Vision and thus to Mega?
- *Micro Results.* What sorts of building-block results will individuals and teams contribute to internal clients (associates)? And will those results add positive value to the Macro and Micro results? (Figure 1.1 shows this progression.)

10. The implications of staying with old paradigms are potentially disastrous for individuals, communities, organizations, and the planet. We can be the victims of past and continuing failures, or we can plan to invent our world and work with others to create and design a better world.

11. The best way to start creating the future is to produce evidence that the present direction is unacceptable. We use a tool called Needs Assessment for this. Include rigorous Needs Assessments as a foundation for strategic thinking and planning.

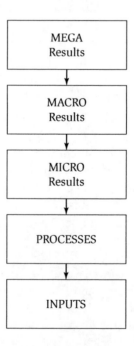

Figure 1.1. Progression from Mega to Inputs.

The Journey of Creation

This book takes you on a journey of discovery and design in order to define practical high payoff results. You will be given the tools and guidance to influence your own evolution and create and design a better world for yourself, your organization, your community, and tomorrow's child.

Notes

1. Don't be taken in by the "been there done that" syndrome simply because the concept received a lot of attention in the 1980s and 1990s. It is as basic and important now as it was then.

2. Success is measured by the problems that are correctly solved using the current rules and regulations.

3. The trick to learning a new paradigm is to set aside your current one while you're learning rather than attempt to fit the new knowledge into your existing model. It won't fit. Joel Barker has influenced our approach to shifting paradigms in the social sciences. We highly recommend the works of Joel Barker and Darryl Conner for straightforward and useful discussions of this vital concept.

4. Like the term paradigm, the term framing is related to how we construct and manage meaning. Whereas paradigms are often out of consciousness, the frames we use can be consciously chosen. Like the photographer captures reality through the lens, frame leaders can construct meaning through language. Gail Fairhurst and Robert Sarr (1996) present this concept in their book *The Art of Framing.* Skillful leaders can use framing to present their paradigms of performance.

5. Peter Drucker notes that we are getting better and better at doing that which should not be done at all.

6. See Pascale, 1990, p. 19.

7. The world economy is presented at a crucial point of transition in the long view scenario. The post WW II boom would be expected to have had an approximate fifty-year cycle with a twenty-five year upswing and a twenty-five year downswing. According to the theory, the new upswing wave and a shift to a new paradigm should be beginning about now. The convergence of communications and computer technology combined with rapid advances in other technologies is helping to create an exploding cluster of continuous change (see Kondratiev, 1935).

8. This article, along with another article by Harold Stolovitch in the April 2000 Special Issue of *Performance Improvement,* notes that less than 10 percent of everything that is learned in conventional training ever shows up on the job. And there are no estimates if what is mastered in training ever really adds value to the organization and external clients and society. These are pretty dismal results for something we know how to dramatically improve.

9. Our thanks to Professor Dale Brethower for this concept.

10. A more detailed description of the New Realities can be found in Kaufman (2000).

11. Malcolm Gladwell's *The Tipping Point* (2000) provides fascinating accounts of how ideas can spread like viruses, and details the attributes of those who are successful in spreading their paradigms. In addition, refer to *Virus of the Mind* by Brodie (1996) for a practical explanation of memes, and for more detailed research on memes refer to the book *Flow* by Csikszentmihalyi (1990).

12. Later, as we focus on the differences between ends and means, we spend considerable time on the conventional and unfortunate use of "need" as a verb. Such phrases that use need as a verb, such as "we need more people" or "we need to fire people," causes people to select the solution before knowing and documenting the problem.

13. These have been developed by Hugh Oakley-Browne with the discussion with Roger Kaufman to replace the conventional "SMART" objectives that fall quite short of helping deliver high payoff results. This is a good example of an older paradigm (SMART objectives) proving to be of little—and perhaps negative—value. SMARTER objectives are discussed fully in Chapter Seven.

14. Thomas and Clegg (1998, p. 369) believe that one of the most difficult paradigm shifts to make in business is to realize that the sole objectives of profit and growth are no longer sustainable as the ultimate objective of enterprise.

15. Some recent attempts to defuse the complexity (and perhaps regain some personal comfort) of Mega is to split off pieces of it, such as "a third bottom line" that is being offered in some parts . . . the third bottom line being the environment. The environment, to be sure, is important. But so also are the other dimensions of Mega, so it is vital to focus on all of the aspects of Mega and assure that they are individually and collectively addressed.

There has been a recent tendency of some to recommend a "third bottom line" of adding environmental impact to organizational accountability. While such a consideration is important, it is deceptive in that it tends to splinter Mega into pieces rather than viewing the societal bottom line as an integrated "fabric" that includes the impacts of environment, health, and economics, among other variables. The use of this suggested "two bottom lines" includes the environment along with other organizational responsibilities instead of simply focusing on one of several important and interacting dimensions.

CHAPTER TWO

Critical Success Factors for Strategic Thinking That Works

CHAPTER GOALS

By working though this chapter, you will be able to answer the following questions:

- ❑ What is strategic thinking?
- ❑ What is strategic planning?
- ❑ What are the six critical success factors?
- ❑ Why is strategic thinking not more of the same?
- ❑ Why distinguish between ends and means?
- ❑ How can the impossible be designed?
- ❑ Should organizations contribute value to society now and in the future?
- ❑ Why are needs not wants?
- ❑ What are the critical success factors?
- ❑ What are the consequences of ignoring the critical success factors?

SIX CRITICAL SUCCESS FACTORS FOR STRATEGIC THINKING AND PLANNING

Table 2.1 shows the six critical success factors for strategic thinking and planning.

Introduction to Strategic Thinking

"Compared to what we ought to be we are only half awake."
—William James

Strategic thinking is the way in which people in an organization think about, assess, view, and create the future for themselves and their associates. It is more than responding to both day-to-day as well as long-term problems, opportunities,

Table 2.1. Six Critical Success Factors.

Critical Success Factor 1

Move out of your comfort zone—today's paradigms—and use new and wider boundaries for thinking, planning, doing, evaluating, and continuous improvement.

Critical Success Factor 2

Differentiate between ends (what) and means (how).

Critical Success Factor 3

Use all three levels of planning and results (Mega/Outcomes; Macro/Outputs; Micro/Products).

Critical Success Factor 4

Prepare all objectives—including the Ideal Vision and mission—to include precise statements of both where you are headed, as well as the criteria for measuring when you have arrived. Develop "Smarter" Objectives.

Critical Success Factor 5

Use an Ideal Vision (what kind of world, in measurable performance terms, we want for tomorrow's child) as the underlying basis for planning and continuous improvement.

Critical Success Factor 6

Defining "need" as a gap in results (not as insufficient levels of resources, means, or methods).

and new realities; it is creating tomorrow. It is not reactive, but proactive. Strategic thinking focuses on how to create a better future by being proactive and adding value to society—through the accomplishment of high payoff results. It is concerned with taking control of the future by developing practical dreams of the results you want to create for tomorrow's child and your clients and partners. Fortunately, it can also be applied any day at any time and is responsive to the new realities and the accelerated rate of change of today and tomorrow's world.

Strategic thinking always involves change, and often, profound personal change. It often requires your present paradigms and your ways of thinking, relating, and performing. It is imagining the results you want to achieve in the future, it is *practical dreaming* . . . creating an ideal future by defining and achieving results that add value.

Strategic Planning

Strategic planning is the formal process of defining the requirements for delivering high payoff results; for identifying what and how to get from our current realities to future ones that add value to society at the Mega level. It is not rigid or lock-step, but rather a self-correcting set of defining requirements and relationships for stating *What Is* in terms of results, and moving ever closer to *What Should Be* results and payoffs.

Strategic planning involves formally asking and answering:

1. What profound shifts are or will influence our future?
2. What is our direction and response to these shifts?
3. What are the elements of Mega that we must address? And why?
4. How will we describe our desired *results* in measurable terms?
5. What are the best ways and means to get there?
6. How will we measure progress?
7. How will we measure success?
8. How will we revise as required?

Strategic planning is the formal process for producing plans documenting the results identified by our strategic thinking. Strategic planning develops, creates, and records at minimum the following results to be accomplished:

1. An Ideal (Mega) Vision for the kind of world we want to help create for tomorrow's child.
2. An organizational (Macro) mission or purpose.
3. Strategic objectives for achieving high payoff results at the Mega level.

4. Tactical objectives for delivering results at the Macro level.

5. Operational objectives for delivering results at the Micro level.

6. Needs Assessment based priorities for the Mega, Macro, and Micro levels. (These define the gaps in results and the costs to meet the needs, as compared to the costs to ignore the gaps.)

7. Tactics/solutions (methods and means) for delivering internal and external (high payoff) results.

Strategic planning formally documents the results and contributions of strategic thinking, namely the results you, your organization, its customers, suppliers, co-workers, and society want to achieve in the long term (five, ten, twenty, fifty, or more years).

Strategic Planning Definition
Strategic planning, properly defined and accomplished, provides the basic directions and rationale for determining where an a organization should head and provides the specifications against which any organization may best decide what to do and how to do it. It is a process for creating and describing a better future in measurable terms and the selection of the best means to achieve the results desired.

IS CHANGE STRATEGIC?

Table 2.2 is designed to help you assess whether the change being considered is strategic or tactical/operational. Check (✓) the relevant column. A "yes" answer is evidence of a strategic issue. Do take the time to complete this exercise; we will use it as a foundation for future activities.[1]

Table 2.2. Checklist for Assessing Strategic Change.

Code	Question	Unsure	No	Yes
1	Is the change concerned with linking and relating results at the three levels of planning (Mega, Macro, and Micro)?			
2	Will the change require the planners to shift their paradigms for planning, thinking, and operating?			
3	Will the change be a response to a set of new realities agreed to by the planners (rather than just more of the same)?			

Table 2.2. (*Continued*)

Code	Question	Unsure	No	Yes
4	Will the change require you to unlearn some things that made you successful yesterday?			
5	Does the change involve contributions to your client's survival, health, and well-being?			
6	Does the change contribute to the quality of life of clients and citizens in the communities you work with?			
7	Does the change require you to set different objectives from the past?			
8	Will the change require changes in your major processes (capabilities)?			
9	Will the change require you to design and select different methods and means to achieve desired results?			
10	Will the change require you to develop new skills and competencies for key roles?			
11	Will failing to respond to the new realities produce unacceptable consequences and increase your risk levels?			
12	Will the change require the whole system to change?			
13	Will change in any one unit, process, or system have implications for other parts?			
14	Is the cost of keeping on doing the same things unacceptable?			
15	Is the change concerned with your balanced score card and does it impact external clients or society?			
16	Is the change concerned with the sustainability of the organization in the long term?			
17	Is the change one of opportunities that will have negative consequences if ignored (for example, fall behind your competitors, go broke)?			

(*Continued*)

Table 2.2. Checklist for Assessing Strategic Change. (*Continued*)

Code	Question	Unsure	No	Yes
18	If you don't change, will you be able to recover in the worst instance?			
19	Will the change have implications for a wide range of people?			
20	Will the change elicit a degree of pain for some?			
21	Will the change elicit high degrees of resistance from some?			
22	Will the change require the previous planners and sponsors to learn new paradigms?			
23	Does the change require shifts in patterns of behavior that define your present culture?			
24	Will the change yield high impact results to help to create a better world for tomorrow's children?			

THE STRATEGIC THINKING AND PLANNING PROCESS

Figure 2.1 is a model of the major steps in the new paradigm for effective strategic thinking and planning, for defining, justifying, and delivering high payoff results. This model will be expanded on in later chapters.

Critical Success Factors for Strategic Thinking, Planning, and Doing

The process of strategic planning integrates all the parts of effective strategic thinking into a results oriented plan. The six critical success factors described below distinguish this model from all others.

1. *Paradigm Shift.* Shift your paradigm about organizations to one that is the largest and most inclusive by beginning with societal good in mind. Move out of your comfort zone and consider two bottom lines:
   - Positive impact on society through improved quality of life.
   - Profit over long term.
2. *Results vs. Methods and Means.* Distinguish between ends and means. Define and plan results at the Mega, Macro, and Micro levels you desire before choosing how to achieve them.

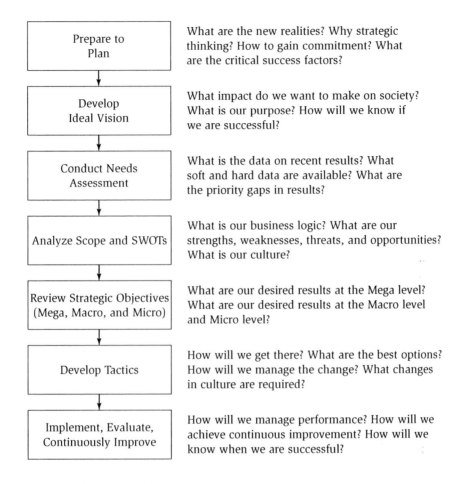

Prepare to Plan	What are the new realities? Why strategic thinking? How to gain commitment? What are the critical success factors?
Develop Ideal Vision	What impact do we want to make on society? What is our purpose? How will we know if we are successful?
Conduct Needs Assessment	What is the data on recent results? What soft and hard data are available? What are the priority gaps in results?
Analyze Scope and SWOTs	What is our business logic? What are our strengths, weaknesses, threats, and opportunities? What is our culture?
Review Strategic Objectives (Mega, Macro, and Micro)	What are our desired results at the Mega level? What are our desired results at the Macro level and Micro level?
Develop Tactics	How will we get there? What are the best options? How will we manage the change? What changes in culture are required?
Implement, Evaluate, Continuously Improve	How will we manage performance? How will we achieve continuous improvement? How will we know when we are successful?

Figure 2.1. The New Paradigm.

3. *Link Mega, Macro, and Micro.* Use all three levels of planning and results, Mega, Macro, and Micro.

4. *Measurable Objectives.* Develop measurable objectives at the Mega, Macro, and Micro levels of results that are linked *systemically* as a *value added chain.* Don't include methods and means in objectives.

5. *Ideal Vision.* Use an Ideal Vision as the foundation for strategic thinking and planning. Don't be limited to your immediate organization or current paradigms.

6. *Needs Are Gaps in Results.* Define "needs" as a gaps in results, not as insufficient resources, means, or methods.

These critical success factors are now explained in more detail.

Shifting Paradigms

"New paradigms put everyone practicing the old paradigm at great risk. The higher one's position the greater the risk. The better you are at your paradigm, the more you have invested in it, the more you have to lose by changing paradigms."
—Barker, 1989

Critical Success Factor One. Paradigms, like mental models, are the ways in which we perceive and filter reality. When the demands and pressures for change within the organization intensify beyond just incremental changes, then it's one indicator that a paradigm shift is imminent. We can and should shift paradigms, even when previous paradigms are not yet failing us. Thinking about the future is not about *"more of the same."* After all, the ways of thinking that led to success yesterday can become a major barrier to creating future success. The new realities require managers and leaders at all levels to change how they think about how the following can or should contribute to results that add value:

1. The elements of organizational performance.
2. The role of the organization in society—there are two bottom lines (and these are high payoff results).
3. The role of leaders (that is, the leader as a steward, not authoritarian or "parent").
4. The process for strategic thinking and planning.
5. The factors that influence human performance.
6. The way problems are defined and the decision process (for example, level of participation).
7. The methods for creating and managing profound change successfully.

Effective strategic thinking and planning require everyone to shift their paradigms and agree on common destinations. This means that many people at all levels in an organization must usually unlearn previous ways of thinking and performing.[2] They then must learn better ways to achieve desired/required performance.

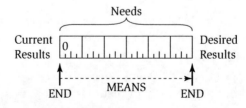

Figure 2.2. Current Results to Desired Results.
Source: From Kaufman, 1992, 1998, 2000.

Distinguish Between Ends and Means

Critical Success Factor Two. Distinguishing between ends and means is another characteristic of a strategic thinker. Results are ends that define in measurable terms the future we want to create. Means are the methods and tactics we choose to achieve the results. It is also good sense, good logic, and good economics to define the future desired state before selecting how you will get there. When methods, means, resources, and tactics are chosen before the problem, opportunity, and result are defined, then we are likely to end up somewhere other than where we desire.

There are many examples of major organizational interventions that failed because a poorly defined problem led to the selection of the wrong solution (just refer back to Table 1.3). Confusing ends and means has profound implications for performance improvement or lack of it. Many times, organizational fads are chosen before the desired results are agreed and defined in measurable terms.

Link Mega, Macro, and Micro

Critical Success Factor Three. Use and link all three levels of planning and results. Each level of results focuses on a different, but related, client category. The chart below shows this relationship. High payoff results are those organizational ends achieved at the Micro or Macro level that yield positive societal contributions at the Mega level, as shown in Table 2.3.

The starting point for strategic planning—unless you aren't concerned with the health, safety, and well-being of your clients and community—is to define the desired results at the Mega level. Planning then proceeds down the chain of results to the Macro and Micro levels. In this way the three levels of results make up a *value added chain* of high payoff results. After all, we want to plan for useful results before selecting any methods or means for accomplishing those results.

Mega level results must be part of all planning if high payoff performance is to be realized at the Macro and Micro levels as well. See Figure 2.3 for this concept.

Table 2.3. Ends Achieved at the Mega, Micro, and Macro Levels.

Planning Level	Client Category
MEGA Results These results are called OUTCOMES	The client is society now and in the future.
MACRO Results These results are called OUTPUTS	These are results delivered to direct clients outside of the organization.
MICRO Results These results are called PRODUCTS	These are results delivered to internal clients—teams or individuals—who add value.

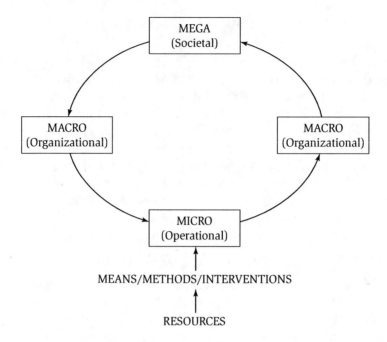

Figure 2.3. The Chain of Results.

Source: From Kaufman, 1992, 1998, 2000.

This model proposes that ethically and professionally we should plan to make useful contributions to society. Lowering toxic pollution levels, eliminating the tragic effects and consequences of war and diseases, and developing self-sufficient citizens (and customers) are all examples of results that can be planned and achieved if we start planning at the Mega level. If we start at the Mega level, the other levels of results will always be linked to a higher order, longer term need. This can give you a competitive edge, help "grow the future," and assure sustainability. This is the new wisdom.

Measurable (and Audacious) Objectives

Smarter Objectives
S = Specific
M = Measurable
A = Audacious
R = Results Focused
T = Time Bound
E = Encompassing
R = Reviewed

Critical Success Factor Four. We create the future twice. We achieve it the first time in our mind through imagining and dreaming, and then again through our external accomplishments.

For any useful results to be accomplished in tangible, measurable forms, first someone has to dream them. Since there are three levels of planning and associated results (Mega/Outcomes, Macro/Outputs, Micro/Products), strategic thinkers develop linked objectives for each of these in measurable terms. To ensure we move out of our present paradigms and break the status quo, we must be bold and audacious when we set and commit to our objectives. These objectives are called *Smarter* objectives. These are objectives that are not based on past processes; they specify the desired future in terms of results that ought to be accomplished, irrespective of the hindrances of today. They invent in the mind's eye and commit to action results that have not yet been achieved (nor perhaps even conceived). As such, they don't include methods and means—the methods and means describe the options for achieving the results, not the results themselves.

Smarter objectives can be used to achieve the seemingly impossible. What you say is possible determines what is possible. That is how we put some men on the moon. And got them back safely. Chapter Seven, Developing Smarter Objectives, covers this critical success factor in more detail.

Ideal Vision

Critical Success Factor Five. It is critical that strategic thinking and planning begin by stepping outside the limits of your organization. This step involves representative stakeholders in answering some fundamental questions about the sort of world you would like to create for tomorrow's child.

The Ideal Vision expresses in measurable terms what we wish to accomplish and commit to design and create.[3] It describes ends and not means, processes, procedures, resources, or methods. In Chapter Four, Preparing to Plan, the Ideal Vision as the starting place for strategic thinking is described in greater detail.

Needs Are Gaps in Results

"Too many organizations are reacting to the future with the mantras (means)
of the past, approaching the task with a frenzy of activity (means)."
—Noer, 1993

Critical Success Factor Six. Define "needs" as a gap between present results and desired results, not as perceived gaps in inputs and/or processes (which are really wants). By defining *needs* as gaps in results, we are thinking strategically, because we are designing the long-term future to be accomplished before deciding what methods and means might create it. Terminology should be precise when describing the world to which we will expect to commit many resources. For example, a *training needs assessment* is not strategic because training is a solution, not a result (see Triner, Greenberry, & Watkins, 1996; Stolovich, 2000). Starting with training as the solution risks being wrong 80 to 90 percent of the time—very, very bad odds but very conventional thinking.

Need is not a verb if you intended to deliver high payoff results. Need is defined as *"the gap between current results and desired results—not gaps in resources, methods, procedures, or means"* (Kaufman, 1992, 2000). This is a critical definition because it helps planners to focus first on what matters—ends and not means. When you use need to mean *"I have to have . . ."* or *"I have decided the solution is . . . ,"* we limit our thinking, planning, and doing to methods and means: we risk selecting solutions that do not go with our problems and opportunities. Alternately, strategic planning and thinking is a proactive process concerned with defining results before selecting among the alternatives to achieve them. It is the role of the leader to maintain a focus on organizational accomplishments through high payoff results, while it is commonly the role of the manager to assist in defining adequate and sufficient means for the accomplishment of required results at the Micro, Macro, and Mega levels. Chapter Five covers this Critical Success Factor in more detail.

The next exercise gives you the opportunity to assess whether the strategic thinkers in your organization have agreed on the critical success factors for effective strategic thinking and planning.

EXERCISE—CRITICAL SUCCESS FACTORS SELF-ASSESSMENT

Use Table 2.4 to assess your present organization to the degree that its strategic planners agree to the six critical success factors and apply them.

Table 2.4. Self-Assessment.

Code	Question	Don't Know	No	Yes
1	Strategic thinkers all agree that strategic planning involves profound change and paradigm shifts from one bottom line to two: societal impact and long-term profit.*			
2	Strategic thinkers all agree that strategic planning must start with describing *results* before selecting means and methods.			

*Or continued funding if you are a governmental or nonprofit agency.

Table 2.4. (*Continued*)

Code	Question	Don't Know	No	Yes
3	Strategic thinkers all agree to develop audacious (or outrageous, extraordinary) objectives that define desired results in measurable terms (that is, Smarter objectives).			
4	Strategic thinkers all agree to include and link three levels of results in their strategic planning (Mega, Macro, Micro).			
5	Strategic thinkers all agree to start their planning by developing and agreeing on a shared Ideal Vision (the world we want to create for tomorrow's child).			
6	Strategic thinkers all agree to define needs as gaps in results at the three results levels—Mega, Macro, Micro.			
7	Strategic thinkers all agree on the negative consequences of ignoring any of the six critical success factors.			
8	Strategic thinkers agree that results at the Mega level of planning are Outcomes, those at the Macro level are Outputs, and those at the Micro level are Products.			

The following exercise will help you identify the consequences of ignoring any one of the factors. Share your results with a colleague.

THE CONSEQUENCES OF IGNORING THE CRITICAL SUCCESS FACTORS

The six critical success factors for strategic thinking and planning are all related. If we ignore one, there are implications and consequences for all others. Here are some example implications of ignoring them.

Paradigm Shifts

"Each age is a dream that is dying. And one that is coming to birth."
—W. B. Yeats

1. If we ignore paradigm shifts, then . . .
    1.1 We get more of the same.
    1.2 We boil slowly to death like the frog in a gradually warming pot of water.[4]
    1.3 Clients miss out on new opportunities.
    1.4 We fall well behind our competitors.
    1.5 We lose control of the future and become its victims.
    1.6 People don't learn to change and adjust.
    1.7 Performance deteriorates at all levels—among individuals, teams, and units.
    1.8 We manage by crisis and become reactive rather than proactive.
    1.9 We become atrophied by the past.

Results Versus Means

"If you don't know what you are building, no tool will help."
—Nirenberg, 1997

2. If we confuse methods and means (processes, activities, interventions, resources) with results, then . . .
    2.1 We waste resources on fads that fail to solve the problem.
    2.2 We spin our wheels without getting anywhere.
    2.3 We encourage managerial incompetence.
    2.4 We lose profits.
    2.5 We lose the trust of clients.
    2.6 We turn off our brains.
    2.7 We work toward solving the wrong problems and don't improve performance.
    2.8 We produce negative results.
    2.9 We waste time debating methods and confusing means with results.
    2.10 We increase the risk of failure.

Develop Audacious Objectives

"Like it or not: the degree to which you speak in abstractions (fuzzies) is the degree to which you abdicate to someone else the power to say what you mean."
—Mager, 1997

3. If we develop fuzzy objectives, then . . .
    3.1 We allow for misinterpretation of the desired results.
    3.2 We create barriers to shared meaning, and thus to shared and useful results.
    3.3 We make it difficult to assess progress and determine success.

3.4 We make it easy to choose costly but ineffective means and methods.

3.5 We create misunderstandings about what results are intended.

3.6 We make it difficult to assess needs.

3.7 We are likely to shift our paradigms too late to respond effectively to the new realities.

3.8 We avoid taking responsibility for measurable results.

Link Mega, Macro, and Micro

"The greatest danger in times of turbulence is not the turbulence.
It is to act with yesterday's logic."
—Drucker, 1993

4. If we fail to link Mega, Macro, and Micro planning, then . . .

4.1 We ignore societal responsibility as an ethic and a source of continuing success.

4.2 We exclude the next generation from our planning efforts.

4.3 We compromise long-term results and sustainability.

4.4 We ignore society as a client.

4.5 We limit our vision to the short term.

4.6 We ignore the benefits of system and systemic thinking.

4.7 We invite failure.

4.8 We leave high payoff results to chance.

Develop Ideal Vision

"The great excitement of the future is that we can shape it."
—Handy, 1997

5. If we proceed without an Ideal Vision, then . . .

5.1 We become victims of short-term planning and mortgage the future.

5.2 We leave the impact in the long term to luck.

5.3 We display lack of caring for the next generation of citizens.

5.4 We ignore the relationships among the three levels of results.

5.5 We increase the risk of failure in the medium long term as well as the long term.

5.6 We limit ourselves to the results within the present paradigm. We ignore the opportunity to start creating "the impossible" for the next generation.

5.7 We choose familiarity over better and more useful paradigms.

5.8 We become reactive to crises in society instead of being proactive.

Needs Are Gaps in Results

6. If we fail to define needs as gaps in results, then . . .

6.1 We increase the risk of "fadaholism"—racing for new means and methods before agreeing on the results to be achieved.

6.2 We waste valuable resources without achieving measurable performance improvement.

6.3 We confuse wants (quasi-needs) with true needs.

6.4 We make it difficult to set and justify priorities for dealing with the real needs.

6.5 We define the wrong problems and waste scarce resources fixing them.

6.6 We waste time debating and discussing quasi-needs . . . we focus on means not ends and consequences.

6.7 We make it difficult to evaluate the worth of our efforts to improve performance and payoffs based on useful results.

6.8 We choose means before defining ends—a triumph of process over consequences.

Think about your own organization and refer to the implications of ignoring each critical success factor. Note those implications or consequences you consider most relevant in the right-hand column on Table 2.5.

Compare your answers with a colleague; then read through the decision chart (Table 2.6) that follows.

Table 2.5. Determining the Implications for Your Organization.

Code	Critical Success Factor	Implications of Ignoring
1	Creating paradigm shift.	
2	Distinguishing means and methods from desired results and Differentiating among the three levels of results and consequences: Outcomes, Outputs, and Products.	
3	Linking results at the Mega, Macro, Micro levels.	
4	Working with *Smarter* objectives rather than vague (fuzzy) objective.	
5	Developing a shared Ideal Vision as the foundation for strategic thinking and planning.	
6	Defining needs as gaps in results at the Mega, Macro, and Micro levels.	

Table 2.6. Decision Chart.

Code	Critical Success Factors	Comments and Guidance
1	Shift your paradigm—move out of your comfort zone and use new, wider boundaries for thinking, planning, doing, and continuous improvement and evaluation.	1. Challenge current wisdom. 2. Challenge assumptions. 3. Search for hard evidence. 4. Identify the new realities and adjust. 5. Reflect on your mental models.
2	Distinguish between ends and means.	1. Define and plan the results before selecting the means and methods. 2. Challenge fads and methods posing as ends. 3. Identify the consequences of rushing to the wrong means.
3	Use all three levels of planning and results—Mega, Macro, Micro.	1. Identify the consequences of results at one level to results at other levels. 2. Learn to think systemically, systemically, and holistically— think in wholes and link results. 3. Identify relationships between parts.
4	Link *Smarter* objectives at Mega, Macro, and Micro levels. *Smarter* objectives are measurable. They should create new paradigms. Don't include methods in the statement of objectives.	1. Challenge vague "fuzzy" objectives. 2. Challenge objectives that maintain the current wisdom and status quo. 3. Contemplate the impossible and make it measurable. 4. Imagine a better future in measurable terms. Use ratio and interval measures.
5	Use an Ideal Vision as the foundation for strategic thinking, planning, and doing—including continuous improvement.	1. Define the world you would like to create for your grandchildren. 2. Think bigger than before—think global and then act locally. 3. Define an Ideal Vision in measurable terms, not vague "nice sounding" platitudes.

(Continued)

Table 2.6. Decision Chart. (*Continued*)

Code	Critical Success Factors	Comments and Guidance
		4. Think wider than just the organization's impact on immediate clients—think about the impact on the whole planet. 5. Plan to move closer to the Ideal Vision.
6	Define need as a gap in results. Needs are not gaps in methods, means, strategies, tactics, or resources.	1. Challenge fads posing as needs. 2. Challenge solutions unsupported by needs assessment evidence. 3. Ask for needs assessment data to support problem solving. 4. Spend sensible time formulating and defining the right problems.

Notes

1. Kaufman (2000) makes the point that not all planning is actually strategic, even if it is called "strategic." Many so-called strategic plans are really tactical or operational, and tend to be continuations of the status quo. Strategic planning should start with the development of an Ideal Vision (Mega level objectives) that is future-focused and concerned with societal impact in the long term (one hundred years). From this should flow the tactical and operational plans.

2. Our thinking on the leadership role in change is influenced by writers including Greenleaf (1977) and Block (1993). Greenleaf (1977) originated the idea of the "servant leader." Block (1993) developed the idea of "stewardship" in his book of the same name.

3. Kaufman (2000) proposes that the Ideal Vision is the best starting place for effective strategic planning. This Ideal Vision should be the foundation for all public and private planning evaluation and continuous improvement.

4. The boiled frog story refers to an experiment in adaptability and data feedback. If one drops a frog into a hot bowl of water it will leap out and survive. However, if the frog is placed in a shallow pan of room temperature water and the pan is heated gradually, the frog adapts to the new temperature. Unfortunately regardless of how hot the water becomes the frog never becomes uncomfortable enough to jump out of the pan. In fact, the frog stays there and boils to death. Some organizations are like the frog—they should leap out of the water and move in a new direction, shift to a new paradigm. Instead, they make adjustments to the status quo when they should be responding to the new realities.

CHAPTER THREE

System (and Systems) Thinking

CHAPTER GOALS

After completing this chapter, you will understand and act on the importance of thinking and acting holistically, not to confuse the parts of an organization with the whole, as well as why you should link what organizations use, do, produce, and deliver to high payoff external results. There is an important difference between system thinking and systems thinking (as trivial as that might sound at first). This chapter will orient you toward defining and delivering useful results, and being able to prove the worth of doing so.

By working though this chapter, you will be able to answer the following questions:

❑ What are mental models?

❑ What is wrong with the traditional organizational chart?

❑ What is a living system?

❑ What are the elements common to *all* organizations?

❑ What is "thinking in networks" (or feedback loops)?

❑ What are the benefits of system thinking? How is it different from systems thinking?

❑ What is "outside in" planning?

THE ORGANIZATIONAL ELEMENTS MODEL

What analogy can we use to describe an organization? There are many different ones to choose from. There is the conventional organizational chart that describes an organization as a formal hierarchy. Alternately, there is a living community model that represents the organization as a naturalistic system. Last, there is a recent model that likens organizations to chaos.[1] We suggest that many of these could describe an organization at different periods of time and from the different perspectives of individuals within the organization.

One story that describes this multiple perspective of an organization is the familiar story of six blind men. When asked what they were experiencing when touching an elephant, they gave six different descriptions, because each was touching a different part of the elephant. They were confusing the parts (subsystems) with the whole. The perspective described in this book is a system perspective, a perspective of not just one organization or just the parts (subsystems) of an organization, but of society as a whole.[2] This perspective is best suited to achieving useful measurable performance improvement. Those who describe the organization by pointing to the traditional organizational chart will find the system model a different paradigm than a conventional systems perspective.

Why Are We Changing?

The process of strategic thinking, and resulting strategic change, is profound. It involves shifting our paradigms and asking the hard questions:

1. What are we changing? And what is staying the same?
2. What are we changing to?
3. Why are we changing?
4. How can we change effectively?
5. How can we measure whether change has occurred?
6. Is it the right change?
7. Have we improved performance and payoffs as a result of the change?
8. Was the change worthy enough to justify the effort?

The first questions require the *sponsors* (or champions) of change to agree on what it is they are changing and why, as well as distinguish what is not changing. This is fundamental.

Before deciding *what* to change, the sponsors require a shared destination, a shared language, and an explicit model of what they are intending to accomplish. If you believe in incremental improvement, you will have different ideas on improving society from those who believe in dramatic revolutions (see Sowell, 1987). We suggest that incrementalism usually is simply a way of denying a reality that changes. Incrementalism is like pulling an impacted wisdom tooth slowly. Sometimes a dramatic change is required *now,* instead of trying to make it happen piecemeal over time. Recall the changes to racism, sexism, and other discrimination—the issue is not the rate of elimination, but that they should be eliminated immediately.

Lol!

Our mental models of an organization will influence our attempts to improve its performance. If we bring science into our models, we can repeat successful improvements and continue to add value based on our successful "experiments" in change; we track our progress and revise as required whenever required. It is one thing to let chance or fate determine our successes. It is quite another to consistently replicate them. A systematic process of documenting our trials and errors—commonly referred to as "research"—is a necessary prerequisite for creating, changing, and innovating repeatedly.

why + how to create success

Applied Mental Models

Beliefs are those things we hold to be true despite evidence to the contrary.

Successful change management is built on sound planning. Since planning both "why to change" and "what results to achieve" requires an agreed-on paradigm, it makes good sense to define explicitly and precisely what the elements of our organization are and what it intends to deliver.

If we believe in incremental improvements, we will describe our destination in very limited terms. If we believe that a chart can best represent an organization, we will describe it in terms of the frames of a traditional hierarchical organizational chart. We bring many deep-rooted assumptions, strategies, tactics, and guiding ideas to whatever we do. We also use a pattern of language to describe what we believe. We share this common language with fellow believers.

We require mental models that are useful and aligned with high payoff results. When working with others to improve organizational performance, we should share a common language and meaning so that we can all agree on "what" we are changing, "where" we are heading, and "why" we are headed there.

The conventional hierarchical organization chart is, at best, a convenient fiction when it comes to mental models. We draw the charts for visitors, but all know that the organization doesn't report that way, doesn't communicate that way, and doesn't produce results that way. Actual reporting and responsibility links are usually networks that jump across the lines and boxes we usually see on an org chart. A newer mental model might portray an organization as a set of concentric circles with individuals and small groups in the center, with major organizational functions around that, immediate external clients surrounding the organization, and society encompassing all of these other "organizational elements." Such a chart would perhaps better show the interactive and interdependent relationships of the organization, along with an acknowledgment that society—as a single common denominator—is a system that encompasses all of our other systems.

The Organization Is Part of a System, Not the System Itself

System thinking[3] enables us to progress beyond simply seeing events as disjointed parts, and instead see patterns of interaction and the underlying structures that are responsible for the patterns. We can also see the purposes. What do we mean by a system?

A system is the sum total of parts, working independently and together, to achieve common results (Kaufman, 1972, 1992, 1998, 2000).

A system is composed of smaller (sub)systems that form a larger system. Each works independently and together. Usually, people who ignore the external client/societal focus of an organization start their planning and doing with one or more of the subsystems, but call each a "system." Thus the confusion between a *system* approach that is holistic and starts with a focus on Mega, and a *systems* approach that looks only at one or more of the *parts* of the overall system. Why is this important (and not just semantic quibbling)? Because simply dealing with the subsystems and not the whole system will deliver failure in the long term. It would be like exercising one part of your body, but not realizing that there are many more body subsystems that make up your health, vigor, and well-being.

The system we are examining in the book is a dynamic system—consisting of organizations and their external environments—with "the whole" being that of society. Subsystems include organizations, agencies, groups, and others who work together to achieve high payoff results—if we plan and deliver correctly.

The Organization Is Not on a Chart

"Everything should be made as simple as possible but not simpler."
—Einstein

System (not systems) thinking looks at the whole, and then the parts, as well as the relationship and connections among the parts. It is the opposite of reductionism (that is, the idea that something is simply the sum of its parts). After all, a collection of parts that are not connected is not a system.

So if our mental model of an organization is an organizational chart, we are ignoring the relationships—interactions—between the parts. We are overlooking what goes on behind or between the boxes (including those partners who are not often shown on the chart such as suppliers, clients, and society). If we think of the organization within society as a *system,* then the real action is happening in the *"white space"* of the organization chart (see Rummler & Brache, 1995). Of course, the organization-as-system mental model typically ignores external clients' and societal survival and well-being. It is not a system model, but a system*s* model.

Most contemporary (and conventional) planning models are of the organization-as-system model. It usually starts and stops with so-called "business needs" and leaves the external clients' well-being to chance.[4]

Unfortunately, the traditional organizational chart can result in silo (or stovepipe) thinking. (See Figure 3.1.) People attend to the parts and ignore or assume the whole. Doing so is a surefire way to get low payoff (or low impact) results.

Comparing a Heap to a System

Table 3.1 compares heaps and systems. The performance of a system depends on how the parts are connected and on how they relate. It also depends on achieving internal and external results that add value to the individuals and the organization, as well as the community. Have you ever seen a traditional organizational chart that includes society as a direct client? Perhaps they should.

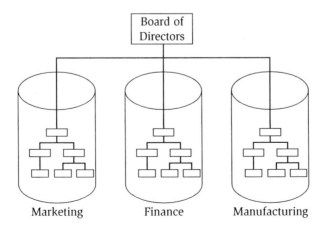

Figure 3.1. Functional Silos or Stovepipes.

Table 3.1. Heaps vs. Systems.

A Heap	A System
A collection of parts.	Interconnecting parts operating as a whole with a common purpose.
Essential properties are unchanged whether you add or take away pieces. When you halve a heap, you get two smaller heaps.	Changed if you take away pieces or add more pieces. If you cut a system in half, you do not get two smaller systems but a damaged system that will probably die.
The arrangement of the piles is irrelevant.	The arrangement of the pieces is crucial.
The parts are not related or connected and can operate separately.	The parts are connected and related and work together.
Its behavior (if any) depends on its size or on the number of pieces in the heap.	Its performance depends on the total structure. Change the structure and the performance changes.
Heaps don't have a purpose. They don't require a direction, and they normally stay in one place. "Do cemeteries move of their own accord?" Heaps are dead parts.	Living systems are purposeful. They have a reason for existing. They can grow and improve. When lacking direction and payoffs, they die. Their growth depends on the quality of the relationship between the parts.

The Silo Model

"As each function strives to meet its goals, it optimizes. . . . However this
functional optimization often contributes to the sub-optimization
of the organization as a whole."
—Rummler and Brache, 1995

The conventional organizational chart may look like the one in Figure 3.2. This vertical model sees the boxes as functions and each function as a separate part. The relationship between the functions is not emphasized. This model encourages a *silo* perspective. At best, units operate in isolation. At worst, units compete against each other. People operating within each focus solely on their own objectives and attempt to capture scarce organizational resources for themselves. Silos discourage people from relating to people in other silos. Any connection is limited to the managers of silos so that people at lower levels are prevented from working between functions to solve common problems. It can even demonstrate

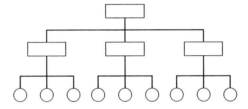

Figure 3.2. Traditional Organizational Chart.

bizarre behaviors . . . such as the leader of a silo directing all communication to be channeled through him or her before distribution to other members of the silo. This can result in what is called "trench warfare" between the different silos in the system. The trench dwellers hide away in their trenches, occasionally emerging to take pot shots at the colleagues (enemies) in the other trenches. This is not a characteristic of strategic or system thinking and planning.

The Organization as Part of a Dynamic System

When we think of the organization as a component of a dynamic (or living) system, adapting and contributing to its external world, we can describe it using the following language:

- Inputs (and conditions)
- Processes (including feedback—revise as required loops)
- Results at three levels: Outcomes, Outputs, Products (each related to levels of planning at the Mega, Macro, and Micro levels)
- Consequences and payoffs
- Customers/clients, internal and external
- Stakeholders, internal and external
- Value added and value subtracted

This language can apply to any organization or unit or part of it. More importantly, this language describes the various elements of the whole system.

If not presented this way, we have a *"mess"—heaps of unrelated things.* We have all of the subsystems tangling and the whole system being ignored. If we depict the *relationships* between these elements, we start to think both *systematically* and *systemically.* We have a useful description of a system if the whole focuses on Mega. We have to relate the parts with the whole, and the whole must be related to adding value for external clients and society—Mega. Consider the many systems that contribute to well-being. Drug interactions? Food allergies causing dizziness? The whole, as the sociologists (and increasingly health professionals) are telling us, is more than the simple sum of the parts.

One practical model for making sense of the many subsystems of the organization is the Organizational Elements Model or OEM (Kaufman, 1992, 1998, 2000; Kaufman, Watkins, & Leigh, 2001). The OEM identifies what an organization uses (Inputs), does (Processes), produces (Products), and delivers (Outputs) and the consequences (Outcomes) for external clients and society.

DEFINING THE ORGANIZATIONAL ELEMENTS

One goal of this book is to provide you with the principles for achieving high payoff results, along with a model and supporting tools to measurably improve the performance and contributions of your organization. We designed it to allow you to define, justify, and deliver useful results.

A successful system defines and demands results that link individuals, teams, and organizations to external clients and society. The language defines what it is we are intending to manage and change, as well as why. We will build the organizational elements one level at a time. These elements apply to all organizational subsystems—and together make a system. Our model is presented in Figures 3.3 and 3.4.

Results: Outcomes, Outputs, and Products

All dynamic (and "living") systems are purposeful. They produce results, ideally desired and useful ones. An organization produces three related but different types of results. These results, if planned and accomplished, meet the requirements of the organization's internal and external clients. Table 3.2 depicts these

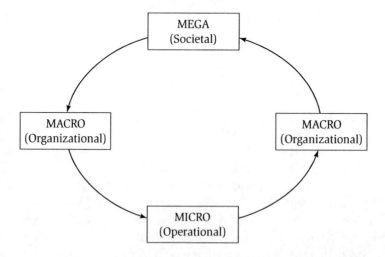

Figure 3.3. The Organizational Elements Model that Flows from Mega to Macro and Micro and then Rolls Up.

Table 3.2. Three Levels of Results.

Type of Result	Definition	Examples
OUTCOMES MEGA–level	The social impact and value added to society.	• Self-sufficient citizens. • Profit in the long term. • Zero disabilities from assaults or rapes. • Zero disabilities from car accidents.
OUTPUTS MACRO–level	Results delivered to external clients.	• Healthy patients discharged. • Delivered vehicle. • Graduate. • Clean water. • Safe road.
PRODUCTS MICRO–level	Results delivered to individuals or teams. Results delivered to internal customers.	• Demonstrated new competencies. • Documents. • A design plan. • Vehicle part.

Source: Organizational Elements Model (based on Kaufman, 1992, 1998, 2000).

three types of results and shows their relationship. All levels of results are part of any organization but unfortunately not all are planned explicitly. Indeed, some results may be negative (for example, the injury of a client; or a faulty tire that cause a car to crash, hurting not only the car's owner, but unlucky others as well).

These results, when planned proactively, are embedded in each other; in this way they can be aligned. Strategic thinking is concerned with planning and aligning these three levels of results to create a better world.

Results should be the focus of planning and doing. Defining and linking results at the Mega, Macro, and Micro levels is one of the critical success factors for strategic thinking and planning. By first describing the desired future at three levels of results (starting at Mega) we are then able to choose the most appropriate solutions and resources and are also capable of justifying their selection.

Results at each level are equally important. This is so important that we'll repeat it: results at each level are *equally* important. Mega is not more important than Micro, nor are those more important than Inputs. They all are equally important and must be linked if we are to be successful.

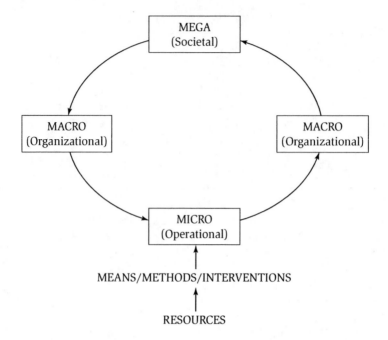

Figure 3.4. Rolling Down from Mega and Up to Align Resources, Means and Methods, Operational, Organizational, then Societal Results.

Source: From Kaufman, 1992, 1998, 2000.

We don't want to assume Mega results; we want to explicitly define and plan them. This is being proactive. We can't achieve Mega results without Macro and Micro results. And we cannot deliver any of those without Process and Inputs. To ignore any level of result is to risk leaving the accomplishment of useful high payoff results to chance.

Inputs (and Conditions)

The first element defined is *inputs*. This refers to those things that an organization requires to achieve its desired results. They are prerequisite starting conditions for an organization to accomplish useful results. To produce results, you require some categories of materials that you convert through a process into something of value to the internal and external customers or clients. Typical examples of inputs include:

- Client needs based on gaps between current and desired performance (not wants)
- Raw materials
- Human capital
- Information capital
- Financial capital

- Equipment
- Facilities
- Requests for proposals
- Laws, rules, regulations
- Products or outputs resulting from other processes
- Existing mores, folkways, beliefs, and values—the corporate culture

Inputs are the resources and requests available or required to produce results for your various customers or clients. They include the *conditions*—the range of internal and external influences (Table 3.3) that affect the use of Inputs and Processes used to accomplish results, as shown in Table 3.4.

Table 3.3. Internal and External Influences.

Internal	*External*
1. The culture of the organization	1. Government regulations
2. Policy and procedures	2. Technology
3. The Mental Models of your leaders, your client	3. Economic trends
4. The physical design and environment of work	4. Competitors
	5. New paradigms

Table 3.4. Examples of Processes.

Examples
• Business processes reengineering
• Customer engagement
• Order fulfillment
• Customer service
• Manufacturing
• Distribution
• Research
• Marketing
• Billing
• Strategic planning
• Performance management
• Information management
• Purchasing
• HR development
• Financial management

Process

"An organization is only as good as its processes."
—Rummler and Brache, 1995

Of course, the processes should deliver internal and external results that are useful. And without first specifying what those useful results are to be, it's unlikely that any process—no matter how "good"—will achieve useful results through chance alone.

The next variable that influences an organization or team performance is called a *process. A process is an end-to-end series or collection of activities that creates a result for a customer, internal and then external (including external clients and society).* A process is what we normally experience as "work." Processes are what the business does (or fails to do), not who performs the work.

A process must meet these six criteria:

1. Produces or manipulates data or physical materials.
2. Impacts (hopefully by adding value) to distinctive organizational results at all three levels.
3. Can be performed or influenced by one or more individuals or teams of people.
4. Is triggered (initiated) by one or more events or cues.
5. Consumes inputs—ingredients and raw materials—and transforms them into results.
6. Can be classified as primary or support, small or big, internal or external.

In summary, a process, including a business process, is a series of steps that translate Inputs into a result in the form of a Product, a result that can then be linked with other products to create an output for the organization and an outcome for external clients and society. Every organization has processes, as does every individual.

Process
A sequence of steps, tasks, or activities that converts Inputs into a result. A work process is a stream of activities that adds value to the Inputs by changing them or using them to produce something new.

In this book we focus on the "big" processes in an organization. The models apply equally well to any organization or personal process. These critical capabilities or processes are value streams that cross functional boundaries such as human resources or accounting processes. Strategic planning is a critical process because it creates the future for all clients, internal and external.

Feedback

System thinking and planning involves thinking and acting in wholes with related feedback loops and networks, rather than in parts, straight lines, or linear relationships. A system approach is not lock-step or linear. The levels of the Organizational Elements Model are all connected directly or indirectly. Like the waves from a pebble in a pond, a change ripples out to affect other parts of a system. In turn, these other parts will change, with this effect rippling back in turn to affect the original part. The original change then responds to that new influence, and so forth. Therefore, the influence comes back to the original part in a modified way, making a dynamic loop, not a one-way street. This idea is referred to as a *feedback loop*.

Feedback loops are like a circle of causality in which every element is both *cause* and *effect*—influenced by some and influencing others, so that every one of its effects, sooner or later, comes back. When you run, your muscles provide feedback to your brain so that you can control rate, balance, and pace.

Feedback is fundamental for any system—no feedback, no system. In this book we are usually focusing on human performance subsystems and how they must add value inside and outside the organization. While most of our work is with Inputs, Process, and Products, we must ensure that they all add value to Macro Outputs and Mega Outcomes. If they don't, you've got a dysfunctional organization.

Feedback
Information or data about performance of individuals, teams, or the whole organization and external clients and society related to inputs, process, or results which allows the system to change its performance to achieve desired results (Daniels, 1989).

Feedback is necessary but not a sufficient condition for accomplishing high payoff results. Feedback must be combined with useful consequences if practical change is to take place. A combination of feedback and positive reward (or reinforcement) is an established approach to improving performance.

Consider the example of an under-performing team. Management might leap intuitively to a training solution without conducting a needs assessment to define the performance gaps in measurable terms when, in fact, no skill gap exists and the team may have performed well in the past. Instead, a training course might be conducted. The trainers could measure the feelings of the team about the course. Not surprisingly, the team scored the course high on the "smile factor" questionnaire, since the course was fun and included river rafting, games, as well as stimulating lectures. This loop is shown in Figure 3.5.

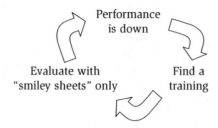

Figure 3.5. Jumping to Conclusions.

Yet, back at the workplace, performance often continues to deteriorate. The real change concerned new objectives expected of the teams. But often teams fail to commit to new objectives because their views and participation are neither sought nor obtained. In our example, the team had the skills to do the job, so training was inappropriate. They understood the objectives, so additional training and team building won't be likely to help.

The Organizational Elements Model feedback loop can (and should) occur at any step. Feedback helps us to stay on target. Without it, the results deteriorate.

Consequences

Contrary to the popular vernacular, consequences (as well as outcomes) can be positive or negative, depending on whether results do or do not add value to internal and external stakeholders. Consequences result from any process. We are concerned with linking and aligning the consequences that occur at the Mega, Macro, and Micro levels. For example, the consequences of delivering a high quality car to a client (Macro result) is that you get repeat business: she tells a friend and your client satisfaction ratings increase. A poor quality car could have negative consequences, such as a road accident—or pollution. The consequences of failing to provide frequent and specific feedback to workers is that people perform to minimum standards, or worse, they perform to the wrong standards.

Consequences must be planned; otherwise they are left to chance. In such cases you are likely to get what you don't want—negative consequences. By linking results at the three levels—Mega, Macro, Micro—we are influencing the consequences in a proactive way. Gilbert (1978, p. 179) showed that increasing the rate of specific feedback has a positive consequence. He pointed out that providing appropriate feedback to the right people never produces less than a 20 percent improvement in performance, often a 50 percent change, and sometimes improvements as high as six-fold.

Keep in mind that every behavior has a consequence. If you want to influence behavior, then plan and manage the consequences and link behavior to people, performance, and payoffs.

Customers (or Clients)

Customers are the people (that is, clients) to whom you deliver results. Physicians call them patients, consultants call them clients, retail stores call them customers, and the computing industry calls them users. In the Organizational Elements Model, each level of results has a corresponding set of customers or clients, as seen in Table 3.5.

This approach to categorizing clients answers a range of questions.

1. Who are the primary (and secondary) clients and beneficiaries of our work?

2. For what purpose(s) does the organization exist?

3. How are our internal and external customers aligned with social responsibilities?

4. Do organizations exist only to meet the desires of their employees? And shareholders?

5. Whose gaps in results (needs, not wants) should receive priority? Why?

6. Who are the primary beneficiaries of planning?

7. Is there only one bottom line—profit? Or are there two bottom lines— profit and positive social impact?

8. What are the different sorts of planning and whom do they benefit?

9. Are stakeholders clients?

10. What does it mean to be market and societal driven?

11. What is ethical for an organization?

From a system perspective, even if you limit your planning to the traditional level of planning results (Micro and/or Macro), your organization, for better or

Table 3.5. Types of Customers and Results.

Types of Customers (or Clients)	Types of Results
1. Individuals or small groups/teams within the organization	1. MICRO-level results; PRODUCTS
2. External clients and the organization itself.	2. MACRO-level results; OUTPUTS
3. Society as a customer.	3. MEGA-level results; OUTCOMES

worse, will have impact on society now and in the future. In short, better to plan for adding value to society, rather than getting sued for subtracting it.

System Thinking Summary

System thinking has emerged over the last several decades as an outgrowth of General System(s) Theory.[5] The organizational elements constitute a "living"/ dynamic system being a *"complex of interacting elements"* and their relationships in terms of adding value to internal and external stakeholders. In this book we frequently focus on human performance systems and how to change and improve them. The purpose of such intents is not casual: it is to measurably demonstrate internal and external value added in the short and long term (ten to thirty years and beyond). We continually focus on internal and external impact and consequences: human performance alone is worthless (and may be destructive) unless it adds value both internally and externally. Thus there must be a link between individual performance, organizational results, and external payoffs.

In Figure 3.6 are all the elements of the organizational elements model (OEM) and their relationships. This system model is a foundation for strategic thinking and planning and defines what we are dealing with when we plan to achieve high payoff results.

THE ORGANIZATIONAL ELEMENTS DESCRIBE A SYSTEM

If we plan and manage the system proactively to plan and create a better future now and in the long term we will start with planning Mega results with our partners.

Defining *What Is*

Table 3.6 is an example of a draft What Is analysis built around the Organizational Elements Model for a manufacturing company that produces tires for the automobile industry.

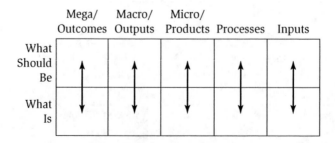

Figure 3.6. Interactions Among Organizational Elements.

Source: From Kaufman, 1992, 1998, 2000.

Table 3.6. Sample Application of OE Model.

Outcomes	Outputs	Products	Processes	Inputs (and Conditions)
Self-sufficient people who contribute	Assembled automobiles	Tire	Organization development	Customer demands and requests
Reduced or eliminated illness due to air pollution	Yearly auto production	Fender	Management techniques	Highly qualified employees (technical skills)
Reduced or eliminated fatalities	Automobiles sold	Production quota met	Manufacturing techniques	Mediocre leadership
Positive quality of life	System delivered	Completed training	Operation production line	Government acts and directives
No welfare recipients	Patient discharged	Trained workers	Training	Adequate equipment
Continued profit	Clients' success	Worker agreement	Reengineering	Adequate access to funds
Stockholder vote of confidence		Course completed	Curriculum	Profit-driven five-year strategic plan
Money for continuation		Operation completed	Quality improvement programs	Budget
Zero crime			Doing	Laws
Zero poverty			Learning	Policies
			Developing	Rules and regulations
			Strategic planning	Existing Products, Outputs, and Outcomes
			Strategic thinking	

EXERCISE—DEFINING *WHAT IS*

This exercise gives you an opportunity to practice a What Is assessment using the Organizational Elements Model. Reflect on your organization and fill in at least two items for each of the elements shown on Table 3.7. You can work with a colleague alone, or with a group. If you are uncertain of the specific figures for the results (Outcomes, Outputs, and Products) guess or insert a question mark (?). Ideally, after reading the remainder of the book you will be able to fill in these items.

Table 3.7. "What Is" Exercise.

Outcomes	Outputs	Products	Processes	Inputs (and Conditions)

The Organizational Elements and Their Relationships

The Organizational Elements Model is a framework for system thinking and planning. The relationship among the parts is critical when thinking about an organization as a subsystem within the larger system of our shared society. A primary goal of this book is to provide you with proven tools to achieve high payoff results. The proven value of system thinking is that it allows us to influence the future state of the system and its parts. It allows us to define, plan, and create a better system. It further allows us to influence our own development as a community and thus create a better world and a better organization for the next generations. Table 3.8 contains some examples.

Table 3.8. Descriptors and Examples.

	Descriptor	*Examples*
1	A system is an entity that maintains its existence and works as a whole through the interaction of its parts to achieve a result. The performance of the system depends on how the parts relate, rather than on the parts themselves. A system is purposeful and self-correcting based on performance feedback.	The organizational elements link, interact, and relate. If you want to manage a system, you must first plan the desired results, then manage the supporting elements to achieve the results. Living systems are purposeful—results define their purpose. Individuals are performance systems, teams are performance systems, as are organizations—all of which operate within a single societal system.
2	Systems form part of a larger system and are composed in turn of smaller systems.	The organization is part of a larger system, for example, a nation or a group of cultures such as the European Union. In turn the organization includes unit performance systems, team performance systems, and individual performance systems.

(Continued)

Table 3.8. Descriptors and Examples. (*Continued*)

	Descriptor	Examples
3	The properties of a system are the properties of the whole. None of the parts has them alone. The more complex the system, the more unpredictable are the properties of the whole system. These whole system properties can be considered *emergent* properties—they emerge when the whole system is working.	Here are some emergent properties: • life • emotions • mental models • music • culture • team morale • memories • dreams • pain You can't find these in the parts of the brain or body or team. They emerge out of the operation of the human system. Similarly, organizational culture emerges out of the working of the parts of the organization.
4	Breaking a whole system into its parts and identifying how the individual parts work independently and together is analysis. You gain insights by analysis. Building parts into wholes is synthesis. When you take a system apart and analyze it, it loses its properties. To understand a system you must look at the whole and determine how the parts function and what each contributes.	To attempt to reengineer organizational processes without first planning the desired results is to ignore the whole system and the relationship of its parts. To improve individual performance you must manage the implications of the whole organization and society. If you train someone but don't provide performance support, performance will deteriorate.
5	Detail complexity means there are a great number of different parts.	Large organizations have many critical processes that interact and influence each other whether we recognize it or not.
6	Dynamic complexity means there are a great number of possible connections between the parts because each part may have a number of different states.	Managing complex change involves assessing the readiness of each unit in the organization for change. Each unit may be at a different stage of readiness to achieve the new results.

Table 3.8. (*Continued*)

	Descriptor	Examples
7	Each part of the system—subsystem—may influence the whole system.	If your supplies are low quality, then no matter how advanced your technology you will have difficulty achieving best results. If you have highly skilled and motivated employees and your processes are poorly designed, you will get minimal results. The process always beats the performer.
8	When you change one element, there are always side effects.	If we increase the frequency and quality of the feedback to the right individual performers, then performance can improve at least 20 percent or more.
9	Human systems resist change; however, when they have enough pain from the existing system, dramatic change can occur.	Manage resistance during periods of profound change. The larger the change the greater the resistance unless there is prior buy-in from all stakeholders. The voice of resistance is a form of feedback. It may tell us a better way to leverage the change. Resistance is energy. It can be redirected into positive change.

Following are some of the benefits of system thinking and planning:

1. You will be able to gain influence over your own life by affecting the patterns that drive events. This means you will have more control over your health, your work, your work team, your finances, and your relationships. You move from being a victim to being a decision maker for your own future. You will become the master of change, not the victim of it. You are not likely to be caught unintentionally by the selfish or ignorant decisions of others.

2. You will have more effective ways of identifying, analyzing, assessing, and resolving performance problems at the various levels of organizational performance.

3. You will have a model for planning the future proactively by envisioning the results and their linkage at the Mega, Macro, and Micro levels.

4. You will have a model with scientific merit and shared language and meaning when talking about how to improve the organization or its parts.

5. You will know how to select appropriate solutions and interventions for improving the system that are clearly linked to measurable results that add value.

6. You will have the ability to identify the implications of changing one element of the system and thus better manage the consequences for the other parts of the system.

7. You will be able to align the Organizational Elements, including the three levels of results, so that you add value to every part of the system, including external clients and society.

8. You will be able to avoid rushing to fad solutions that may well add no value to the results desired—or even make things worse.

9. You will be able to reduce the risk of failure caused by only dealing with one part of the system in isolation from the other parts.

10. You will be able to identify priority needs based on gaps in results at the Mega, Macro, and Micro levels.

11. You will be able to respond to the new realities well by defining and delivering high payoff results and continue to deliver added value in the long term (ten to thirty years and beyond) to your various clients.

12. You will be able to demonstrate strategic thinking and planning skills that make a measurable difference because you are influencing and orchestrating all elements of the system. This is holistic and proactive strategic thinking. The primary focus is on external clients and society.[6] It is a competitive advantage. In fact, one indicator of your success in delivering high payoff results might be if others come to benchmark you and your organization.

13. Finally, you will be able to repeat and replicate effective performance at all organizational levels because you understand the cause-effect streams based on the relationships among the various elements of the system.[7]

Ask *"If I do this and accomplish it, what will that improve?"* Ask again and again. By doing so you will push yourself and others from a concern with only Inputs and Processes to the three levels of results: Mega, Macro, and Micro.

The Organizational Elements are a model of a system. They are not the system. As Bateson (2000) has stated, *"The map is not the territory,"* but it does help us to navigate the territory. The OEM framework is a practical and theoretically sound framework for strategic thinking and planning. It has been successfully applied almost worldwide. This approach has several advantages:

1. It ensures we consider all parts of the system and especially their relationship when planning to design a better future, based on linking results at three levels: Mega, Macro, and Micro.

2. It emphasizes the interaction between the parts. If you change one part every other part changes . . . for better or worse.

3. It emphasizes that before fixing gaps in resources, means, methods, and processes (quasi-needs) you must assess the gaps in results. And then prioritize these needs on the basis of the costs to meet the needs as compared to the costs of ignoring them.

THE ORGANIZATIONAL ELEMENTS—USEFUL APPLICATIONS

The OEM shows the relationship among the various organizational elements, plus the feedback loops, conditions, and consequences. What appears to be a maddening "mess" does have a methodical logic when we look behind and between elements of the traditional organizational chart.

The practicality of a system view is that it can be applied to any organization, any unit, any team, and any individual who wants to consciously create, design, plan, and deliver a better future. The model helps planners to distinguish between desired organizational results and the organizational efforts required to produce the results at three levels, Mega (Outcomes), Macro (Outputs), and Micro (Products).

PLANNING FROM A HELICOPTER VS. PLANNING FROM THE GROUND

If we plan from the "ground," we start with an "inside the organization" view in which the primary client is only the organization and we tend to limit our future focus to more of the same—we limit the future to the present paradigm, seeking only to make it better.

If we take a "helicopter" (or holistic) view, then we start outside of the organization and can better see society as a primary client. This encourages us to explore the new realities and to seek new paradigms that will add more value to all client groups. The helicopter view gives a wider perspective and more options for the future. This system view of change is the only way to best guarantee high payoff results. It is taking the "big picture" overview that does not get lost in details; it keeps us from being so busy looking at trees that we don't realize we're in a forest.

Notes

1. The writings of Margaret Wheatley (1992) on chaos theory, naturalistic systems, quantum mechanics, and physics explore ways of thinking about an organization

in more scientific ways. Realities change shape and meaning because of our relationships, and even if we plan the future we must still learn to deal with uncertainty. Newer thinking is moving toward "complexity theory" that overcomes some of the untenable assumptions of chaos theory (such as "everything is unpredictable," which of course, is a prediction).

2. Kaufman (2000) uses the word *society* as an inclusive term. It includes the immediate clients plus the communities (near and far) in which the immediate clients use the product or service. For example, a high-energy transmitter installed to give range to TV users might be placed close to a school, putting the schoolchildren at risk to potentially harmful high energy waves.

3. Senge (1990) again popularized systemic and system thinking and reintroduced the concept of the learning organization. (Garratt, 1994, wrote about learning organizations and noted the even earlier work of Argyris). However, five other systemic thinkers influenced the development of systemic thinking, including von Bertalanffy's open systems theory, Beer's organizational cybernetics, Ackoff's interactive planning, Checkland's soft systems approach, and Churchman's critical systemic thinking. In his writings, Kaufman has developed an integrated strategic planning plus model that emphasizes societal impact as the start point for system thinking applied to organizational performance. All these writers emphasize that we require planning approaches to deal with uncertainty, although there is common confusion of system and systems approaches.

4. Many contemporary models ask about and collect data on customer satisfaction and assume that is enough attention to external consequences. But a happy customer is not necessarily a well-served customer. In the extreme, drug pushers have very happy clients, as do those who sell other quick fixes such as training or fad models for organizational change.

5. See von Bertalanffy, 1968. Interestingly, and much to the confusion of readers, this author uses "system approach" and "systems approach" interchangeably. We wish he had not. Our reading of his work is that he was not altogether clear about societal results—Mega.

6. This is the basis for Strategic Planning Plus (Kaufman, 1992) that we now call "Mega Planning."

7. Richard Clark, a professor at the University of Southern California, refers to one-shot solutions that cannot be replicated as being a "craft."

CHAPTER FOUR

Preparing to Plan

Ensuring You Do the Right Thing and Not Simply Do Things Right

CHAPTER GOALS

By working though this chapter, you will be able to answer the following questions:

- ❑ Why strategic thinking and planning?
- ❑ What are the critical process steps in strategic planning?
- ❑ What are the key tasks in preparing to plan?
- ❑ Is your organization ready for strategic planning?
- ❑ What are the objectives of a sponsor's brief?
- ❑ What level of strategic planning is appropriate?
- ❑ What are the criteria for selecting members for the planning project team?
- ❑ Who are the clients of strategic planning?
- ❑ Why is Mega level planning the best place to start?
- ❑ What are the common barriers to strategic planning?
- ❑ What level of needs assessment is relevant?
- ❑ What data do we require and how will we collect it?
- ❑ What are the benefits of preparing to plan?
- ❑ Has your paradigm shifted to Mega level planning and why?

At this stage we hope that you have decided that strategic thinking and planning is better than relying on good luck (or bad habits) for designing and achieving a better future. Planning organizational success is complex because it should involve representatives from your partners, internal clients, external clients, and society. Before any major adventure, such as climbing a mountain, experts agree that there is a process of preparing to plan, including considering whether you should climb the mountain in the first place. This step mitigates the danger of rushing into action without thinking about implications, consequences, and potential scenarios. This preparatory step for strategic thinking and planning is critical to success. This chapter provides you with a series of checklists and guides to help you do this step well. Interestingly, the emphasis continues on useful results: it is more important, as Peter Drucker reminds us, to "do the right thing" rather than just doing things (whatever we are now doing) right. So we should focus on the ends (results)—useful and high payoff ones—before carrying out our processes better.

A Responsive Approach

Strategic planning is a dynamic and responsive process. But it is also a responsible approach. It is not a rigid lock-step approach because it does not always follow a fixed sequence. The steps presented in this chapter should therefore be treated as guidelines, not rules. However, to be dynamic and flexible does not imply that the planners can ignore any step. It means that all steps must be considered and completed at some time during the thinking and planning process.[1]

The readiness of the organization will have an influence on which steps have already been done and how well they have been done. As a change agent you will have to be patient and sensitive. Your sponsors (and/or clients) may not at first value the degree of rigor that you advocate, and they may just want to "get on with it" without a thorough Needs Assessment (or a results/impact basis for planning and doing). In the first few applications, the strategic planning process may be hesitant and slow but, like most new practices, the processes will get better with experience and appropriate feedback. The Strategic Planning Implementers Checklist below is designed to help you consider the human side of the change process.

Is the Change Strategic?

In Chapter One you learned to recognize the new realities. At the end of Chapter One you were provided a questionnaire to complete. The questionnaire helped you to assess whether the change you are considering is strategic, tactical, or operational. As part of this chapter, you should revisit your responses to that questionnaire. For change to be strategic it must be targeted at the societal value added level: at Mega. Other types of planning and doing are actually "tactical" or "operational." Does it make sense to do tactical or operational planning if it does not add value to the organization and to external stakeholders?

The Strategic Planning Implementers' Checklist

❑ Remember that one of the most painful things you can ask anyone (including yourself) to endure is change. Profound change elicits strong emotions. If it doesn't, then the change must indeed be trivial.

❑ Be attentive, objective, and caring. Listen—at first with your ears open and mouth shut, later with both functioning. Share the possibilities and positive consequences that can and will evolve. Don't be a bull in the china shop. Never accuse, never abuse, and never blame. Instead, use data for fixing, rewarding, and learning. Take the old approach of "Come, let us reason together."

❑ Get people away from the security of their offices and the built-in, run-and-hide excuses of being too busy to plan, having to answer phone calls or respond to memos, having to crank out the overdue report, putting out "fires." Go to a neutral area and break the ice before getting down to the realities of proactive planning.

❑ Realize that proactive planning often carries an implied (even if unintended) criticism of the current regime and approaches. State that possibility very early, and get it up on the table. Discuss the group's likely defense mechanisms and ways to circumvent them.

❑ Bring to everyone's attention that proactive planning is *their* tool, their opportunity to make the kind of contribution, individually and together, they really want to deliver. Show them how they, by using proactive planning, can be in control—the masters of change, not its victims.

❑ Ask, don't tell. Don't be accusatory in your questions. Such phrases as "Isn't it possible that . . ." or "I feel . . ." often reduce the possibility of sending an unspoken, unwittingly accusatory message.

❑ Be clear. Use the language of the group, but don't change meanings in order to have them accept you. Often people use words that are fuzzy or have too many alternative meanings. Don't water down the precision of your words and message or continually shift your meanings to fit with current biases. Doing so risks falling into the "We already do that" trap. Be precise, be comfortable, maintain rigor. Get common working definitions.

❑ Be patient. When people react, get defensive, start throwing off blame, or attack you, recognize and acknowledge their frustration. Listen actively.

❑ Don't affix blame on others (and don't claim all the credit yourself—even if it's deserved). Steer clear of the "we/they" divisions. Help others to envision new contributions, to set fresh horizons, and to reaffirm current useful purposes.

❑ Resistance is a likely and natural part of the learning process. Identify it and support the clients in openly expressing the resistance. Don't take it as a personal attack on you or your competence. Resistance is an emotional response to the challenge of stepping out of one's comfort zone. Remember that resistance is really a form of commitment—to old ways and means.

❑ Don't take it personally when you, the "messenger," are attacked. If you have followed the above guidelines, if you are without hidden agendas, and if you really do care about the people, organization, and community you are there to help, the right results and approach will evolve.

THE STRATEGIC PLANNING PROCESS

Formal strategic planning is a process. The process steps shown in Figure 4.1 provide a logic that still allows for responsive application.[2] We are concerned with the first step in this chapter.

Why Strategic Thinking and Planning?

In the previous chapters the rationale and logical foundation for strategic thinking and planning were built. New paradigms, new realities, and new research findings demand new responses; new problems can rarely be solved by the paradigms that created them. Key questions that should be asked and answered by planners if they are to commit to proactive thinking and planning follow.

Why Strategic Thinking and Planning?

1. What are the new realities of our business and world?
2. Am I satisfied with the results I deliver to our stakeholders and clients?
3. Am I committed to making a positive impact on society?
4. Do I want to create a better world for tomorrow's child?
5. Do I want to improve? Do I know how?
6. Do I want satisfied, happy, and contributing employees?
7. Do I want to increase my ROI?
8. Do I have a shared language and meaning about where I'm headed?
9. Do I have an explicit model for the strategic thinking and planning process?
10. Are my present practices (paradigms) working and will they still work tomorrow?
11. Do I want to stay ahead of my competitors?
12. Do I want my competition to benchmark us?

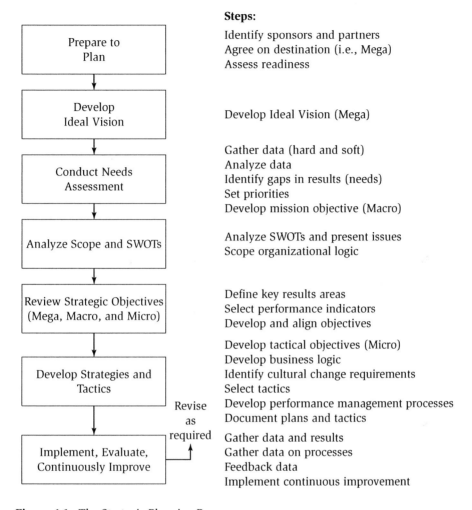

Steps:

Identify sponsors and partners
Agree on destination (i.e., Mega)
Assess readiness

Develop Ideal Vision (Mega)

Gather data (hard and soft)
Analyze data
Identify gaps in results (needs)
Set priorities
Develop mission objective (Macro)

Analyze SWOTs and present issues
Scope organizational logic

Define key results areas
Select performance indicators
Develop and align objectives

Develop tactical objectives (Micro)
Develop business logic
Identify cultural change requirements
Select tactics
Develop performance management processes
Document plans and tactics

Gather data and results
Gather data on processes
Feedback data
Implement continuous improvement

Figure 4.1. The Strategic Planning Process.

Who Is the Sponsor?

The sponsors are those who have the legitimate power as well as authority to initiate and support the strategic planning process. Usually the sponsors will include a CEO or board member of an organization (or their nonprofit/government/institutional equivalent). Because they are the sponsors and the planners, they should invite appropriate others to participate in the planning process. Involving important partners in planning will result in what Drucker calls *transfer of ownership*—transfer of owning the plan and its consequences from "me" to "us."

The preparation of the sponsors is dealt with in detail in Chapter Eight, Creating Change. The first set of questions the sponsors should address are those covered under the question: *"Why strategic thinking and planning?"*

What Questions to Ask First?

The sponsors of change work with the facilitators and change agents to answer the following questions:

Preparing to Plan

1. Why do we require strategic planning?
2. What results do we want to deliver to internal and external customers? To what extent are we currently delivering those results?
3. What data exists to tell us we require strategic planning?
4. Are we ready for this intervention? (See the Readiness Assessment Questionnaire in Table 4.1.)
5. At what level will we start—Mega (Ideal Vision), Macro, or Micro? Why is it vital to start at Mega?
6. Who will participate? How will we select project team members?
7. How will we gather data on needs (gaps in results)?
8. What time frames are realistic?
9. When will the planning team be briefed?
10. What resistance can we expect, and how will we manage it?
11. What are the implications of ignoring gaps in results?
12. What is our level of strategic thinking skills?
13. What process will we follow?
14. How ready is the planning team for change?

What Data Exist?

If your organization has already conducted a valid Needs Assessment (identifying gaps in results at the three levels of results) you may have data enough to go ahead. Recall, however, that most commonly so-called Needs Assessments will only have identified desired Processes and resources, not specified current and required results. This data, when available, is the evidence for making a decision to think and plan strategically. When not available already, then we must collect it in order to make rational decisions. Additionally, if the data is based only on gut feeling and intuition (that is, soft data), then this is insufficient to justify stepping into a strategic planning process.

Some entrepreneurs and small businesses have difficulty with this rigorous approach. However, this step is essential to future success in the long term unless the sponsors can live with the implications of moving on without sound evidence.

Are We Ready?

Strategic planning and the accomplishment of high payoff results requires a high level of commitment. It involves changing paradigms that can often require profound change by all those involved. Even if the sponsors are ready, there is a requirement to identify potential stakeholders who could sabotage the process. This step also requires the sponsors and facilitators to predict resistance and decide how it will be dealt with. Organizations, like individuals, must be ready to learn and to perform. Readiness is demonstrated through a strong "felt requirement," often accompanied by a high degree of discomfort with the status quo. This pain is an indication that expectations have changed and the status quo and present paradigm are no longer acceptable. Without clearly defined needs (gaps in results) there is no rational or emotional case for change. As Daryl Connor (1992) reminds us, reactive change is usually motivated by pain. True as this may be, recall that being reactive is only part of the change picture. We encourage you to be proactive and create change so that pain does not come to us in the first place.

The assessment of readiness helps to avoid the risk of failure. If the organization is not yet ready, then a planned "tutoring" program supported by a Needs Assessment process will be more appropriate, before commitment is achieved. A Readiness Assessment follows (Table 4.1). The sponsors and change facilitators should complete this questionnaire before deciding where to go next.

At this stage of the process, change agents have:

1. Identified a sponsor who wants to start the process of strategic planning.

2. Assessed the readiness of the organization for change (refer to Readiness Assessment).

3. The sponsor has agreed to the step of "preparing to plan" in more detail.

If the organization is not yet ready, the sponsors should prepare a "plan to plan." This plan addresses the items on the Readiness Assessment that received a "No" rating. This questionnaire is designed to help the sponsors and change agents assess the readiness of the organization for formal strategic planning. The scoring key and interpretation are in Table 4.2.

Table 4.1. Formal Strategic Planning Readiness Assessment.

	Item	No	Not Sure	Yes
1	The sponsor(s) have a shared perspective on the new realities (new paradigms).			
2	The sponsor(s) agree that the status quo is no longer acceptable.			
3	The sponsor(s) agree on the implications of not responding to the new realities.			
4	The sponsors recognize and accept that strategic thinking requires them to step out of their comfort zones.			
5	The sponsors agree that planning is first a process that designs future results and second that selects the methods and means to achieve the results.			
6	The sponsors recognize that a need is a gap in results, not a gap in resources or methods.			
7	The sponsors are committed to the long-term survival and sustainability of the community.			
8	The sponsors are committed to delivering worthwhile contributions to external clients *and* society.			
9	The sponsors are committed to delivering organizational contributions that have the quality desired by their *external* partners.			
10	The sponsors are committed to delivering internal results that have the quality desired and required by the *internal* partners.			
11	The sponsors are committed to proactive planning before reactive planning is required.			
12	The sponsors are committed to adding or deleting organizational objectives if the evidence supports the change.			
13	The sponsors are committed to the measurable improvement of all individual and team performance.			

Table 4.1. (*Continued*)

	Item	No	Not Sure	Yes
14	The sponsors are committed to the involvement of a representative range of planning partners.			
15	The sponsors are committed to selecting or designing efficient internal processes only after the results have been defined.			
16	The sponsors are committed to continuous improvement built on rigorous measurement and evaluation.			
17	The sponsors agree that evaluation data is to be used only for fixing and improving, not for blaming.			
18	The sponsors agree that single issue concerns will not be tolerated.			
	Total Scores			

Table 4.2. Scoring and Interpretation Sheet for Readiness Assessment.

Scoring Key and Interpretation	
Determine the total score by counting each "yes" response as 1 point. While neither "no" or "not sure" responses receive any points, each provides you different data: "not sure" responses indicate data that you don't know and should obtain prior to making a decision about your organization's readiness for strategic thinking and planning.	
High probability of success	13 to 18
Medium probability of success	8 to 12
Organization not yet ready	0 to 7

PREPARING TO PLAN

Critical Tasks

The detailed tasks of preparing to plan are listed as a checklist in Table 4.3. The sequence is not fixed, but all tasks should be completed before the project team starts its planning process.

You may wish to add further tasks to the list, but leaving any out will have negative consequences for the success of the strategic planning initiative.

Table 4.3. Checklist for Preparing to Plan.

Task	Person Responsible	Date Completed
❏ Identify and select sponsor(s)		
❏ Assess readiness		
❏ Brief sponsor(s)		
❏ Gain agreement to process		
❏ Select planning partners		
❏ Identify barriers and resistance		
❏ Commit to the Mega level of Needs Assessment		
❏ Decide on what data to collect		
❏ Decide on how to gather data		
❏ Select project team		
❏ Develop project plan		
❏ Communicate plans		
❏ Define time frames		
❏ Assess skill levels of planning team		
❏ Assess existing data on needs		
❏ Collect needs data		
❏ Reduce and analyze data		
❏ Identify needs		
❏ Prioritize needs		

Brief the Sponsors

This step can and typically should be repeated. Initially it could be done with the CEO (or chief officer) in the first meeting. It could then be repeated if the number of sponsors is expanded. It could also be conducted with boards of directors or councils, as well as the planning project team. A sponsor must demonstrate being a champion and being engaged in both the process and owning the results.

The following is a guide to the topics that are important for briefing sponsors/change champions and gaining their commitment to the process:

Sponsor's Briefing Guide

1. The new realities and the impact now and in the future. Implications of muddling on (Chapter One).
2. Why strategic thinking and planning (Chapters Two and Three).
3. Needs Assessment and what data already exists (Chapter Five).
4. Readiness for change (this chapter).
5. The process of strategic planning (Chapters Five, Six, and Seven).
6. The preparing to plan requirements (this chapter).
7. Cost and consequences (Chapter Nine).
8. The six critical success factors (Chapter Two).
9. Dealing with resistance and barriers (Chapters Eight and Nine).

Items from this list can be used to brief other planning partners.

Gain Agreement on the Process

In this step the sponsors are influenced to accept the critical steps of the strategic planning process. Gaining agreement on the process is essential before beginning any planning and assessment initiatives.

Select the Planning Level

There are three possible planning levels, each corresponding with a level of results and client group, as shown in Table 4.4.

Table 4.4. Three Planning Levels.

Level	Type of Result	Clients and Beneficiaries
Mega	Outcomes	Society and future citizens, including tomorrow's child
Macro	Outputs	Delivery to external clients
Micro	Products	Internal clients, both individuals and teams

You are thinking and planning strategically only when you begin planning at Mega and link all three levels of results. We urge Mega planning as the starting point because:

1. It demonstrates we are committed to the survival and improvement, and possible sustainability, of our customers and clients over the long term.

2. It shows we care about tomorrow's citizens, including tomorrow's children.

3. It ensures we align the Macro and Micro results with the high payoff results we want to accomplish. These linkages create synergies among all the elements of the organization because they are linked to a higher purpose at the Mega level. This is practical, holistic, system, and systemic thinking in action.

4. It increases the certainty that society will perceive your organization as adding long-term value. This is a distinct competitive edge compared to competitors who don't yet care about positive societal impact, or simply referring to it in fuzzy terms—while not delivering it in measurable terms.

5. It gives meaning to daily task performance because what people do can be linked to a Mega level Ideal Vision that has relevance today, tomorrow, and in the long term. From a system perspective, everyone has the potential to make a positive difference to their team, their organization, community, and society. (See Table 4.5.)

Select Planning Partners

Ideally, every organizational member should be invited to be a partner in planning the future. The higher the level of involvement, the higher the level of commitment by individuals. However, there are a number of alternatives for participation by relevant stakeholders. The alternatives are influenced by the type of organization, its size, the values and skills of its leaders, and the resources available. There are three human groups in planning: (1) executives/managers/leaders; (2) employees/associates (internal clients); and (3) external customers/society/community.

The human partner groups should be made up of people who are representative of the actual constituents. These partners provide perspectives and perceptions about reality as they experience and sense it. They also lend credibility to the process because they are seen as representative. Participation of groups may occur at various stages in the planning process, and not all partners have to be involved in every step.

Who Are the Clients?

"Who are the clients?" is a key question for all organizations. Initially, we often believe that we can easily define our clients, but a system perspective requires that we reexamine our old assumptions. Who are the primary beneficiaries of the planning and its consequences? Who are the secondary clients and beneficiaries (i.e., client's clients)? Figure 4.2 illustrates this concept.

Table 4.5. How to Discriminate the Planning Level.

Question	Planning Level	
Are you *uncertain* whether society and tomorrow's citizens will benefit in measurable terms from what you deliver? Do you want to be proactive and plan the difference?	Then choose to implement Mega level strategic planning. Develop (or ratify) an Ideal Vision. (Refer to Chapter Seven.) This is the only level that is strategic.	STRATEGIC
Are you *uncertain* whether you are delivering high quality and useful Outputs in measurable terms to your external clients and society? Do you want to?	Then choose to plan at the Macro level of tactical planning and link the results to the Ideal Vision.	TACTICAL
Are you *uncertain* about whether individuals and teams are turning out high quality and useful products for internal clients? Do you want to be certain that all add value to the organization and society?	Then choose Micro level operational planning and link the results to Macro and the Mega Ideal Vision	OPERATIONAL
Do you want to be holistic, systemic, systematic, and integrated in your planning?	Then start at the Mega level outside the organization and develop an Ideal Vision; then link Macro and Micro to the Mega.	INTEGRATIVE

There are many espoused values by managers, leaders, and politicians that sound good and have popular support, but they are not supported by measurable objectives or responsible action. After all, we are what we do and accomplish, not just what we say. Examples taken from public comments and glossy values charts hanging on the walls in the reception area include:

- "Client Focused"
- "High Quality Products"
- "Integrity"
- "World Class"

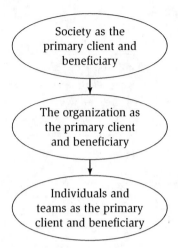

Figure 4.2. Categories of Clients (They Are Best Linked).

However, these espoused values get lost in the daily applied practice of what is really valued (and what is often really behind the slogans above):

- "Irrational decisions based on personal agendas"
- "Personal power"
- "Wants rather than needs"
- "Act first, think later"
- "Just give them more of whatever they want"
- "Find a good motivator to change their attitude"

If we define who the groups are that should benefit from the results of organizational undertakings, then this will influence how we approach planning the future and who should be involved. Three different planning orientations relate to who the basic clients are. Who benefits from the use of the plan:

1. The society and/or community that the organization serves.
2. The organizational itself (owners/shareholders).
3. Individuals, teams, and units within the organization.

When we proactively plan with all of society as the essential client, we include consideration of what is beneficial to the organization and individuals as well. This is also a positive approach to sensible globalization. By emphasizing that we being planning at the Mega level of results (planning for high payoff results), we are demonstrating practical societal responsibility, concern for the long-term survival of our organization, as well as concern for our grandchildren and tomorrow's citizens.

Large Scale Participation

One step of strategic planning suitable to large scale participation is Strategic Planning Step 2—Develop (or ratify) an Ideal Vision. Every citizen, in a sense, is a stakeholder in every organization if you believe that organizations should make a positive contribution to society. A large scale intervention is a method for involving the whole system, internal and external clients, in the strategic thinking and change process.[3]

Developing an Ideal Vision can incorporate many other organizational processes, including whole system change, large scale change, the Conference Model, Future Search, Work Out, Open Space Technology, Simu-Real, and Scenario Building.

Mega Level Intervention—Develop (or Modify, or Ratify) an Ideal Vision

This guidebook proposes a holistic and Mega level intervention that emphasizes linkages among the three levels of results. Other large scale interventions lack this results focused emphasis. The benefits of involving representatives of all three client groups in developing the Ideal Vision include:

1. Learning and paradigm busting occurs when people assemble to examine assumptions and are open to feedback (Argyris, 1982; Argyris & Schon, 1978).

2. Creating and designing an ideal world is an essential but often a daunting task, which no one person should sensibly define alone. Shared knowledge, purpose, and meaning comes from collective effort based on a common destination. This common destination is, in turn, based on the kind of world, in measurable terms, we want to help create for our collective future.

3. Everyone has a chance to influence the design and the achievement of a better future.

4. Positive emotions about a shared Ideal Vision can be elicited by skilled facilitators. This creates new expectations—the impossible becomes possible if we simply shift our mental models.

5. *Practical* empowerment can occur when representatives of all three stakeholder groups are brought to the discussion table. When facilitated, people are given equal "air time" and can have opportunities to influence decision making. Every voice can be heard.

6. The method speeds up the process of sharing perspectives and gaining commitment on common objectives (for example, most good citizens would like to create a world free of war and violence and other negative Outcomes of human activities). Many of the exercises found in this book and the companion CD can be useful in gaining commitment to the accomplishment of high payoff results.

MEGA LEVEL VISIONING: COMMITTING TO THE LONGEST VIEW

Busting Your Time Paradigm

Mega level planning is a step out of one's comfort zone for many planners. After all, many compensation systems are built around short-term wins based on cost cutting, quarterly profits, beating the competition, dominating market share, and/or increasing the short-term book value. Because of this short-term planning paradigm, many strategic planning approaches seldom plan beyond three to five years, and rarely accomplish high payoff results.

If we are habitually looking back, then we are either historians or poor planners. The short-term view of existence is demonstrated through the experience of the fellow who fell off the fifty-story skyscraper. He is reported to have said as he rocketed past the second floor "I'm OK so far."

Handling Complexity

Contemporary researchers have established a key relationship between long-term planning competencies and the ability to cope with complex tasks. It appears that the farther into the future one can visualize oneself functioning, the more competent one is at handling complexity, parallel processing, the juggling of multiple tasks, and coordinating performance.

A person's "time horizon" is defined as the maximum time span that a person can plan and execute specific, measurable, ongoing results focused activities. This "time horizon" is an indicator of a person's strategic thinking and planning potential. Horizons are continually outside of one's reach, but that does not prevent opportunity seekers from voyaging toward them. Those who commit to the possibility of the future require commitment in the long term, despite knowing full well that they may never realize their Ideal Vision. The shorter the time frame of planning, the more likely it is that you are dealing with non-strategic issues. Strategic thinkers, then, have a long-term mind-set.

Elliot Jaques,[4] a professor of social and management science, has spent many years studying the task complexity of leadership and management roles. His research indicates that one of the brain's most important mental models is its window on *time.*

If you determine what a person thinks about time, you can determine the extent of a person's work capacity, the kind of work he or she is suited to and how far into the future the person is capable of imagining and visioning. People who only think short term are unable to recognize the consequences and implications of their actions in the long term. In Jaques' (1989) book *The Requisite Organization,* he defines "time stratum" as the distance into the future that the person can see himself or herself committing to the development of objectives and the engagement of time and effort toward the accomplishment.

The implication of this is that there is a correlation between our ability to envision into the future and operate within it despite complexity.

Short View Implications

Here are some of the implications of restricting planning to the short view:

1. Limiting yourself or the planning team to the short view reduces the potential to explore new paradigms, possibilities, and/or research and to deliver high payoff results. The short view restricts the paradigm to more of the same. The danger here is of creating another "vision" just as restrictive as the old one.

2. If you concern yourself solely with the short view, then you only deal with the perceived realities of the present and past. In turn, you focus narrowly on existing responses and objectives. Such practices leave you vulnerable to becoming a victim of emerging realities and rapid changes.

3. Taking the short view can be perceived as irresponsible. You neglect society by refusing to attend to anything other than the here and now. "Who cares if people get injured by our products—it's not my responsibility to create a better world for tomorrow's citizens. They can solve their own problems." Short timers act with no thought to the long-term consequences of their actions—and as we've learned from dramatic examples in the energy trading and accounting industry, the results of this can be disastrous.

4. Short timers are liable to choose short-term objectives, methods, and means that could have an adverse effect on the long-term sustainability of their organizations. Short timers commonly rearrange the deck chairs on the Titanic instead of defining the right destination, course, and obstacles.

Assessing Your Time Span Commitment

Tables 4.7 and 4.8 provide exercises that will help you to assess your ability to commit to a long-term horizon. Table 4.9 provides some common mistakes. These exercises can also be used to assess potential team members for the Planning Project Team. These challenge the common short-term strategic planning paradigm that ignores the societal impact of an enterprise now and in the future. Read through the questions and then answer each one. Don't be surprised if these take you out of your comfort zone. Mega planning considers the achievement of high payoff results in the long-term future, as well as in the here and now. It incorporates the benefits of long-term planning with the shorter term Macro and Micro planning results. Table 4.6 summarizes the different levels of planning and results and emphasis that Mega is the only truly strategic level of planning.

Table 4.6. Planning Levels.

Level of Planning	Results	Time Frame
Mega Results delivered to society now and in the long term.	OUTCOME	STRATEGIC (10–30+ years)
Macro Results delivered to external clients that are beneficial to the organization.	OUTPUTS	TACTICAL (3–10 years)
Micro Results delivered to internal individuals and teams.	PRODUCTS	OPERATIONAL (6 months to 2 years)
Process Improvement	EFFICIENCY	OPERATIONAL (Today or next week)

The exercise in Table 4.7 is an opportunity for you to assess whether you have shifted your paradigm to a Mega, Macro, and Micro approach. We urge you to realize that these questions are ones that all organizations must consider and answer as part of preparing to plan.

At this stage, consider your commitment to answering these questions by placing a check (✓) in the appropriate column. You will assess your own commitment and the commitment of your colleagues.

Table 4.7. Assessing Your Paradigm.

Code	Questions	Self-Assessment			Assess Colleagues		
		No	Not Sure	Yes	No	Not Sure	Yes
1	Do you commit to deliver organizational results that add value for your external clients AND society?						
2	Do you commit to deliver organizational results that have the measurable quality required by your external clients?						

Table 4.7. (*Continued*)

Code	Questions	Self-Assessment			Assess Colleagues		
		No	Not Sure	Yes	No	Not Sure	Yes
3	Do you commit to produce internal results that have the measurable quality required by your internal partners? (Micro/products)						
4	Do you commit to having efficient internal processes?						
5	Do you commit to acquire quality human capital, information capital, and physical resources? (Inputs)						
6	Do you commit to evaluate: 6.1 How well you deliver Products, activities, methods, and procedures that have positive value and worth? (Process performance) 6.2 Whether the results defined by your objectives in measurable terms are achieved? (Evaluation/continuous improvement)						

EXERCISE—ASSESSING ORGANIZATIONAL COMMITMENT

This exercise is a continuation of the Readiness Assessments completed earlier. It provides a tool for assessing the commitment of your organization to the Mega level strategic thinking and planning paradigm:

1. Which of your internal and external clients can afford not to address each of the results formally? (This means identifying and dealing with each in measurable performance terms.)

Table 4.A. Addressing Levels of Planning: You and Your Organization.

Level of Planning and Type of Results	Can afford not to address formally and rigorously	Must address formally and rigorously
Mega (Outcomes)		
Macro (Outputs)		
Micro (Products)		
Processes (activities, means, methods)		
Inputs		
Continuous Improvement		

2. Which of the organizations that you interact with (airlines, grocery stores, and so forth) should not address these questions? Which would you prefer to address each level of planning and assessment formally?

Table 4.B. Addressing Levels of Planning: Other Organizations.

Level of Planning and Type of Results	Do not now address formally and rigorously	Must address formally and rigorously
Mega (Outcomes)		
Macro (Outputs)		
Micro (Products)		
Processes (activities, means, methods)		
Inputs		
Continuous Improvement		

3. What are the risks for starting at the Mega level?

4. What are the risks for not starting at the Mega level?

5. In what ways are you adding value to your organization? To your external clients? To your community? To society? What could you be doing and contributing?

Barriers and Resistance

Contingency planning is concerned with *"what if"* scenarios. Identifying barriers and resistance to change, like contingency planning, is practical, proactive, and makes good sense. The identification of barriers and resistance to change is best done during the preparing to plan stage. Resistance is the emotional response of people when faced with new paradigms (or new ways of doing and thinking). It is a natural response to new paradigms and requires each of us to step out of our comfort zone.[5]

Since resistance is an emotional response within a person, it may often not be a reflection of the rational, objective, and logical discussion taking place. Certainly, this does not make emotional resistance to change any less of a reality for those experiencing it. William Bridges reminds us in his seminal *Managing Transitions* that, while change is external to us and exists only situationally, our emotional readjustment to change—our transition from the old to the new— is intensely personal, and thus internal and psychological. We become more resilient—able to bounce back from external changes with minimal dysfunction—if we are open to the possibility of what could be, unhindered by the perceived impossibility of surmounting "What Is."

Barriers are those external events (for example, lack of skills or poor practices) that can contribute to the failure of the strategic planning process. Barriers and potential resistance points should be identified with the sponsors in this step so that they can be addressed and resolved.

Indicators of Resistance

It is important to be able to recognize the indicators of resistance so that you can develop tactics to deal with them. Here are the major expressions of resistance:

1. *Confusion.* Resistance can create a barrier to learning the change message. The change agents must repeat the message in different ways. People will process the message in different ways. This can take the form of inaction where the shock immobilizes people.

2. *Immediate Criticism.* Even when the "reason why" is well explained, people will often criticize the change because they are experiencing a range of feelings from distrust to anxiety to fear.

3. *Denial.* People can put their heads in the sand and deny the data that justifies the change. It is often easier to ignore the data about how bad it is, rather than face the fear of the future.

4. *Malicious Compliance.* People can smile and appear to go along with the delusions while hanging onto the past and "playing the game" of change without actually changing.

5. *Sabotage.* Overt sabotage is easy to identify. People take purposeful action to stop you from progressing. Of course, rarely is sabotage an overt act, making it all the more difficult to identify, discuss, and rectify.

6. *Easy Agreement.* People may not have sufficient information to challenge the logic of the change process. They may comply too early, only to discover later the implications for them. The "easy agreement" can turn to active resistance.

7. *Deflection.* People may talk about anything other than the change and its implications.

8. *Silence.* This is a difficult form of resistance because people are withholding from you what they think and feel.

9. *Anger.* When people feel threatened by change, they can experience intense anger. The shift from anger to sabotage is not a difficult one for many to justify.

10. *Depression.* Clinical depression is not usually triggered in organizational change, but it can occur. On the other hand, it is not uncommon for resistance to manifest as grief, and the sponsors of change must be ready to deal with it in a healthy way.

11. *Acceptance.* This involves facing and coping with the change. It does not necessarily mean people like the change, but rather that they are willing to recognize it as "the way things are now," and are open to the possibility of it making a positive difference in their lives.

ASSESSING RESISTANCE TO CHANGE

The exercise in Table 4.8 allows you to assess the frequency of these indicators in your organization during deep change. Resistance does not have to be bad; after all, it is a natural response. Instead, it should be identified and managed by being sensitive to peoples' feelings.

If your organization is undergoing deep change at present, assess the frequency of the resistance indicators occurring.

Deep Change

Deep change in an organization means change that involves all parts of the system, not just superficial increments, in delivering high payoff results. Deep change is profound change that involves significant paradigm shifts.[6] Kaufman and Lick (2000) define deep change as change that starts at the Mega level and then extends down through Macro, Micro, Processes, and Inputs. Deep change

Table 4.8. Assessing Resistance to Change.

	Resistance Indicators	Nil	Seldom	Sometimes	Often	High Frequency
1	Confusion—inaction					
2	Immediate criticism					
3	Denial					
4	Malicious compliance					
5	Sabotage					
6	Easy agreement					
7	Deflection					
8	Silence					
9	Anger					
10	Depression					
11	Acceptance					

is not just changing the furniture; it means moving to a completely new framework and reality that you have to design yourself.

BARRIERS—COMMON MISTAKES MADE BY STRATEGIC PLANNERS

Table 4.9 shows some examples of frequent mistakes made by strategic planners.

Commitment to the Mega level of Needs Assessment

Needs Assessment is the identification and prioritization of needs (gaps in results) for selection and elimination or reduction on the basis of costs to meet the needs versus the costs to ignore them. The level of planning chosen by the sponsors will influence the level of needs assessment data that is gathered. There are three levels of results and thus three levels of Needs Assessment, as shown in Table 4.10. After all needs are gaps between present results and desired results at three levels, Mega, Macro, and Micro.

The differences among these three are in degree not kind. In each the same assessment and data collection tasks are performed. The major difference is in the starting place and the type of data gathered.

Table 4.9. Common Mistakes.

Mistake	Description
1. Plan only at the team, unit, section, or project level and ignore the linkages between Mega, Macro, and Micro levels.	Organizations are required to be agile and responsive to the faster changing world or they will become extinct. If they don't plan to make a positive impact on society, and fail to change their paradigms for thinking and performing, they are assuming and hoping that what they do will add value. By planning and linking all three levels of results, they become the designers of change rather than the victims.
2. Prepare objectives for activities, means, and methods rather than results.	Objectives should be Smarter (see Chapter Seven). They should be measurable and written for results and include criteria for success. If we spend most of our time on processes, activities, and resources (quasi-needs), we are putting the methods cart before the expected results horse. Objectives must identify ends not means, methods, or resources.
3. Develop plans without participation from internal and external partners.	Although it appears quicker and easier to put a plan together with a small group, there is a strong likelihood that it will not be supported by those who made no contribution. The higher the level of participation, the higher the level of ownership and commitment.
4. Select solutions before defining the problem clearly and setting the desired state.	One of the most frequent management errors is the rush to solutions before clear definition of the problem and the desired state. Too often human performance problems are given the "pill" of training before the gap in results has been defined in measurable terms. Fadaholism is a frequent symptom of this error. The fad of rushing to process reengineering or downsizing has been estimated to fail at least 75 percent of the time.

Table 4.9. (*Continued*)

Mistake	Description
5. Spend time developing values statements before (or instead of) developing a results-oriented measurable Ideal Vision.	Many values prescriptions look the same as one's competition. Espousing values is seldom the same as practicing the values through action. By defining objectives at the Mega, Macro, and Micro levels then choosing appropriate means to achieve them, we show our true values in action. Beliefs and values are best considered in the context of an Ideal Vision. Then the individuals have the opportunity to re-think their beliefs and values in a societal results context.
6. Define and identify needs as gaps in resources, methods, or techniques. (Wants and Quasi-Needs)	When "*need*" is used as a verb (for example: • "We need more buildings." • "We need more money." • "We need more training."), you are selecting solutions that are not based on a rigorous diagnosis of the problem based on real needs. If you first identify gaps between present results and desired ones, true needs are then defined and you are in a better position to choose efficient and effective methods to meet the needs.
7. Ignore some of the steps in the strategic planning process.	Leaving out any of the critical steps will diminish the quality and value of the plan. There are ways of accelerating the process, but leaving out steps typically produces a flawed plan.
8. Assume that all strategic planning approaches are the same. Assume that the process is nothing more than common sense and intuition.	All models are not the same. Many are reactive and start at a low level or spend much time strategizing without having defined results at the three levels (Mega, Macro, Micro). Many approaches start with the decision to implement a new fad that is expected to be magic. These fads are seldom if ever preceded by a rigorous Needs Assessment.

(*Continued*)

Table 4.9. Common Mistakes. (*Continued*)

Mistake	Description
9. Conduct annual rituals of strategic planning but fail to think and act strategically throughout the year.	Many people think strategic planning and thinking takes place only at ritual retreats, induced by good wine and lectures that produce a glossy plan. This plan is then summarily ignored until the next annual ritual. Strategic thinking can be done any day of the week. It is the ability to identify and respond well to the daily new realities. It is about linking methods and means to desired results at the three levels—Mega, Macro, and Micro.
10. Focus on short-term profit planning while ignoring the new paradigms.	It is easy to be misled by short-term profit. It looks good and pays well, and any method is OK as long as the profits grow in the short term. The "Balanced Score Card Plus" (BSC+) paradigm (Kaufman & Forbes, 2002) and Mega level objectives are moves away from the profit-only measure of success. There are two bottom lines—profit and societal value added. The inclusion of Mega on any balanced score card is vital.
11. Use a planning process from last year and fail to challenge present assumptions, paradigms, and cultural norms. "Just do it the way we did last year." Don't challenge the planning process itself. Stay within your comfort zone.	The power of existing paradigms is that they screen out new paradigms, new realities, and new data. The present paradigms filter out other options. Our personal mental models and group paradigms are mostly unconscious. We often don't know what we don't know. Blissfully ignorant, we cruise along planning to solve tomorrow's problems with yesterday's paradigms. If yesterday's paradigms were so good, why do we still have people getting injured and killed by some organization's products? If given the opportunity, would we create the world like we have it today?

Table 4.10. Questions by Level of Result.

Level of Results	Key Questions
Mega (Outcomes)	What are the gaps in results in terms of our society? What impact of self-sufficiency? What impact of safety and security?
Macro (Outputs)	What are the gaps in results in terms of what your organization delivers to external clients? What are your levels of customer satisfaction? What are your short-term profit levels? What is your share/stock value? What are the levels of emitted toxic substances? What are the accident and disability rates of our Outputs?
Micro (Products)	What are the gaps in results in terms of what individuals and teams deliver to internal clients? What are your staff satisfaction levels? What are your wastage levels?

What Data?

The data gathered at each level of needs assessment can be "hard" or "soft." Hard data is about independently verifiable performance and specifies required results. Soft data is about opinions and perceptions and is characteristic of desired results. Here are some of the questions you will want to answer through the data:

Preparing to Plan—What Data?

1. What are our present results at the Mega level (Outcomes)?
2. What are our present results at the Macro level (Outputs)?
3. What are our present results at the Micro level (Products)?
4. What is the organizational culture?
5. What distinguishes our culture?
6. What are our present missions and our purpose?
7. What are the present customer satisfaction ratings?
8. What are our staff satisfaction ratings?
9. What are our stakeholders telling us?
10. What are our present financial results?
11. How is value added defined for our society (external/internal clients)/ community?

How to Collect the Data

There are ten major data gathering methods, shown below:

Major Data Collection Methods

1. Observation
2. Individual interviews
3. Group interviews
4. Literature/documents
5. Telephone interview
6. Questionnaire surveys
7. Criterion tests
8. Assessment centers
9. Critical incidents
10. Artifacts/work products

Choose from this list the most effective mix of methods for the level of needs you are assessing. For more information on these approaches, see Chapter Five.

Select the Project Team

The sponsors should select members for the project team that will produce the strategic planning documents. The criteria for selection to the project team should include:

1. Level of position power and authority.

2. Level of strategic thinking and planning skills and competencies.

3. Level of long-term commitment to the organization.

4. Level of technical expertise relevant to the core capabilities of the organization.

5. Level of authentic leadership skills and competencies.

6. Commitment to Mega and the accomplishment of high payoff results.

7. Open, with no hidden objectives or single issue agendas.

These are just some of the criteria for placement on a strategic planning project team. We believe strategic planning cannot be delegated to a strategic unit. It should be owned, practiced, and sponsored by the CEO, his or her selected team, and all other stakeholders (both internal and external).

The project team must define each member's role in terms of the unique contribution that each member can make. See the listing of possible roles below. A good team is comprised of players who play their own roles with distinction while avoiding the diminishment of others' roles.[7] In addition to this internal team, it is also critical to include representatives from the clients' organization or division, as well as members from the surrounding community in which organizational results are to be delivered.

The Nine Team Roles

- Plant
- Resource
- Investigator
- Coordinator
- Shaper
- Monitor–Evaluator
- Team Worker
- Implementer
- Completer
- Specialist

Tying Up Loose Ends

The following tasks complete the preparing to plan process. The sponsor could assign these tasks to appropriate people to complete.

1. Write the preparing to plan document.
2. Define the time frames and project schedule.
3. Communicate the plan to all partners in planning.
4. Conduct the Needs Assessment (including data collection and reporting).
5. Prepare venues and supporting resources.
6. Brief various groups of participants.

The Benefits of Preparing to Plan[8]

In summary, here are the benefits of preparing to plan:

1. A high level of commitment can be elicited early in the strategic thinking and planning process.
2. The possibility of failure is reduced by assessing the readiness of the organization instead of racing to resource allocation.
3. Shared meaning is achieved on the *script* before the director and actors start rehearsing.

4. The criteria for selecting project team members are agreed on early in the process. The sponsor starts with the *right* team to drive the process.

5. Realistic time expectations are set early in the process (often ten to twenty days in year one is realistic).

6. Coordination issues are identified early in the process, allowing all participants to plan their time. A realistic budget is allocated.

7. The risk of failure is reduced. Preparing to plan is a proactive step. The barriers and potential resistance can be identified early and contingency plans developed to deal with them.

Reminder:

If you can't plan on the basis of the parts of Mega, you commit to deliver and move ever closer to, you will likely not be successful or practical.

Notes

1. There may be shortcuts (although we don't recommend them), but first ensure that they work by evaluating your success or lack of it, and be prepared to revise as required. Sometimes quick-fix shortcuts are suggested to those who want to dodge the rigor of defining and delivering high payoff results. Beware of shortcuts.

2. Kaufman (2000) presents a variation to the steps presented in this book. The basic Kaufman model assumes the preparing to plan step has been completed. This book emphasizes the requirement to complete the preparing to plan stage before any other. They actually are both part of the starting step of "scoping."

3. Bunker and Alban (1997) describe the history of large group interventions and the concept of getting as many planners as possible in the same room to design and create a better world. Their book *Large Group Interventions* is a detailed examination of the various planning techniques. They emphasize process; we emphasize process is necessary, but unless the results desired are agreed then we can suffer from paralysis by process analysis.

4. For more detail on time perspectives and their influence on planning refer to *The Requisite Organization* by Jaques (1989).

5. Peter Block (2000), in his book *Flawless Consulting*, devotes a chapter to the subject of resistance.

6. The term "deep change" was first introduced in Kaufman and English's *Needs Assessment* (1979). Englewood Cliffs, NJ. Educational Technology Press.

7. Meredith (1995) has done extensive research on the roles that emerge in high performing teams. Teams that have nine discrete team member roles represented performed better than those with a narrow range of roles represented.

8. Preparing to plan is part of the first step in strategic planning. It is broken out here to show the importance of the steps suggested for planning.

CHAPTER FIVE

Assessing Needs

*Defining the Critical Gaps in Results . . . and
Putting Them in Priority Order*

CHAPTER GOALS

By working though this chapter, you will be able to answer the following questions:

- ❏ What is a valid need versus a want?
- ❏ Why is it important to distinguish between means and ends?
- ❏ What is a Needs Assessment?
- ❏ What are the three levels of Needs Assessment?
- ❏ What are quasi-needs?
- ❏ What is a problem and what is a strategic problem?
- ❏ What are the benefits of Needs Assessments?
- ❏ How do you use the OEM (Organizational Elements Model) structure for Needs Assessments?
- ❏ What are the critical steps of Needs Assessments?
- ❏ What is the difference between hard and soft data?
- ❏ What data gathering methods work?

❑ How does cause analysis point to the best solutions and interventions?

❑ How can you prioritize needs?

❑ What are the critical gaps in results?

NEEDS ASSESSMENT OR WANTS ASSESSMENT?

Have you read the newspaper or followed the news recently, especially after the following sorts of events?

- The CEO of a large corporation falls from grace and fails to increase shareholder value.
- The CFO of a large corporation fails to meet accounting and reporting standards.
- The sports team that many expected to win loses the final.
- An organization that many people purchased shares in collapses.
- Dangerous products are allowed to stay on the market, even though the organization is aware of the consequences to its clients.
- The political leader is discovered to have a hidden past.
- A teenager kills fellow students at school.
- A school principal receives low marks on the school's success factors.

What happens is that citizens become pundits at diagnosing the causes ("reasons why") and analyzing the contributing factors for the event. Sports team failures elicit high levels of diagnosis. In addition to high levels of analysis, we observe many solutions being prescribed to fix the perceived problem. These problem definitions, diagnoses, and solutions fill a lot of copy space, air time, and talk-back sessions.

Unfortunately, few informal diagnostics and well-meaning cause analyses have scientific merit. All too often individuals are blamed without any thought given to how to rectify the problem. This chapter gives you guidance on how to approach human performance problems and opportunities with a more proactive scientific approach through Needs Assessment and problem analysis. Effective Needs Assessment ensures that the right problem is clearly defined in measurable terms before appropriate solutions are selected. Defining and selecting the "right" problems are essential to delivering high payoff results.

DEFINING NEEDS AND WANTS

This one word, need, is critical to creating a better world. How we define the word, and then how we use it, is vital for defining and delivering high payoff results. Strong statement? We think not.

Needs are gaps in results—gaps between current results and desired results at three levels, Mega (Outcomes), Macro (Outputs), Micro (Products). (Kaufman, 2000)

If you want to solve any problem, it is important to get the language and precise definitions right. If we fail to define our terms, we will fail to communicate. Shared meaning about a significant problem, its causes and solutions is based on well-defined terms. Gilbert (1978) exhorted us to be scientific in our approach to solving human performance problems; he believed science is careful of its language.[1]

"What Should Be" indicates our desired result. "What Is" is defined by the data regarding the current status of those results. The *need* is thus the results gap between What Is and What Should Be.[2] (See Table 5.1 and Figure 5.1.) It is only sensible and rational to select our methods and solutions—our interventions and activities—after we have defined the desired result in measurable terms. To do otherwise is irresponsible, wasteful in resources, and too often fails to solve the

Table 5.1. Levels of Need.

Need Level	What Is?	What Should Be?
MEGA (Outcomes)	Two million die from famine annually	Zero deaths due to famine
MACRO (Outputs)	Wheat and barley production below U.N. levels for African states annually	Wheat and barley production at least achieves U.N. levels annually
MICRO (Products)	Communities growing techniques unable to produce annual gain quotas; Farmers do not have skills to maintain equipment, therefore 75 percent goes unused	Communities at least meet quotas; All farm equipment is required to meet quotas

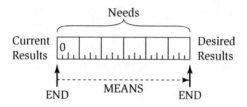

Figure 5.1. Gap Between Current and Desired Results.

Source: From Kaufman, 1992, 1998, 2000.

problem. And while we are defining our terms, *problems* are the gaps in results chosen for elimination or reduction. No *needs* (gaps in results), no *problems*.

Wants

Wants are solutions—including resources, methods, procedures, and activities—that may have been selected before the problem has been clearly and precisely defined. By confusing wants and needs, we will likely get locked into one solution and ignore potential alternatives. See Table 5.2 for some differences.

When a person says, "I want," we often ask the question "Why?" Yet, when a person says, "I need," we commonly assume that he or she has identified the best solution for the problem (although it is rarely the case). Sometimes a person uses the word want to imply a need. This is not simply semantics, but important differentiations between ends and means, between wants and needs.

However, if we confuse preferred solutions, means, and methods with desired closure of gaps in results, we are at risk of "fadaholism," which is the most frequent waste of money and resources in many organizations. "Fadaholism" is

Table 5.2. Confusing Wants and Needs.

Wants Stated as "Needs"	Needs
We "need" more training.	Increase my leadership ratings by at least five points.
We "need" more police on the beat.	Decrease petty crime to zero from one per three hundred citizens.
We "need" more F16 fighter jets.	Decrease the incidence of cross border incursions to zero from three hundred per month.
I "need" a new family vehicle.	Provide a vehicle that doesn't break down from one that is inoperable three times a month.

the serious error of leaping to a solution before defining the problem in rigorous terms or labeling a solution as "a need" when it is a method looking for a problem.

Identify the need in the list in Table 5.3 below by placing a check in the appropriate column.

Table 5.3. What Are the Actual Needs?

We Want	Means and Methods	Results and Ends
1 Self-directed teams		
2 Empowerment for our people		
3 Process reengineering		
4 Systems thinking and the learning organization		
5 To reduce youth suicides to zero		
6 Situational Leadership training		
7 Open Book management		
8 Knowledge organization		

Potential for Confusion Between Means and Ends

When we use the word need as a verb, we ignore other solution possibilities and means, thus restricting ourselves to a solution that may not be the best one or the right one to achieve the desired result (end). This type of behavior is a good way to avoid delivering high payoff results.

Consider the case of the city in which there was a strong political lobby to build another bridge across a harbor. This received strong emotional support from many uninformed citizens and politicians who frequently stated, "We 'need' another bridge." Was the proposed bridge really a want? Roads were congested, traffic jams were frequent, and road rage had increased. The true requirement was the reduction of safe transit time from its current to desired levels (this related the perceived problem to economic as well as personal quality of life). Racing to the new bridge solution by calling it a "need" when it was just one of a number of options, cost the citizens hundreds of millions (and possibly billions when projected over time and what else could have been done with the money) and didn't solve the problem.

Other options included:

1. Build a tunnel.

2. Increase ferry facilities and resources.

3. Limit personal cars to defined zones.

4. Build a rail bridge.

5. Improve public transport resources.

6. Increase use of home offices.

The habit of using *"need"* as a verb to prescribe one single solution is widespread. The use of the word is meant to make our wants, wishes, and biased solutions sound important. We often use "need" as a verb or in a verb sense, and jump from unwarranted assumptions to foregone conclusions. Here are more examples: "We 'need' more computers." "We 'need' more money." "We 'need' to get a positive audit report this year . . . or else." "We 'need' more teachers." "We 'need' fewer teachers." "We 'need' more sex and drug education." "We 'need' to restructure health care." "We 'need' more aircraft carriers for defense." "We 'need' more money for youth at risk." "We 'need' more social welfare funds." "We 'need' to improve schools." "We 'need' more gun control." "We 'need' to eliminate gun control."

These are all examples of potential methods to meet (assumed) real needs (that is, gaps in results). Yet they are not the needs. They are often biased solutions chosen before the desired results had been defined and agreed upon.

Needs Assessment—A Definition

Needs Assessment is the process for identifying and prioritizing needs for selection, elimination, or reduction on the basis of the costs to meet the needs versus the costs to ignore them (Kaufman, 1998, 2000; Kaufman, Watkins, & Leigh, 2001). Needs Assessment is an essential process that is closely tied to pragmatic strategic thinking and planning process. The process includes:

1. Gathering data on gaps in results at three results levels, Mega, Macro, and Micro.

2. Analyzing and interpreting the data and defining the implications of ignoring the gaps in results.

3. Selecting which gaps have the highest priority.

4. Linking the needs to higher level results by answering the question "If I fix this (Micro) need what impact will it have on Macro and Mega needs?"

Quasi-Needs

A quasi-need is defined as a gap in methods or a gap in resources, not a gap in results (Kaufman, 1998, 2000; Kaufman, Watkins, & Leigh, 2001). Common examples of quasi-needs are shown below.

Frequent Quasi-Needs

- We have to have more training to . . .
- We must get more computers for classrooms.
- We require more effective buildings.
- We should have more speed cameras to lower the road toll.
- We require more drug and alcohol programs for youth at risk.
- We have to hire XYZ consulting firm to . . .

If you are saddled with a quasi-need by an enthusiastic "fadaholic," keep repeating the key question suggested by point 4 above: "If we applied this solution, what results would we get in measurable terms?"

Repeat this question until specific results has been identified at all three levels of results. Table 5.4 below identifies how the questions we ask differ when considering needs from quasi-needs.

Table 5.4. Different Questions to Ask.

		Key Questions
Needs	Mega Results (Outcomes)	Am I concerned with closing the gaps in results (needs) related to the impact that my organization makes on society and the improvement or sustainability of the planet?
	Macro Results (Outputs)	Am I concerned with closing the gaps in results in client satisfaction related to the quality of what I deliver to immediate clients?
	Micro Results (Products)	Am I concerned with closing the gaps in results related to the quality of what teams and individuals deliver to internal clients?
Quasi-Needs	Processes	Am I concerned with the gaps in process performance and the quality of resources available?
	Inputs	Am I concerned with the gaps in availability and or quality of the resources used?

A Word on "Training Needs Assessments"

The implication of defining need as a gap in results is that it renders the term "training needs assessment" as inappropriate (Triner, Greenberry, & Watkins, 1996). Training is one of many solutions (a method, means, or process) for fixing (closing) a performance gap. Training is not a gap in results; it is one of several possible solutions to a specific performance gap caused by a lack of skills, knowledge, abilities, and/or attitudes. When an individual is unable to achieve the desired results (objectives) of the role and the cause is proven to be due to a skill gap, then the sensible solution could be training. The process for analyzing performance gaps that can be fixed by training is better called a *Training Requirements Analysis*. Of course, those performance gaps would have to be first identified through a Needs Assessment.

Problems (and Opportunities)

A "problem" is simply a need selected for closure or reduction. Just as a machine is not a problem until there is a measurable variance between its present performance and the performance defined by its specifications, a "problem" does not exist until there is a results gap (a need) that is selected for reduction or elimination.

A problem can be defined as any situation in which it is decided that a gap in results should be closed between What Is and What Should Be. If current and required results are identical, then no problem exists, other than the maintenance of existing results. In this book we define a problem as a need that has been selected for reduction or elimination. A Needs Assessment should be the first step in any problem identification and solving process. If it is not, where then should objectives come from? A Needs Assessment provides the rigorous basis for objectives.

The following preconditions must exist to begin the problem solving process.

Problem Solving Preconditions

- The existence of a results gap (need) between What Is and What Should Be.
- A recognition that a gap in results exists.
- The desire to decrease or eliminate the gap.
- An ability to measure the size of the gap and the implications of ignoring it.

If any one of these conditions is absent, then the problem solving effort may be neither justified nor successful. Needs Assessment, then, is critical to effective problem solving and decision making. It ensures the problem is defined in measurable terms and that the implications of ignoring the problem are explicitly examined as part of the decision process. A detailed problem solving process is introduced later in this chapter.

Defining Need Precisely

To be precise, a *need* is only the documented gap between current and desired/required results. It is a gap in results, not a gap in resources, methods, or solutions. When we state a purpose, such as "We shall reduce the water pollution levels," there is an assumption that a costs-consequences prioritization has been completed and the need has been selected for resolution. Setting priorities for needs on the basis of the costs to meet the needs as compared to the costs to ignore them helps make cost-efficient and cost–effective decisions about which needs to be resolved first.

Discriminating Needs from Wants, Wishes, Methods, Means, and Fads

The exercise in Table 5.5 gives you practice at discriminating some common fads and means statements from needs statements. To gain a check (✓) in the third column the statement must be measurable, clearly identify a gap in end results, and not include a means. After you have completed the exercise, check your answers with those given in Table 5.6.

Table 5.5. Differentiating Needs from Wants.

	Statements (Unedited)	Not Sure	A Want	A Need
1	We "need" a larger army.			
2	We "need" more values based educational programs.			
3	We want to reduce deaths due to unclean water to zero by 2020 from thirteen per year.			
4	We want more scenic roads.			
5	We "need" more speed detection devices on main roads.			
6	We want faster trains between major cities.			
7	We especially "need" more leadership training.			
8	We "need" more computer networks.			
9	We want to reduce burglaries in our town by at least 75 percent over the next year from a current level of 2.5/week.			
10	We "need" to implement the process reengineering plan by the end of the year.			
11	We want to lift our customer satisfaction ratings currently 84 percent by at least 5 points by 2005 to 89 percent or beyond.			

(Continued)

Table 5.5. Differentiating Needs from Wants. (*Continued*)

	Statements (Unedited)	Not Sure	A Want	A Need
12	We commit to reduce accidents due to machine defects to zero by the year 2044 AD.			
13	We "need" to implement the *learning organization* tactic to improve our culture significantly.			
14	We "need" to restructure the organization to improve our performance.			
15	We must introduce self-managed work teams to support our team.			
16	We must introduce a balanced score card to our measurement approach.			
17	We should reduce the water pollution levels, currently two million, to levels defined by the water council by 2005.			
18	All team leaders should achieve at least 75 percent of their Smarter objectives from a present average of 37 percent.			
19	We "need" more technically competent staff.			

Table 5.6. Answers to Exercise.

Code	Statements	Answer
1	We "need" a larger army.	This is a means. Why is a larger army required? What result would be achieved? What is the problem that a larger army will fix? This is a want proposed as a solution, but it is not an end.
2	We "need" more values based educational programs.	This is a want, a possible solution to an undefined problem. It is not a result. What is the desired result expected from values based education? What result will be increased or decreased by introducing values based education?
3	We want to reduce deaths due to unclean water to zero by 2020 from thirteen per year.	This is a clear definition in measurable terms of a need. This is a need even though the word "want" is used. This adds value to society. This identifies a gap in results.

Table 5.6. (*Continued*)

Code	Statements	Answer
4	We want more scenic roads.	This is a want, a potential solution to a problem. This is a means without an end attached, and even falls short of specifying "how many" more roads are desired. This is not a need.
5	We "need" more speed detection devices on main roads.	This statement is not a result. This is a means. In one state, this solution was introduced at great expense and removed two years later because it failed to achieve any measurable results.
6	We want faster trains between major cities.	Why? What is the desired result? This is a means not an end.
7	We especially "need" more leadership training.	This is a solution to an unstated problem. It is not a need. Training is a common solution stated as a need. The term Training Requirements Analysis is better than Training Needs Assessment because training is not a gap in results, but is a solution to one type of gap in results—a skill gap.
8	We "need" more computer networks.	Why? This is not a result; it is a method to achieve an unspecified result. This is a want rather than a gap in results.
9	We want to reduce burglaries in our town by at least 75 percent over the next year from a current level of 2.5/week.	This is a need, although it uses the word "want." This defines a result in measurable terms using explicit measurement criteria.
10	We "need" to implement the process reengineering plan by the end of the year.	This is a want, a means, a method. 75 percent of process reengineering projects fail. This is a potential fad looking for a problem. What is the result the method hopes to achieve?
11	We want to lift our customer satisfaction ratings, currently 84 percent, by at least 5 points by 2005 to 89 percent or beyond.	This is a need stated in measurable terms. Although the word "want" is used, it describes a result. But it's reasonable to additionally ask why only 5 points?

(Continued)

Table 5.6. Answers to Exercise. (*Continued*)

Code	Statements	Answer
12	We commit to reduce accidents due to machine defects to zero by the year 2044 AD.	This is a need. It defines a desired end result.
13	We "need" to implement the *learning organization* tactic to improve our culture significantly.	This is a tricky one. The first statement is a want, a method, a means. The part about improving culture could relate to a need if it was defined in measurable terms.
14	We "need" to restructure the organization to improve our performance.	This is a method, a means not a need. What result will be accomplished through restructuring? What is the problem that the restructuring "pill" is expected to fix?
15	We must introduce self-managed work teams to support our team.	This is another fad proposed strongly as a need. It is a method looking for a result. By linking it to a strategy, the proposer is hoping to have the one solution accepted.
16	We must introduce a balanced scorecard to our measurement approach.	Another "must" proposed as a need. It is not a need. It is a means to an unspecified result.
17	We should reduce the water pollution levels, currently two million, to levels defined by the water council by 2005.	Although the word "should" is more often a want, in this case it is a need. Why? The result implies that a precise measure is available. A water treatment plant would have this as a Macro-level need.
18	All team leaders should achieve at least 75 percent of their Smarter objectives from a present average of 37 percent.	This is a need. It measurably describes the results to be accomplished in terms of What Is and What Should Be.
19	We "need" more technically competent staff.	With some word crafting and performance data, this could be developed into a need for an HR department. However, at present we should ask the question "why?" What problem will be solved by having more technically competent staff? At present this is a means not an end.

NEEDS ASSESSMENT BENEFITS

Based on the previous discussion, you should now be able to recognize the difference between needs and wants, results (ends) and methods (means)—tools and interventions. You are now better prepared to understand the potential benefits of Needs Assessments and the implications of ignoring the process.

Why Do Needs Assessments?[3]

There are a number of compelling reasons for conducting an effective Needs Assessment. We'll consider several of these below. Some of the reasons will apply to the level of results being addressed: Mega, Macro, or Micro.

The Right Solution. Needs Assessments define problems (selected needs) and state them in measurable performance terms. Based on these gaps, priorities are derived on the basis of the costs to meet the needs, as compared to the costs to ignore them. Doing so ensures that the right solution will be selected for the right problem. Too often solutions are selected before the actual problem has been defined. The major implications of ignoring Needs Assessments include: the underlying problem doesn't get solved; money and human resources are wasted; and people become frustrated and performance continues to deteriorate.

Clear Direction. Needs Assessments bring rigor to the identification and solving of organizational and human performance problems related to strategic, tactical, and operational directions. Needs Assessments help to get shared meaning on direction and the means to get to the destination on the basis of empirical evidence.

Proactive. Needs Assessments are the foundation for proactive planning. If we stay reactive we will become the victims of change. Rather than react to crisis (and resulting "pain" and "presenting symptoms") and rapidly changing situations, we can choose to create What Should Be. If a gap exists or is emerging, we can preempt the barriers to success and plan to overcome them. Similarly, we can seek the opportunities arising out of new paradigms and take action to realize the opportunities to create and accomplish high payoff results. Designing future results that define What Should Be is a function of proactive Needs Assessment. Using Needs Assessments at the Mega, Macro, and Micro levels allow you to participate in "change creation" and not always be in "change management" mode. *Change creation* is a proactive approach that allows you and other stakeholders to define the world and organization you all want to create rather than simply reacting to imposed change (Kaufman & Lick, 2000).

Shared Commitment. When people are expected to display high levels of commitment about future direction, it is critical that there is shared meaning about where they are headed, why they want to get there, how to tell when they have arrived, and how they will best get there. Needs Assessments develop data-based shared meaning and commitment to useful results.

Conflict Resolution. On the road to shared commitment, all organizations, teams, and communities have conflicts over future direction, allocation of resources, and methods and means. Needs Assessments ask the critical questions that help to resolve these conflicts. The following questions clarify what the priorities should be.

Questions to Identify and Resolve Conflicts

- Do we want to design a better world for our future children?
- What would a better world look like? How would we measure it?
- What business are we in? Who are our clients? Who benefits?
- What is our primary mission or purpose? How does it add value to tomorrow's child?
- How do we add value?
- What results do we want to deliver to our immediate clients?
- What levels of satisfaction would we like for our employees?
- What are the critical gaps in our performance?
- How can we agree on how to improve performance?
- What should we change and why?
- What resources should we allocate?
- Can we agree on our priorities?
- Can we get beyond our current beliefs and values?

Costs of Poor Performance. Poor performance can have multiple negative consequences, for example, lost clients, decreased profits, low morale, increased staff turnover, or reduced share values. These decreases in desired results can continue unless the right solutions are selected and implemented. When the gaps in results are serious, wrong solution(s) continue the spiral of poor performance. Needs Assessments, when using the definition of "need" as a gap in results, provides the data for calculating the costs of ignoring the problem versus the value of resolving it. Serious problems require valid estimates of costs and the value added of fixing the problems as compared to ignoring it.

Most cost-analysis models only compare costs with results for Processes, Products, and sometimes Outputs. With our suggested definition of need, one may also estimate costs and consequences for delivering versus ignoring Outcomes (Kaufman & Watkins, 1996; Kaufman, Watkins, & Sims, 1997; Muir,

Watkins, Kaufman, & Leigh, 1998). Estimates of return on investment for defining and delivering high payoff results are important. Increasingly, we must prove the value of what we used, did, produced, and delivered in terms of returns to external clients and to the organization.

Proposal Acceptance Rate. If you are in a role where you have to seek funds and resources to meet needs, solve problems, and seize opportunities, then Needs Assessments increase the probability that your proposals will be accepted and funded. Needs Assessments produce the requisite evidence to justify a proposal. They also avoid getting locked into one solution prematurely, since they allow for committing to accomplishing required results, rather than committing to one particular ways or means.

By using "Need" as a gap in results there is a triple payoff: (1) The What Should Be dimension provides the performance specifications (objectives) for planned change; (2) The What Should Be dimension provides all required criteria for evaluation and continuous improvement; and (3) Data are available to justify both the cost to meet the need as well as the cost to ignore it. With both costs computed, anyone rejecting the proposal would then "own" the consequences for non-support.

Define Priority Gaps. Most organizations have multiple gaps in results. However, not all are equally important. Needs Assessments help to clarify which gaps really matter by examining the costs of meeting the need versus the costs of ignoring them. This is accomplished by sorting needs in priority order based on these costs and consequences. The important gaps can then be selected for needs analysis and *causal analysis* that identify why the gap exists and that in turn assists in selecting the most appropriate solutions.

Reduce Confusion. Organizations are complex. They produce large amounts of information about performance. Everyone in the organization has an opinion about what is going on and how well the organization or part is performing. Part of this confusion is the confounding of ends and means, results and methods, problems and solutions. Needs Assessments cut through the confusion by producing results-referenced evidence to highlight What Is versus What Should Be. We can replace confusion with agreement and acceptance, resulting in greater effectiveness and efficiency. And demonstrate useful results.

Ethical. The three suggested levels of Needs Assessments are linked so that if you choose a "fad" solution to a Micro problem, there will be a ripple effect on Macro and Mega results. This ripple may come back to attack the decision maker who made a poor decision. A business that intentionally pollutes a river because of the costs to install a filtration system will suffer in the long term because society will often receive reparations when such wrongdoing is discovered. The consequences in the future will be more often the extinction of the organization, because it is damaging society as a client. Needs Assessments force organizations to face the positive and negative consequences of their short-term solutions and include a consideration of long-term results in organizational thinking, planning, and doing.

Fad Busting. Needs Assessments are a prescription for avoiding selecting solutions before we know the problems. New methods, new paradigms, and new tools are produced daily, and they often have dramatic claims to success based on opinion and false evidence. What appears glossy and attractive on the surface often turns out to be a costly disaster. Some fads can be like viruses, invading quickly, doing their damage until the organization detects their negative effects. The cycle then starts again, as the same process that selected the fad is used to select another solution. Needs Assessments can break this cycle of anti-performance fads by applying the rigor of sound assessment and diagnosis before selecting the appropriate prescription.

Needs Assessments generate a range of interventions and solutions, breaking paradigms that didn't work in the past and providing better options for fixing the selected problem.

A Needs Assessment is not an activity that replaces the other management tactics you read about (benchmarking, balanced score cards, quality management, and the like). Rather, Needs Assessments allow your organization to justify the selection of these "solutions" based on data instead of flavor-of-the-week diagnoses.

The exercise in Table 5.7 gives you an opportunity to identify which benefits appeal to your organization. Rate each benefit of a Needs Assessment by checking (✓) in the column that represents how much each of the items appeal to your organization. You may have to refer back to the explanation of each benefit above.

If you are not sure, then we highly recommend you find out—it may be the difference between future success and mediocrity.

THE ORGANIZATIONAL ELEMENTS

Needs Assessment and the Organizational Elements Model (OEM)

The Organizational Elements Model (Kaufman, 1992, 1998, 2000; Kaufman, Watkins, & Leigh, 2001) provides a framework for Needs Assessments at three levels and places quasi-needs as subordinate (refer back to Chapter Three).

The results are depicted here as value added chains. High payoff results and payoffs are those that will add value for the "entire results chain," from

Table 5.7. Assessing the Benefits of Needs Assessments.

Benefit	Not Sure	Low Value	Medium Value	High Value
1. The right solution				
2. Clear direction				
3. Proactive				
4. Shared commitment				
5. Conflict resolution				
6. Costs of poor performance				
7. Proposal acceptance rate				
8. Define priority gaps				
9. Reduce confusion				
10. Ethical				
11. Fad busting				

individual performance accomplishment to organizational and external/societal contributions. A Micro result should add value to the Macro level result that in turn should add value to Mega level results. Similarly, a Process should contribute worthwhile results at reasonable cost.

The OEM also depicts the three levels of valid Needs Assessment and their relationship to quasi-needs. By starting planning at the Mega level of gaps in results (needs) we ensure that we are heading in the right direction before selecting the means and methods to get there. Problem solving and decision making should start with a clear measurable definition and justification of What Is versus What Should Be. (See Figure 5.2.)

Needs Assessment and the OEM

When we have defined the needs in precise "interval" or "ratio" scale terms, we are in a better position to evaluate the various interventions and solutions before choosing the best one or mix (see Kaufman, 2000, p. 36). Needs defined with data calibrated on a *ratio* scale of measurement are defined by their *equal* scale distances with a known zero point (for example, zero defects or temperature in Kelvin where matter stops moving), while data at the *interval* scale of measurement also shares *equal* scale distances, data does not utilize a known

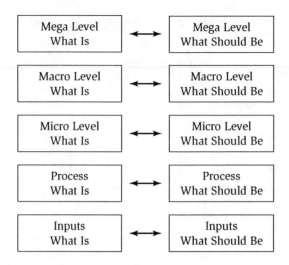

Figure 5.2. From Present to Desired Results.

and fixed zero point (for example, average test performance). Data at both the interval and ratio scales of measurement are commonly derived from performance data and ratings.

Data at the nominal (naming or numbering) and ordinal (rank order) scales of measurement can also be useful in conducting a Needs Assessment. Data at these scales, however, offer decision makers less precision and can be misleading if not examined carefully within the context of their collection. Objectives are always provided in interval or ratio scale measures, while goals, aims, or purposes are measured in nominal or ordinal scales (Kaufman, 1972, 1992, 1998, 2000).

Quasi Needs Assessment

The OEM does not exclude doing a quasi Needs Assessment, it only places such in its most useful perspective—as an assessment of gaps in means and resources, not gaps in results and consequences. What the OEM indicates is that you should not choose to close gaps in process performance, resources, methods and Inputs before you link them to precisely defined objectives—based on gaps in results—at the Mega, Macro, and Micro levels. To select methods and means related to processes and inputs before defining the desired results in interval or ratio terms is to be guilty of picking a solution before we know the problems or wishful thinking. Instead, if quasi Needs Assessments are to be conducted, they are best done only after a full Needs Assessment at each of the three levels of results.

What Should Be?

What often happens in a Needs Assessment is you discover there are no precise measurable statements of the desired results. A need exists and requires further analysis and closure when there is a proven and important gap between desired results (What Should Be) and present results in interval or ratio scale terms (What Is). We urge that the desired results should be specified as Smarter objectives (Chapter Seven). Too often the desired result is stated as a "fuzzy" vague goal. For example—we want to: "Improve customer satisfaction." "Achieve greater market share." "Increase profit." "Put people first." "Become the best." "Provide outstanding government." "Increase our growth potential."

It is risky reasoning to believe that these vague general purposes or intentions will improve performance. Success is best calculated through measurable objectives stated in non-fuzzy terms. A need should be measured as a gap between present results and desired results if you expect to define and deliver useful high payoff results. See Table 5.8 for the difference.

Table 5.8. Fuzzy vs. Useful Examples.

Fuzzy Example	Useful Example
WHAT IS Customer complaints are unacceptable	WHAT IS Customer ratings are down 25 percent from last year
WHAT SHOULD BE Customer satisfaction must improve	WHAT SHOULD BE Customer ratings should achieve at least a 25 percent increase over last year

The appropriate intervention, when there are no rigorous measurable results stated as Smarter objectives, is to develop objectives for the areas of performance under study. Until the performance is stated in measurable terms, there is no clear definition of a problem (a selected need).

Three Levels of Needs Assessments

There are three levels of Needs Assessment and two quasi-needs options. Your role in the organization will determine the level you will usually be asked to deal with and then assure that they link all three levels of needs, as shown in Table 5.9.

The model shown in Figure 5.3 depicts the strategic approach to Needs Assessments. It suggests that strategic Needs Assessment must always start with the Mega level of gaps in results in the Ideal Vision. Macro and Micro levels are then addressed.

Table 5.9. Three Levels of Needs Assessment.

Mega Needs	Common Result Areas
Gaps in Outcomes Society as the client	Reduced self-sufficiency Deaths due to violence Disabilities due to accidents Unsafe transport Unsafe accommodation Levels of discrimination-based levels of non self-sufficiency Environmental sustainability that continue profit levels
Macro Needs	Common Result Areas
Gaps in Outputs Immediate clients	Customer satisfaction levels Health levels Return on investment (ROI) Outputs returned Non-delivery Profit levels (short term)
Micro Needs	Common Result Areas
Gaps in Products Internal clients	Staff satisfaction levels Share values Accident levels Staff turnover Absenteeism Production reject levels Health levels Skill levels

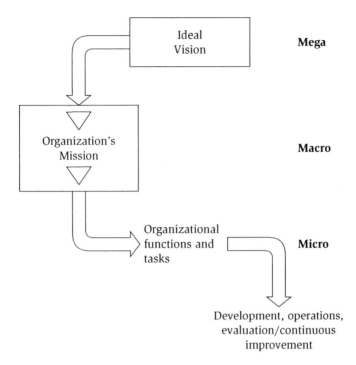

Figure 5.3. Relating and Rolling Down Needs Assessment by Level.
Source: From Kaufman, 1992, 1998, 2000.

THE NEEDS ASSESSMENTS PROCESS

It should be evident at this point that the Needs Assessment process is a purposeful part of formal strategic thinking and planning. In this rational situation Needs Assessments will be conducted at three levels starting at the Mega level of results and linking Macro and Micro followed by quasi Needs Assessments as necessary. Whatever level you are working at, there is a process that should be followed which we call the *Scope, Obtain, Collect, Evaluate,* and *Report* (or SOCER) model.

The SOCER Model

The five steps of the SOCER process for Needs Assessments are described below and shown in Figure 5.4.

In all good projects, success is built on a sound plan to which all those involved have committed. Each step is outlined in terms of the key questions that must be answered to complete the step.

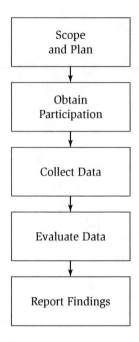

Figure 5.4. The SOCER Model.

Starting at any other level than Mega is impractical and dangerous to your organizational health!

Scope and Plan. The overall purpose of Needs Assessments is to provide the foundation for improving performance at all levels of the Organizational Elements Model. The following questions must be addressed in this step.

Scope and Plan Questions

- Why do needs assessments?
- What are the potential payoffs of needs assessments?
- Is the organization ready for change?
- What are the implications of proceeding without data from a needs assessment?
- Do we have hard (independently verifiable) data about organizational performance? Soft data?
- Do we have hard data about individual and team performance? Soft data?
- Who is/are the sponsors and partners, champions?
- Why must the Mega level be addressed first followed by Macro and Micro?
- Who will develop the detailed plan and implement it?
- What is the level of commitment?

- Who will be affected by the results?
- Who will benefit from the results?
- What will be delivered to immediate customers?
- What will be delivered to society?
- What societal value will be added?
- What societal value might otherwise be subtracted?
- What process will be followed?
- What language will be used (shared meaning)?

All the key partners must be committed to the scope (hopefully committing to Mega, Macro and Micro level results) and plan (that begins with Needs Assessment). The key partners are those affected by the results and those who will have to implement the change.

Obtain Active Participation. There are a number of potential partners in any Needs Assessment. The following questions will help screen potential participants in the assessment process.

Obtain Participation Questions

- Who will be affected by the Needs Assessment?
- How can you actively involve all interested parties?
- Who is the initiating sponsor of change?
- Who are the cascading sponsors of change?
- Who are the change agents?*
- Who are the targets of change? Why?
- Who are the clients? Who are the client's clients?
- What level of participation is required for each group affected?
- Who will resist the effort?
- How will the plan be communicated effectively to all interested groups?
- What group benefits the most? Why?
- Who will be on the project team?
- When will you have the first meeting and who will attend?
- What support will be provided for the various partners and contributors?
- How will the Mega level be integrated and linked with the level under study?
- Who will do the needs analysis (aka, cause analysis, including the identification but not selection of alternative methods and means)?
- Who will collect the data?
- How will partners who do not contribute be handled?

*One useful source for more information regarding this topic is Connor (1992).

Collect Data. Collecting data can be easy or difficult, usually depending on whether the organization has historically recorded and captured data in measurable terms. Here are questions to address in this step.

Collect Data Questions

- What data already exists?
- Is existing data both hard and soft?
- What level of data exists for Mega, Macro, and Micro?
- What mix of data gathering methods will be used? Why?
- What sample size provides verifiable evidence?
- What internal data about individual and team performance gaps will be collected?
- What external data will be collected about gaps and discrepancies in client results and expectations? In societal consequences?
- Does both hard and soft data have to be collected?
- How will the data be translated into evidence of needs?
- Who will collect the data?
- How will the data be captured and recorded?
- Will you use a Needs Assessment questionnaire to collect soft data?
- Is there a suitable questionnaire available? Can one be usefully modified?

Evaluate Data. Before identifying priorities and analyzing the needs to establish the causes of the results gaps, you will first want to gain agreement on what needs the data has uncovered. There will be disagreements at times. Some questions to use are provided here.

Evaluate Data Questions

- Is the data about results (and not just about means, methods, and resources)?
- What level of results data: Mega? Macro? Micro?
- Is it hard or soft data?
- Does the soft data support the hard data? And vice versa?
- Is there enough data?
- Is the data consistent?
- Was the data collected using valid (and reliable) measures and mean?
- Is the data relevant?
- Does the data raise confidentiality issues?
- What are the conclusions that can be drawn from the data?
- Does the data point to causes for the gaps in results?
- Is more data required?
- Is the data biased? Is your interpretation of the data possibly biased?
- Does the data include solutions?
- How will you remove solutions from the data?
- Are you confident in the data?
- Does any of the data confuse Needs with Wants?
- Does the data cover all the common important result areas?
- Is the data in interval or ratio terms?
- Do the clients/partners agree with the interpretation of the data?

A number of conflict resolution methods are available for reconciling the differences:

- Compare the soft data (sensed needs without externally veriable data to support them) with those based on hard data. If they don't match, gather more data, perhaps through qualitative rather than quantitative methods.

- Check that the data is about results. If it is not, translate it into results and then check with the partners in Needs Assessment. Resolve debates over means, methods, and resources by pointing out the results data. Avoid quasi-needs discussions that have no results links established.

- Establish linkages between Mega-level needs data and the impact on Macro and Micro needs. *Don't assume the linkages will turn out well if you don't define them formally.*

- Special interest groups will often have a "pet solution" that they strongly assert is a "need" by words such as: "We 'need' more building space." "You 'need' more training." "We 'need' better computer software." "You really 'need' more training." "You really, really 'need' more training."

These are solutions for unspecified and assumed problems. Refer the partners to the agreed language. As demanding as it might seem that we keep pleading to define need as a gap in results, it is absolutely vital that need be defined and treated in this way. We keep repeating this plea to help overcome years of us all having used need as a verb and suffering the consequences of selecting solutions before defining and justifying the problems.

Challenge those who consistently favor a special "want" by asking *"What result will we get if we successfully did this?"* And keep asking that question until you get to Mega.

The SOCER process for Needs Assessments can be applied at the three levels of results: Mega, Macro, and Micro. There will be some differences by level; however, your basic behaviors in the process remain the same. Some of the differences are noted in Table 5.10. There are repeats of the common ones for the *Scope and Plan* step between the levels. Use the table to develop your own checklists for the levels at which you are working.

The SOCER process can also be applied to quasi Needs Assessments that concern gaps in processes and inputs. A series of sample questions that should be answered for each step of the process is shown in Table 5.11.

Report Findings. When the data evaluation is complete, you are then in a position to list the needs and define priorities. The definition of priorities is based on an analytic technique called *costs-consequences analysis* (Kaufman, 1996; Kaufman & Watkins, 1996). This is a process for calculating and estimating a return on investment for each listed need.[4]

Table 5.10. Comparing Needs Assessments by Level.

SOCER	*Mega* Outcomes	*Macro* Outputs	*Micro* Products
S Scope and Plan	Who is the sponsor? Who else is responsible? What is the organization's purpose? What is the impact on the Ideal Vision? Are we ready? What data already exists?	Who is the sponsor? Who else is responsible? Who will gather the data? Are the standards of quality defined in measurable terms? How can we link this level to Mega?	Who is the sponsor? Who else is responsible? What is the performance under scrutiny? Is the target individuals or a team? What level of influence do we have? How can we link to Mega and Macro?
O Obtain Participation	Who are the community partners? How will we involve the greater number in large-scale change? What is the level of commitment?	How will we involve external clients in the process? Who will make up the project team? Who will do what by when?	Can we engage the target groups in generating the data? Is the culture committed to continuous improvement?
C Collect Data	What data exists about present impact on society? What data are not available? Does soft data verify hard data? Is there agreement?	What are the present client satisfaction ratings? What are the best data collection methods? Who will collect the data?	What "off the shelf" instruments are available? Are task lists or competency models available?
E Evaluate Data	What are the priority needs? What are the costs to ignore the problems? What are the costs to fix the problems? What are the Smarter objectives?	Are the links with Micro results and Mega results obvious? Made? What criteria will be used to set priorities?	What are the causes of the problem(s) (identified though needs analysis)? What are the possible solutions?
R Report Findings	Who can authorize action? Who will approve the needs definition? What methods and means (strategies and tactics) will you recommend? Are the options compared?	How urgent is the solution? Are there any obvious solutions? How will the findings be presented?	Who can approve the solutions? Is training a solution? Has a training requirement analysis been completed? What other possible interventions can be considered?

Table 5.11. Applying the Model to Quasi Needs Assessments.

S Scope and Plan	O Obtain Participation	C Collect Data	E Evaluate Data	R Report Findings
Who is the sponsor? What is/are the presenting problems? Who will be involved? What is the purpose? Are the links with Micro, Macro, and Mega established? What data already exists—hard or soft? Who will gather the data? What major processes are involved? What resources are the concern? Who will lead the project? What data gathering methods will be used?	How ready are the participants? What are the implications for the target group? What if we don't do anything? Is it worth the effort? What is the level of pain? Who wants to fix it the most?	What are the gaps in process performance? What are the gaps in resources? What methods could be improved? What are the opportunity gaps? Have we enough data?	Can we align the quasi-needs with Micro, Macro, and Mega levels of needs? What are the causes of quasi-needs? What solutions are indicated? What are the restraints? How will we overcome the restraints? What are the priorities? Do we have agreement on the priorities?	Who gets the report? Who approves change? How will the report be presented?

The key questions in this approach are:

- "What will it cost to eliminate or extinguish the need?"
- "What will it cost to ignore the need?"

Each group involved in the Needs Assessment process can be encouraged to use the cost-consequences analysis to establish a priority list of needs. The various priority lists can then be compared and common priorities established for further causal analysis. Nominal group techniques and other consensus building approaches may be used to formulate the priorities of the organization. Without the data of the Needs Assessment, though, priorities are too often determined by the one(s) who speak the loudest and the most. See the list of questions below.

Report Findings Questions

- Have the needs been clearly documented as gaps in results?
- Has a costs-consequences analysis been completed?
- Has agreement been gained on priority needs?
- Is there a requirement for cause analysis* at this stage?
- Do the clients expect suggested solutions at this stage?
- Does the report include What Should Be objectives?
- How do the clients expect the report to be presented?
- Are the needs stated as problems for resolution or opportunities? Or both?
- Are the problems all stated in interval or ratio terms? If not, can they be?
- Where cause analysis is required is there a management plan?
- Where there is insufficient data is this reported and a recommendation made?
- Are there any major unresolved disagreements?

*Cause analysis is part of needs analysis.

GATHERING THE DATA

If you are committed to performance improvement, you will have three major levels of Needs Assessment data to work with: Mega, Macro, and Micro. If your project, based on the needs data from the Mega and Macro levels, is focused on the Micro level you will require data about individual and team performance. However, even if you are limited to the Micro level, you had best identify the link between Micro level performance and Macro and Mega level performance.

Whatever level you are dealing with, you will require rigorous evidence. Evidence is developed by gathering data on the problem as it is presented to you by the client, as well as from the client's environment. As physicians know well, the perceived problem is not necessarily the real one. Data provides the evidence to:

1. Be certain a problem or opportunity exists.
2. Decide whether it is worth fixing.
3. Select the right solution(s).
4. Evaluate whether the solutions(s) worked and revise as required.

Performance Improvement

Data gathering should be the first step in the following processes.

1. Developing strategic plans.
2. Developing tactical plans (and this should be linked to number 1 above).
3. Developing operational plans (and this should be linked to 1 and 2 above).
4. Identifying and solving problems.
5. Improving the performance of individuals, teams, groups, organizations, and communities.
6. Troubleshooting performance problems.
7. Reviewing performance and audits.
8. Creating change—simple or complex.
9. Managing change—simple or complex.

Collecting, analyzing, and interpreting data ensures decisions are made with sound evidence.

Soft Data and Hard Data

Data can be classified as *soft* or *hard*.

Soft Data. Feelings, perceptions, and opinions are soft data. They are important, but data such as this that cannot be independently verified should not be the only source of evidence for rigorous Needs Assessments. Soft data must be supported by hard data to make the evidence robust.

Hard Data. Data that is independently verifiable through external sources is hard data. Hard data is often quantified in interval or ratio scale terms because it is dealing with verifiable measurable results at the three levels.

Effective planning, problem solving, and decision making should not be based on soft data alone. Perceptions and hard evidence have to be compared and merged such as:

- How accurate is the data on present results?
- How valid is the data?
- Have the desired results been stated in measurable terms?
- What are the opinions and perceptions of the people involved about both present results and desired results?
- Do the hard and soft data agree?

Why Collect Soft Data?

You should apply the following rules to help you decide why and when to collect soft data.

Soft Data—Why and When?

- *IF* hard data are not available, soft data is better than no data.
- *IF* you have hard data, gather soft data to support and verify the hard data, and find new hard data to be collected.
- *IF* you want to gain commitment, gather "needs sensing" data on those performance gaps they *perceive* as important, and relate with hard data.
- *IF* you want to communicate that people's feelings are important also, gather soft data about how they feel about performance gaps and opportunities.
- *IF* you want to clarify apparent conflicts in the hard data, gather soft data to resolve the conflict.
- *IF* you are short on time and want to narrow down the data search, first collect soft data on the performance gaps then gather hard data in specific areas.

Sources of Hard Data

The following are some examples of hard data sources.

Hard Data Sources

- Highway accident rates
- Rape cases prosecuted and adjudicated
- Deaths from violence
- Deaths from AIDS
- Deaths from diabetes
- Deaths from heart disease
- Deaths from war and riots
- Miles of safe roads
- Sales
- Stock/share value
- Profit levels
- Unemployment levels
- Safe accommodation

- Attendance at art events
- Attendance at sporting events
- Truancy levels
- Minor crime levels
- Number of complaints
- Level of taxes paid
- Prison inmates
- Recidivism rates
- Customer satisfaction ratings
- Skill test results
- Honors and awards
- Swimmers saved (lifeguards)
- Medals gained at Olympics
- Patients discharged as well
- Accident levels in organization

This is a mixed bunch from a wide range of organizations. Each organization will develop its own data sources for hard data. These sources are verifiable (and usually quantifiable) if the data has been captured and documented.

Sources of Soft Data

The following are some of the possible sources of soft data.

Soft Data Sources

- Exit interview notes.
- Feelings about what is important, especially intensity of feeling about the problems or gaps in results.
- Opinions or morale levels—high or low.
- Anecdotal stories about critical incidents.
- Perceptions of key partners.
- Questionnaires and surveys.
- Culture surveys.
- Stories from the past.
- Perceptions of future trends.

The usefulness of soft data is that it can corroborate (or disconfirm) the hard data through people's feelings about the situation. We often construct our own reality based on inferences drawn from a merging of both hard and soft data. In addition, soft data often reveals areas for which the hard data has not (yet) been collected.

Before moving ahead, be sure that there is agreement between the hard and soft data you collect. The following checksheet in Table 5.12 is intended to help you develop a data collection plan for Needs Assessment activities in your organization.

Table 5.12. Essential Questions.

Code	Questions	Notes
1	What hard and soft data will we collect?	
2	How will we collect the data?	
3	How much time is available? How urgent is the project?	
4	How much money is available?	
5	What people are available? How many?	
6	What are the skill levels of the people?	
7	What are the confidentiality issues? What questions will be resisted?	
8	Are there cultural issues which impose restraints on what is gathered and how?	
9	Are there any methods that are unsuitable or suitable?	
10	What level of rapport exists between the data gatherers and the target groups?	
11	What influence tactics and methods are required to overcome resistance?	
12	Are the sponsors fully aware of their role?	
13	What sample size? How is the sample to be identified?	
14	Are people geographically spread? How widely?	
15	What special resources and logistics are required?	
16	What level of support can be expected from the target groups?	
17	What data collection methods are preferred by the sponsors? The change agents? The HR department?	
18	How important is confidentiality for the target group?	
19	How will the data be captured and documented? Will the methods of collecting data be both valid and reliable?	
20	Who will compile the data?	
21	How will the data be reduced?	
22	How will the needs data be presented?	
23	How will questions be answered?	

DATA GATHERING METHODS

The task of gathering data is demanding. It should be rigorous because the cost of solving the wrong problems or selecting the wrong solutions can be extremely high. No single data gathering technique alone is suitable for all Needs Assessments, and any mix selected will be influenced by the level of Needs Assessments that you are dealing with (Mega, Macro, and Micro).

As introduced in Chapter Four, a range of methods for data collection exist, as shown in the listing that follows. Each of these will be summarized below.

Data Gathering Methods

- Observation
- Individual interview
- Group interviews (focus groups)
- Document search
- Telephone interview
- Questionnaires/surveys
- Criterion tests
- Assessment centers
- Critical incidents
- Artifacts/work products
- Review of public data
- Accessing research and statistical data bases

Observation

Individuals and teams demonstrate the results of their skills (work) and the way they accomplish the results through observable behaviors (actions). These actions or behaviors result in performance. Further, performance can be positive or negative; it can add or subtract value. High payoff results are desirable because they add value not only within the organization, but outside of it as well. Thinking, feeling, and imagining are cognitive behaviors (processes) that as yet are not directly observable but the evidence of thinking, feeling, and imagining can be verified through observable behaviors and accomplishments.

These observable actions and accomplishments can provide sound verifiable evidence for use in Needs Assessments. Observation provides an opportunity to get straight to on-the-job performance and results. Observing a surgeon operating allows the observer to link both critical behaviors and the accomplishments. The major disadvantages include the requirement of some level of expertise and the potential ethical issues of unobtrusive observation. Observing people and teams at work requires considerable skill. The unobtrusive observer is more likely to perceive errors, problems, creative applications, consequences, and results than a participant observer, such as a co-worker. Good observers are able to pinpoint behaviors that consistently produce superior results. Table 5.13 summarizes the advantages and disadvantages of observation.

Table 5.13. Observation Advantages and Disadvantages.

Pros	Cons
The observers can pinpoint behaviors and performance directly.	They can be difficult to interpret where cognitive tasks are performed.
Often the behaviors can be linked directly to desired and or undesired results.	You may not always be able to link the behaviors directly to results or consequences.
The behaviors can be monitored for frequency over time.	Sampling the people and time can give biased "one shot" data.
It is suitable for both Micro and Macro level observations.	The observer can influence a change in performance, both good and bad.
They are not screened through hearsay evidence.	The observers can create bias through their own emotional reactions.
They can reveal opportunities for improvement.	It can be costly.
They can verify data collected through other methods.	

Individual Interviews

The interview methods allow analysts to gather information directly from all categories of clients and stakeholders. Interviews are suitable for soft data collection, as they solicit people's opinions or personal experience (see Kaufman, Watkins, & Leigh, 2001). This method requires a high degree of competence and commitment from the interviewer, as seen in the listing below.

Interviewer Skills

- Active listener
- Note taking
- Rapport building
- Empathy
- Discriminate opinions from facts
- Self-management

- Questioning
- Attention to detail
- Presentation skills
- Observation
- Time management
- Detachment

Interviews can produce large quantities of information that can be difficult to manage and analyze. Also, interviewees will typically have a number of concerns or issues that ought to be discussed prior to the interview, as shown below.

Interviewee Concerns

- What is the purpose of the interview?
- What is the reason for the interview and "why me?"
- Who are you? (the interviewer)
- What are your skills? What credibility?
- What's in it for me?
- How will confidentiality be dealt with?
- What will happen to the data?
- Will anything change based on my suggestions?

Group Interviews

Focus groups are a popular form of the group interview. A focus group can be thought of as an interview with several people at the same time. It is a structured approach with specific questions to be discussed by a representative group of clients (internal and external).

Well-facilitated focus groups can be used to elicit soft data about needs. Where no hard data is readily or immediately available, you can design a questionnaire to give structure to the interview and openly discuss respondents' replies. Questionnaire data, such as the mockup in Table 5.14 below, may be quantified, but it is still not hard data since the opinions it represents are not independently verifiable.

Select a number of result areas at Mega, Macro, or Micro levels and design a simple rating scale. Ask respondents to rate both What Is (in their perception) and What Should Be. Be sure to anchor/label the results dimensions. This technique influences people to start defining needs as gaps in results. Focus groups can be especially helpful in gaining agreement on desired results.

Table 5.14. Rating Scale for Group Interview.

What Is?				Important Result Areas	What Should Be?				
Hi				Low		Hi				Low
1 2 3 4 5					Profits	1 2 3 4 5				
1 2 3 4 5					Customer ratings	1 2 3 4 5				
1 2 3 4 5					Staff ratings	1 2 3 4 5				
1 2 3 4 5					Share value	1 2 3 4 5				
1 2 3 4 5					Complaints	1 2 3 4 5				
1 2 3 4 5					Sales	1 2 3 4 5				
1 2 3 4 5					Accidents	1 2 3 4 5				
1 2 3 4 5					Staff turnover	1 2 3 4 5				
1 2 3 4 5					Competency levels	1 2 3 4 5				
1 2 3 4 5					Rejects	1 2 3 4 5				
1 2 3 4 5					Returned Outputs	1 2 3 4 5				
1 2 3 4 5					Safety of what is delivered	1 2 3 4 5				
1 2 3 4 5					Societal impacts	1 2 3 4 5				

Document Search

Organizational documents, especially electronic records, can be a rich source of data and evidence for performance gaps, desired results, trends, and cycles.

Good analysts are not limited by organizational documents; they also search documents outside the organization to access relevant data. Data for Mega level Needs Assessments generally come through documents outside of the organization. Document data can be both hard and soft. The analyst requires the following skills:

Document Search Results

- Accessing data files
- Classification skills
- Attention to detail
- Data analysis and graphic depiction
- Statistical skills
- Presentation skills
- Structured writing, for example, information mapping
- System thinking (relating everything to Mega)
- Objectivity

Table 5.15 shows the pros and cons of searching. The method is suitable for gathering data at all levels of Needs Assessment.

Table 5.15. Pros and Cons of Document Searches.

Pros	Cons
Numbers and evidence tend to be robust and easy to understand and communicate.	It is difficult to discriminate the relevant documents and reports.
Bias can be reduced.	People enter the data and they can also enter their bias.
Accurate benchmarks can be elicited from the documents.	It can be difficult to rigorously quantify some important aspects of performance.
Units can be compared.	It can be time-consuming.
Changes in results can be tracked.	The data may be out-of-date.

Telephone Interviews

Telephone interviews are a variation on the skills of individual and group interviews. You must have a clear purpose. Before using the telephone, answer the following preparation questions:

Telephone Interview Preparation

- Have I done my preparation to scope the target group?
- Who is the best possible person(s) to interview?
- Am I getting relevant information?
- Am I talking with the right person?
- How do the responses of various people compare?
- Is anything being implied and not stated explicitly?
- What are the critical questions I want answers to?
- Am I getting the answers I want?
- How will I deal with resistance?
- Am I getting hard data/soft data?
- How will I record the data?
- What is missing?
- Is my telephone voice "agreeable"?

If you decide to use telephone interviews, use the questions above for preparing your data gathering format.

Questionnaires/Surveys

Questionnaires appear to be the most frequently used method at the Micro level. There are many instruments designed to collect mostly soft data about individual and team performance. Effective questionnaires are difficult to develop and getting an acceptable range of responses is also difficult. But if you want to obtain data from a wide dispersed sample, then they are efficient. Competent analysts often use interviews as the first step in designing a valid questionnaire; it gives them some insights into the presenting and actual problems to be defined. However, soft data alone is insufficient for a robust Needs Assessment. Personal opinions and perceptions must be compared to the reality of the hard data. At the end of this chapter a guide is provided for designing Needs Assessment questionnaires.

Criterion Tests

Criterion tests are sometimes called performance tests. If you want to gather data on mountain bike riders, then ask them to ride the mountain bike over a representative multiple terrain course. This is the most valid test of mountain bikers' performance. The performance test allows an observer to gather data on both skill gaps and results (accomplishments). Not only is this data gathering method useful at the Micro level because you can establish a direct link between the key behaviors that produce the high value results, but you will also collect some Mega and Macro level data as well since it is linked directly to performance.

Assessment Centers

Assessment centers have gained popularity as a means of gathering data about leadership and management performance. They are expensive to set up and require highly skilled facilitators. Like questionnaires, they can be suitable for collecting high quality data at the Micro level of results. There are some complex skills and behaviors that lend themselves to assessment center review, especially where social skills and simulations are important.

Critical Incidents

Critical incidents are those situations, behavior patterns, or result patterns that can be shown to have a substantial impact on performance and organizational (Macro) and societal (Mega) consequences. Many things happen in the work setting, but not all are directly related to gaps in results or opportunities for improved results. By searching the records for critical incidents or by recording critical incidents and their results, we can generate evidence about good and bad performance that can indicate needs.

Artifacts/Work Products

If one wants to check out the gaps in a potter's performance, we will check his ceramics. If 50 percent of them are cracked and he requires a 100 percent to meet his standards, then we have a need, a gap in results. This can be a suitable data source at the Macro level and the Micro level. At the Mega level there may be a time delay for the impact to surface in terms of artifacts, although typically such evidence will become available.

Summary

The ten major data gathering methods all have advantages and disadvantages. The "secret" is not to rely on only one method, but select the methods on the basis of the questions you are asking. Use an appropriate mix of methods to serve the purpose of the Needs Assessment project. Useful analysts take an eclectic-yet-results-focused approach. A checklist for developing a Needs Assessment questionnaire follows.

Needs Assessment Questionnaire Design Guidelines[5]

❏ Ensure the questions are about the result areas at the Mega, Macro, and Micro levels (refer to Chapter Seven).

❏ Ask about perceptions of gaps in the result areas for both What Is and What Should Be.

❏ Ask questions about the three levels of needs and the three associated levels of results.

❏ Obtain evidence of the validity and reliability of the measures to be used.

❏ Make the questions clear in order to get reliable responses, but short enough that people are likely to respond.

❏ Use an approach that makes it clear to respondents exactly what is wanted. People don't want to write long answers, so when appropriate use a checklist or multiple-choice format to reduce the inconvenience level while making the questionnaire easier to score.

❏ Don't ask questions that reveal, directly or indirectly, a bias. Don't use the data collection instrument to bias the responses you really want.

❏ Ask several questions about each result area. Ask about each concern in different ways to increase validity. Basing any decisions on answers to one question is risky.

❏ Test the data collection instrument on a sample group. Identify problems in meaning, coverage, and scoreability. Revise as required.

❏ When collecting performance ("hard") data . . .

Make sure the data collected relates to questions about the result areas.

Assure yourself that the data collected relate to important questions for which you want answers.

Assure yourself that the data are based on enough observations to make them reliable, not a one-time happening.

Make sure that the data can be independently verified and cross-checked.

Turning Reactive into Proactive

Even if your position power is limited and you are only able to define needs at the Micro level, you can be proactive and link your work with potential impact on Mega and Macro levels of results. Pointing out these linkages to your sponsor can strengthen your proposal. Often you may be saddled with "wants," methods, fads, and pet solutions that are stated as "needs." Even though you know they are means, you are expected to react promptly to these solutions. What you can do is gain permission to ask the proposer for some clarification through questions such as:

1. What would happen if we ignored your proposal (for example, "We 'need' more vehicles")?
2. What was the process that led to your conclusion?
3. What evidence exists for the problem you wish/want/require/desire (not "need") to solve this way? Why is it a priority? What results will we get if we do? What high payoff results will we get?
4. Could you help me to understand the events that lead to your conclusion?
5. What would success look like if we applied this solution?
6. Is there any evidence to justify your solution as being the best one?
7. What is the desired result in measurable terms if we do it this way?
8. Can we revisit the problem definition?
9. Could this problem be a symptom of a larger problem?
10. Could we explore some alternatives?
11. What would it cost if we applied the solution and it did not work?

This "inquiry" approach allows you to be proactive and diplomatic at the same time. You can engage the person in a conversation that explores the accomplishment of high payoff results in relation to potential means and resources.

System Thinking: Relating All the Parts

The three steps of Needs Assessment, needs analysis, and solution selection are linked and related. Good analysts become involved in all three. When we talk of a *system* approach, we include all three steps, but *always* start with creating and designing the desired results for the team, organization, and society.

Note that in the beginning we are imagining, or picturing, a better world, a better organization, a better team, and a better self—all in measurable terms. This is proactive planning. This is strategic thinking.

We can then gather data about the present results, compare it to the desired results, and identify whether there are gaps. This is Needs Assessment. The system approach captures the *"biggest picture"* and is *"holistic"* because it recognizes the relationships among society, organization, teams, and individuals—and proactively seeks opportunities to improve all the interacting parts. Some tools for applying a system approach are shown in Table 5.16.

Table 5.16. System Approach Tools.

Code	System Approach Steps	Example Tools
1	Identify Target What are we seeking to improve? What external future do we want to create?	Strategic planning and thinking
2	Define opportunities and needs (gaps in results).	Needs assessments (results-gap analysis)
3	Prioritize gaps (needs) and opportunities. (Select problems for fixing.)	Needs assessments Cost consequences analysis Risk analysis Smart thinking (Mitroff)
4	Analyze the cause of needs and opportunities.	Cause analysis (Gilbert) Performance analysis (Mager & Pipe; Rummler & Brache) Front-end analysis (Harless) Goal analysis (Mager)
5	Identify possible methods and means—solutions and interventions—to meet the needs and opportunities.	Methods—means—media analysis. Brainstorm Scenarios Consequences analysis
6	Select solutions, interventions (methods and means).	Cost/results analysis Advantages/disadvantages analysis Battelle method Panel consensus Simulation
7	Design/purchase solutions, interventions, methods and means.	System(s) design System(s) development Instructional systems design (ISD) Criterion referenced instruction (Mager & Pipe) Human performance technology SWOT (strengths, weaknesses, opportunities, threats) analysis Competency modeling Process redesign

(Continued)

Table 5.16. System Approach Tools. (*Continued*)

Code	System Approach Steps	Example Tools
8	Implement selected methods and means.	Performance management Planning tools (e.g., PERT, CPM) Human performance technology Instructional system design models Criterion referenced instruction
9	Evaluate process performance—for efficiency and effectiveness.	Formative evaluation
10	Evaluate accomplishment of results.	Summative evaluation Goal-free evaluation
11	Revise as required.	All tools in steps 1 to 10 could be applied

SELECTING PRIORITY NEEDS

We are now close to completing the Scope, Obtain, Collect, Evaluate, and Report (or SOCER) process and have collected the data through a mix of methods. We now want to evaluate the data and elicit the needs so we can place them in priority order for fixing or eliminating.

Gain Agreement on Data

When you have recorded your own data in a SOCER matrix such as that provided in Table 5.10, it will be easier for the various partners to evaluate the data so that it can be determined whether there is sufficient data and whether the soft matches the hard data. In the process, there may be conflict and disagreement over the data. Data can create pain and people can become defensive and unpredictable about the data. Be patient and resolve disagreements by way of a mix of the following actions:

1. Get more hard data.

2. Separate any methods and means that have crept in as "needs" when they are really solutions and pet "wants."

3. Challenge and win over the difficult partners who have personal agendas.

4. Challenge old paradigms served up as "needs" when they are tools, techniques, and methods that have failed in the past.

Weighting Methods

Listing the needs in priority order can be achieved by ranking the list against the following criteria:

Criteria for Rating Needs

- Is it an important result area?
- What is the cost of ignoring the need? High? Medium? Low?
- What is the cost of meeting the need? High? Medium? Low?
- Is the need (gap in results) an ethical issue?
- What level of agreement exists on the priority?
- Are the linkages and relationships between Mega, Macro, and Micro level needs evident?

Whatever mix of weightings are used, you will require a high level of agreement from the partners in the process before moving on to select solutions and interventions (methods and means).

Group Techniques to Gain Agreement

There are a number of powerful techniques for influencing groups to agree on priorities. Some of these methods are listed below:

Techniques for Gaining Agreement

- Group discussion
- Nominal Group Technique
- Scenarios
- Simulation and gaming
- Delphi techniques
- Polling
- Card sorts
- Dialogue followed by rating
- Advantages/disadvantages analysis
- Decision balance sheet
- Electronic voting
- "Need" advocate
  (role play the advocates for the gaps in the results)
- Panel consensus
- Weighting values

Always relate means to ends, and all ends to the Mega level.

WILL THE NEEDS ASSESSMENT WORK?

Overview Needs Assessment Audit

As we have discussed, you can waste a lot of money on fads, methods, means, and solutions that don't work. They don't work because they are presented as "needs" when they are really wants or solutions. We emphasize that effective Needs Assessments will ensure that you connect solutions to the "right" well-defined measurable results.

It is good practice to evaluate your own Needs Assessments to ensure they deliver added value. You can bust paradigms and "fads" which don't work by using effective Needs Assessments. The checklist in Table 5.17 is a Needs Assessment audit (Kaufman 1998, 2000). Use it to check and review a Needs Assessment process and to plan a highly effective Needs Assessment.

The format in Table 5.18 provides you with a way to record the needs. It also highlights gaps in the data and areas where you will have to gather more data.

The next table (5.19) expands this format to include possible methods and means (quasi-needs). Use this format to record the Needs Assessment data and possible methods, means, solutions, or interventions.

Table 5.17. Needs Assessment Checklist.

Code	Criteria	Yes	Unsure	No
1	Are the needs stated as gaps in results (a gap between What Is and What Should Be?)			
2	Is there a clear distinction between ends and means (results versus methods or resources)?			
3	Is there a linkage established between Mega results, Macro results, and Micro results?			
4	Are the Mega level results identified (payoffs for society)?			
5	Are the Mega level results clearly imbedded in the Ideal Vision (which is the driver for the organizational purpose or mission)?			
6	Are the Macro level results identified (payoffs for the organization)?			
7	Do the Macro level results move the organization closer to the Ideal Vision (Mega)?			

Table 5.17. (*Continued*)

Code	Criteria	Yes	Unsure	No
8	Are the Micro level results identified (payoffs/consequences for individuals and small groups/teams in the organization)?			
9	Does every need statement exclude methods and means for achieving them?			
10	Are needs listed in priority order on the criteria of what it costs to meet the need versus what it costs to ignore it?			
11	Are interventions/solutions selected on the basis of a cost-consequences analysis for each need or cluster of related needs?			
12	Are continuous improvement (evaluation) criteria taken directly from the "What Should Be" dimension of the selected need?			
13	Do continuous improvement (and evaluation) results report the extent to which needs or clusters of related needs have been reduced or eliminated?			
14	Are continuous improvement results used for improvement and not for blaming?			

Table 5.18. Format for Recording Needs.

Types of Results	Current Results	Desired Results
MEGA (Outcomes)		
MACRO (Outputs)		
MICRO (Products)		

Table 5.19. Recording Needs Assessment Data and Possible Solutions.

Types of Results	Present Results	Possible Methods and Means to Close the Gap in Results	Desired Results
MEGA (Outcomes)			
MACRO (Outputs)			
MICRO (Products)			

Assessment and Evaluation—Related but Different[6]

Evaluation and Needs Assessments are related but different. Both deal with gaps in results, but each has a different function to perform. When you evaluate you compare, after the fact, the obtained results with your intended results: a comparison of "what results were accomplished" with "what results were intended." When you conduct a Needs Assessment, you are, before the fact, finding the gaps between current results and desired ones: a comparison of "What Is" with "What Should Be."

Evaluation is reactive; while Needs Assessment is proactive. Both, however, should use data concerned with gaps in results.

Evaluation and Needs Assessment ask different—yet related—questions. Needs Assessments provide the data for determining where you should head, while evaluation assumes you knew where to head and the data would tell you the extent to which you have arrived at your intended destination. Based on the questions you want answered, select those that you should answer, and then select the appropriate tools to do so.

Notes

1. Human performance improvement should be driven by sound evidence for methods chosen and be built on a scientific foundation to justify its efficacy. Gilbert (1978) emphasized the requirement for shared language. Interestingly, Gilbert suggested that "value" is found "at the next level of results." He did not specify Mega

as the ultimate value level (perhaps suggesting that such would be a "philosophical" level. In language and in implementation everything—everything—must be focused on measurable adding value at the Mega level.

2. Frances Hesselbein, in *Hesselbein on Leadership* (2002), states this in inspirational terms: "How do we move from where we are to where we are called to be?"

3. See Kaufman, 2000, p. 71.

4. Another related approach is Leigh's (Leigh, Watkins, Platt, & Kaufman, 2000; Kaufman, Watkins, & Leigh, 2001) CUDA Analysis.

5. See Kaufman, 2000, p. 53.

6. Based on Kaufman (1990), Relating evaluation and needs assessment. *Human Resource Development Quarterly, 1*(4), 405–408.

CHAPTER SIX

Solving Problems

Closing the Priority Gaps

CHAPTER GOALS

By working though this chapter, you will be able to answer the following questions:

- ❏ What is the definition of a problem?
- ❏ What is a *simple* problem?
- ❏ What is a *complex* problem?
- ❏ What do simple and complex problems have in common?
- ❏ What are the common errors in problem formulation?
- ❏ What are the simple problem solving steps?
- ❏ What are the *key questions* to ask for each step?
- ❏ What are the complex problem solving steps?
- ❏ What are the key questions to ask for each step?

SOLVING PROBLEMS—AN OVERVIEW

A problem is a need selected for resolution. No need, no gap. No gap,
no problem . . . and no new intervention.

In the previous chapter you learned how to conduct Needs Assessments. A
need was defined as a gap in results, not as a gap in resources, methods, or
means. Needs can be identified at three levels, whereas quasi-needs are gaps
in resources and methods. Quasi-needs are important but subordinate to real
needs.[1] Strategic planning and thinking starts with Mega and then links
Macro and Micro to the accomplishment of high payoff results, as shown in
Figure 6.1.

A Needs Assessment identifies gaps in results and then places them in priority order, based on agreed criteria. When a decision has been made to fix or
resolve a need, we have identified a problem.

In this book a problem is defined as "a need selected for resolution." A problem is therefore a gap in results that has been selected for closure by either an
organization or through partnership of organizations. A problem does not exist
until there is evidence to demonstrate that there is a priority gap between present results and desired results.

Needs Assessment is therefore an essential precondition for effective problem solving. Needs Assessments gather the data to establish that there is a

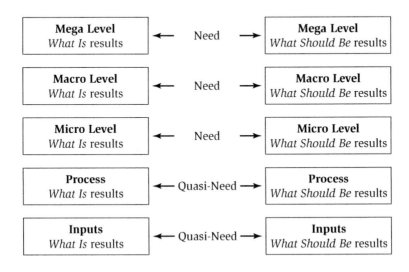

Figure 6.1. Needs Link What Is with What Should Be.

situation worth fixing. Some of the preconditions to problem solving are listed here.

Problem Solving—Preconditions

- The existence of a gap in results between What Is and What Should Be.
- A recognition that a gap exists.
- The commitment to close, eliminate, or decrease the gap.
- The tools to measure the size of the gap and the implications of ignoring it.
- The competencies and resources to fix the problem.

If these preconditions don't exist, then you probably haven't got a problem worth fixing or you haven't defined the problem clearly enough to adequately solve it.

There are three levels of planning and results, Mega, Macro, Micro. Problems can exist at all these levels when needs are selected for closure. Needs Assessment data defines problems and assists in prioritizing gaps in results.

Problems can be grouped as simple or complex. You can have simple problems and complex problems individually or working together at all three levels of results.

One of the major obstacles to effective problem solving is the development of an adequate problem definition. That is why a Needs Assessment is critical to both good planning and good problem solving. We want to gather the evidence to show that a problem exists and whether it is simple or complex and at what level of results.

If a problem is poorly defined, the probability of achieving a solution will be diminished. Since this initial stage of problem solving will influence how all other stages are approached, this step must be done right the first time (and every time). As a rule a thumb, the complexity of the problem will increase in relation to the level of results at which it operates. For example, reducing deaths due to war to zero is a substantially more complex problem to solve than improving the performance of a junior assembly line worker. In turn, the benefits to the individual, organization, and society derived from solving problems are similarly greater at higher levels of results (although just because a problem is less complex does not always mean that it is easy to define and solve). Regardless of whether it is simple or complex, the process you use to solve problems contains similar steps. Use the following questions to help you decide whether the problem is "simple."

Is It a Simple Problem?

- Is it a gap in results at the Macro or Micro level?
- Do you have all the data?
- Is the problem obvious as presented?
- Is the cause(s) of the problem obvious?
- If the problem was solved would it be immediately obvious?
- Can the solution be implemented in a short time frame (1 minute to 1 year)?
- Is there a high level of certainty?
- Are there few people who have to be involved in agreeing on the solution?
- Are the consequences of ignoring it immediately obvious?
- How many people are affected?

If it is a simple problem, use the six-step process from Figure 6.2, which is explained later in this chapter.

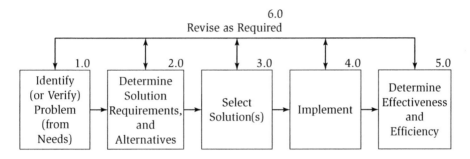

Figure 6.2. The Six-Step Problem Solving Process.

Source: From Kaufman, 1992, 1998, 2000.

Use the following questions to help you decide whether the problem is complex.

Is It a Complex Problem?

- Is it a gap in results at the Mega or Macro level?
- Are you uncertain about what the real problem is?
- Do you have incomplete data?
- Are the boundaries of the problem unclear?
- Do you have to get a number of people to agree to the problem statement?
- Are you confused between symptoms and the problem?
- Do all the important people agree on the problem statement?
- Does the problem appear messy?
- Are there unknowns?

- Is there an ethical issue with the problem?
- Is there difficulty in formulating the problem in interval or ratio terms?
- Is there confusion about results and methods?
- Are many people unclear about the desired results?
- Does it appear to require a mix of solutions to fix it?
- Are many people affected?
- Are the consequences of ignoring the problem only appearing after long time frames?

If you answer yes to most of these questions, then you probably have a complex problem. In solving complex problems we will use a similar framework as we do with simple problems; additional steps will just be added to address issues related to the complexity.

Defining the Problem

The most frequent error in problem solving is the failure to define the problem as a measurable gap in results. This leads to unresolved problems, wasted resources, and often bad feelings between stakeholders.

Think of five or six problems as they are presented in your life. Note them in the box below.

Note Some Problems

1.

2.

3.

4.

5.

6.

Consider these perceived problems as you progress through the next few pages of the text.

Needs Assessments identify multiple needs that in turn raise multiple problems for fixing. Before you move to fix the problems, each one should be screened through the process shown by the flow chart in Figure 6.3.

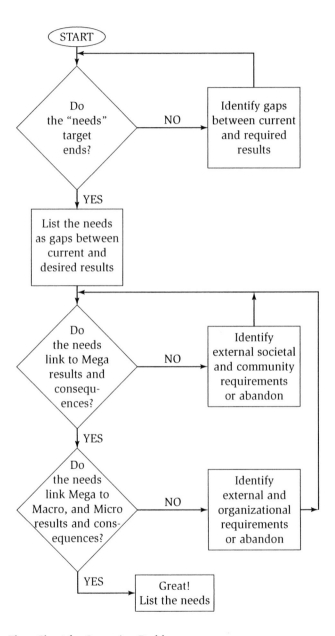

Figure 6.3. Flow Chart for Screening Problems.

Source: From Kaufman, 1992, 1998, 2000.

TWO COMMON PROBLEM SOLVING ERRORS

Flawed Leadership

"The conventional wisdom is indeed very conventional but not very wise."
—Nirenberg, 1997

In Chapter One (Busting Old Paradigms and Using New Ones), you completed an exercise that asked you to assess the impact on performance of a wide range of management and leadership tools. The tools have at times been presented as the best answer to managers' problems. The evidence, unfortunately, does not support their espoused benefits. Too often, action oriented leaders have raced to the latest tool, lacking a complete Needs Assessment and diagnosis of the problem. This has turned many potentially helpful tools into fads—too often the tool has been linked to the wrong problem or to no problem at all. Commonly, popular methods or tools (means) are strongly sold as a "needs"— even though gaps in results have not been defined or agreed on.

Trivialization

The tools, concepts, and models that might help leaders (if they were applied to the right problem) are sometimes trivialized. Sound familiar? Someone attends a guru-of-the-day seminar and gains a little knowledge. The complex tool gets reduced to a parlor game status such as "dialogue." Dialogue is a very powerful tool, but if an adequate Needs Assessment is missing it will fail to achieve performance improvement.[2] The application of quality management is riddled with examples of simplifications that didn't lend to improvement. Very sound concepts like learning from errors and revising as required have been degenerated to shortcuts such as continuous process improvement, micromanagement, quality teams, and other techniques to defuse this otherwise valuable tool. And while each of these "shortcuts" to quality can make valuable contributions, they do not lend themselves to the rigor required of achieving high payoff results.[3]

Simplifying the complex can often be like expecting vitamin pills to cure nearsightedness. We can avoid this trivialization of potentially powerful tools by ensuring we plan results before rushing to selecting means to get there. John Nirenberg, in his book *Power Tools* (1997), critiques a wide range of these management tools. The following quote from his book summarizes so called current wisdom well:

> "Trial and error management embraces each new concept with a fervor
> unknown outside cult circles. Even the most inglorious examples of the tools
> enter the bestiary of management techniques with only the slightest critical
> examination. These events result in groundless incantations of current buzz
> words rather than real understanding and implementation with intentionality."
> (Nirenberg, 1997, p. 64)

ERRORS IN FORMULATING THE PROBLEM

The previous errors were concerned with a "rush to action," which is the myth of performance improvement based on the idea that leadership is action, and by implication, not really intellectual nor reflective.

However, although management is action oriented at times, we would expect the action to be preceded by clear definition of the results desired and the problems to be resolved in achieving the results. One of the most frequent errors in problem solving is solving the *wrong problem* precisely. There are five types of this error:

1. Picking the wrong stakeholders and partners.
2. Selecting an artificially narrow set of options for problem formulation.
3. Phrasing a problem incorrectly (quasi-problems based on quasi-needs).
4. Setting the boundaries or scope of a problem too narrowly.
5. Failing to think systemically (thinking in parts instead of wholes).

We will explain each of these in detail below.

Picking the Wrong Partners

This involves selecting a small group of non-representative partners to define the problems. Planning the future should involve those affected as partners, or at least have them involved in the Needs Assessment and problem formulation. Never make an important decision about the problem without challenging and then clarifying the various perceptions of the problem. Involve partners in challenging the formulation of the problem.

Considering Options Too Narrowly

Selecting a limited set of problem solving options includes working on only one definition of the problem initially, and often results in options that lack any real alternative. This can also include the selection of only one solution for a complex problem. Never accept a single definition of an important problem; it is important to produce at least two very different formulations of any problem considered important. In the case of solutions, the more alternative solutions considered the better the quality of the final solution.[4]

Stating the Problem Incorrectly

Phrasing the problem incorrectly is a common error. This can take a variety of forms:

1. The problem is mistakenly stated as a gap in methods, means, resources, and processes (quasi-needs).

2. Stating the problem in vague terms rather than in precise measurable terms.

3. Stating the problem around symptoms rather than results.

Strive to gather data through a rigorous Needs Assessment so that the problem is stated as a gap in results.

Setting the Boundaries or Scope of a Problem Too Narrowly

In the absence of hard measurable data, problems can be defined too narrowly. A narrow definition can lead to wasted effort, wasted resources, and failed solution(s). A system perspective can be beneficial in overcoming this barrier to success. Unfortunately, the application of a "systems approach" often does not include subsystems later found to be critical. It confuses a system with systems, or the parts with the whole.

Failure to Think Systemically

When one thinks in parts, then one is ignoring the relationships and linkages between the elements and the parts. Never attempt to solve any important problem at any level without relating all the Organizational Elements Model (Kaufman 1997, 1998, 2000).

Use the checklist in Table 6.1 to assess your problem formulation.

Table 6.1. Checking the Problem Formulation.

Code	Question	Yes	Unsure	No
1	Has evidence for the problem been gathered through a rigorous needs assessment at the Mega, Macro, and Micro levels?			
2	Have those affected by the problem been involved in generating data about the problem?			
3	Do all the important partners agree on the formulation of the problem?			
4	Is the problem stated as a selected gap in results?			
5	Are the gaps in results stated in rigorous measurable terms, namely ratio or interval?			
6	Are you sure of the problem level? Mega? Macro? Micro?			
7	Are you sure the problem statement is not a gap in methods and/or resources (quasi-needs)?			

Table 6.1. (*Continued*)

Code	Question	Yes	Unsure	No
8	Has the problem been defined too narrowly?			
9	Has the problem statement been challenged by various partners?			
10	Has the problem been stated at the appropriate level, Mega, Macro, and Micro?			
11	If the problem is a quasi-need, has it been linked to key results areas at the Mega, Macro, and Micro levels?			
12	Is there agreement that this is a priority need?			

SIMPLE PROBLEM SOLVING

One way to view a simple problem is to think of it as passing the following criteria:

1. One or very few people are affected by it.
2. The problem formulation (definition) is agreed on by all.
3. It is probably at the Micro level.
4. You have sufficient data to define the problem as a measurable gap in results.
5. The correct solution(s) is obvious.
6. It doesn't require a lot of time, effort, or resources to gather the Needs Assessment data.
7. There is a high degree of certainty.
8. The consequences are short-term.
9. All stakeholders agree about items 1 through 8 above.

The problem-solving process is a planning process to get from present results to desired results.

Formulate Problem Based on Needs

Problems are selected needs—gaps in results stated in measurable terms. We can use the problem solving process to fix the problem. Here are the sorts of questions that must be answered in this step.

1 Problem Formulation Questions

- How is the problem presented?
- Is it stated as a gap in results?
- Are the results important?
- Is the gap stated in measurable terms (for example, best in ratio or interval scale)?
- Do all the parties seriously affected agree on the problem formulation?
- Has the needs assessment identified this as a priority?
- Is this a one-time problem?
- Is this part of strategic planning, that is, one of a cluster of related problems?
- Has a cost-consequences analysis been done?
- Is it primarily a people problem?
- Is it primarily a process problem?
- Is it a machine problem?
- Does enough data (hard/soft) exist?
- What would happen if we ignored the problem?
- At what level is the problem—Mega, Macro, Micro?
- Is it a simple problem?
- What are the symptoms?
- How will we know it's solved?
- Are there any policy restraints?

Determine Solutions Requirements and Identify Solution Alternatives

In this step we are looking for the various means that will help us solve the problem. We have defined the ends in the previous step and can now analyze the alternative ways to get to the desired result. One of the common errors in this step is to leap to one solution without considering other options. Here are the questions to consider in this step.

2 Solutions Questions

- Have we completed a causal analysis?
- Does the cause analysis indicate appropriate solutions?
- Is there obviously more than one solution?
- Could we use solution generation techniques?
- Are useful ready made solutions available?
- How much time is available?
- How urgent is the requirement for a solution?
- How can we compare the solutions?
- Is the acceptance of others critical?

- Do we have the skills to develop worthwhile alternatives?
- Who can help us find alternatives?
- Is the problem complex?
- What are the things we cannot do?
- What are the costs of each alternative?
- Who else will be affected by each solution?
- Do we have the resources for each alternative?
- Which one will get the greatest resistance?
- If we choose one what else could go wrong?
- Do we require more research? What are the risks?
- Which solutions give the quickest result for least cost?
- Will it require a mix of methods?

Note that a solution is not selected at this problem solving step. Steps 1 and 2 are only problem identification and problem detailing. The balance of the steps relate to problem resolution. Only in step 3 do we select the solution(s) that will be implemented.

Select Solution(s)

Now we can take action. This step is a major decision step. You will select the best alternative to get you to where you want to be. Here are some of the questions to be answered as part of selecting the right solutions.

3 Select Solutions Questions

- How will we decide to decide?
- Who will make the final decision?
- Can the decision be delegated to one person?
- Must it be a group decision?
- What group technique could be used to make the decision?
- When is the decision required by?
- Who must be informed of the decision?
- How must the decision be communicated?
- What is the latest time?
- What is the earliest time?
- Who is accountable for the decision?
- Are you confident about the decision?
- Is the decision based on: A formal causal analysis? A formal costs consequences analysis?
- Which solution(s) have the better ratio of cost to consequences?
- What are the possible unintended consequences?
- Was this solution selected from a system perspective?

Implement

In this step we plan and manage the detailed steps to apply the selected solution(s). This step requires attention to detail. Details include:

1. What results must be accomplished.
2. Who will be responsible for accomplishing the results.
3. How many people will be involved.
4. How much coordination is required.

Here are some of the key questions to answer in the implementation of almost any solution.

---

4 Implementation Questions

- What are the stages in implementing the solution(s).
- What are the critical tasks to be completed?
- Who will do the tasks?
- What are the progress checks and time frames?
- Will PERT* or Gantt charts help plan the steps?
- What skills are required? Do we have them?
- How can we get skills we lack?
- What training is required?
- What performance support is required?
- What resources are required?
- What is the budget?
- If a detailed plan is required, who will write it?
- How will we deal with resistance and barriers?
- What methods and procedures must be followed?

*Program Evaluation and Review Technique

Determine Effectiveness and Efficiency

In this step we are concerned with evaluation. We want to know whether we are still on target, whether we have arrived, and/or do we have to change our destination. Often the world (or paradigm) in which we first formulated the problem changes suddenly and the problem changes. We can also make mistakes along the way, and these should be reflected on to help us avoid them in the future. Here are some of the questions to consider in the evaluation of the effectiveness and efficiency of solutions:

---

5 Determine Effectiveness

- How are we progressing?
- Are we on target?

- How far off target are we?
- Is the objective (result) still relevant?
- Are we better off? Worse off?
- Are we within budget?
- What have we learned?
- What could we do better?
- Is the problem solved? How do we know?
- Have the symptoms disappeared?
- How much did it cost? What are the payoffs?
- Are the problem owners satisfied?
- Have there been any adverse consequences?
- Has the problem changed?
- Did we use the time well?
- Did we solve it fast enough?
- Do we have to go back to the needs assessment and collect additional data?
- Should we try other means?
- Should we quit?
- Should we celebrate?
- Do we now decide what to keep, what to continue, what to stop?

Revise as Required

You may not have to use this step in simple problem solving—remember, no need, no gap. No gap, no problem—and nothing to continuously improve. However, sometimes we don't solve the problem fully or we might come up with a similar problem in the future and want to solve it right the first time. Here are some continuous improvement questions:

6 Revision Questions

- Should we revise our objectives?
- Should we change the performance indicators?
- Should we revise the implementation plan?
- What could work better next time?
- Should we involve more people?
- Why were we successful or why did we fail?
- What would we do the same way again?
- What have we learned about our own styles, filters, and biases?
- Should we revise our solutions?
- Should we replace our solutions?

Use the worksheet in Table 6.2 to note your answers to each step. Refer to other worksheets for detail.

Table 6.2. Simple Problem Solving Worksheet.

1. Define and Formulate the Problem	
What is the present result?	What are the desired results?

2. Determine Solutions Options

Refer to your responses to the Solutions Questions to compare the alternatives.

3. Select Solutions

Note the selected solution or intervention(s).

4. Implement

Note the key tasks, who will be responsible, and by when they are to be completed. Use more detailed planning sheets if necessary.

5. Determine Effectiveness and Efficiency

6. Revise as Required

What Simple and Complex Problem Solving Have in Common

All problem solving processes, simple or complex, are a form of the six-step problem solving model (Figure 6.2). The complex problem solving process presented next is an expansion of these same six steps. Because problem solving is so important to building the bridge between planning and delivering high payoff results, the general six-step problem solving model is discussed again in detail in Chapter Ten.

COMPLEX PROBLEM SOLVING

Complex problem solving includes a wider range of factors to be considered. On the surface the steps appear the same, but experts tend to consider more steps in the complex problem solving process. Examples of complex problems could include:

- Reforming education
- Finding a cure for cancer
- Achieving peace in our time
- Bringing a failing company back to a competitive position
- Resolving leadership problems

Figure 6.4 outlines the twelve-step process for solving more complex problems (which extends the basic six-step process provided earlier).[5]

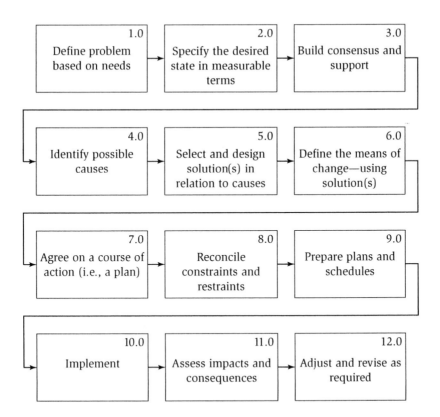

Figure 6.4. Key Steps in Complex Problem Solving.

Source: From Kaufman, 2000.

Complex problem solving is more like assembling a jigsaw puzzle than painting by numbers. Expert problem solvers check each of the twelve steps, but they don't always follow the purely logical numbered sequence. The whole process relies on information, and at times you don't have all the information to complete a step. The process is like detective work or intelligence gathering. You might do parts of one step, move on, do parts of another, and then return to complete a step because you have more data. You may also come into the process at different steps.

Someone else may have done a prior Needs Assessment but not involved enough people. So you may have to spend time on step 3 (building consensus and support) for the problem formulation with many partners.

Use the steps to ensure you consider all the elements of the jigsaw puzzle, but don't feel constrained to follow the numerical sequence. You may follow a different sequence for each problem selected in the Needs Assessment. What follows are some notes and key questions for each step.

Define the Problem Based on Needs

It is often easy to sense that something is wrong based on a clear set of symptoms or indicators. A crisis may suddenly occur. A vaguely stated problem of enormous proportions may be presented, and so on. The key in this step and step 1 is to gather enough data (hard and soft) to define the problem. A Needs Assessment can be used to define one problem or many. This step is closely related to step 2. This is where the most effort should go before moving around the other steps. Some additional questions to ask are shown here:

---

1 Define the Problem

- At what level is the apparent problem, Mega, Macro, Micro?
- How valid and reliable are the data?
- Should more data be collected? Hard? Soft? Both?
- How are the customers, clients, partners affected?
- How widespread is it?
- How many are affected?
- How serious is it?
- Who owns the problem?
- What are people's perceptions of the problem?
- What priority should be assigned even if it is poorly stated? And/or if the data are insufficient?
- What methods will give us quality data?
- What would tell us the problem is solved? The problem is getting worse?
- What are the implications of ignoring the problem?

Specify Desired State

"If we can't define a problem so that it leads to ethical actions that benefit mankind, then either we haven't defined or are currently unable to define the problem properly."
—Mitroff, 1998

It is often easy to state what is wrong with an individual, a team, a community, or an organization based only on perceptual data. We don't, however, have a need until there is a demonstrated gap between desired results and present results stated in measurable terms. And this, of course, requires that the organization define its desired destination in relation to results to be accomplished for the society, clients, and individual employees.

As more people become involved in the problem definition, more personality types become introduced to decision making. While this is essential for an accurate definition of "What Should Be," more voices can make it more difficult to gain agreement on desired results. Questions for specifying the desired state follow:

---

2 Specify the Desired State

- Have we created a *Smarter* objective for the desired state/result?
- What are the best performance indicators for success?
- Do all the key partners in planning agree on the statement of the desired state?
- What level is the desired state, Mega, Macro, Micro?
- Can we link the desired state level with other levels?
- What will be the impact on the Ideal Vision?
- What paradigms for success will we have to challenge?
- Are there ethical issues in the statement of the desired state?
- Have the assumptions underlying the formulation of the problem been discussed?
- Is the problem worth fixing?

Build Consensus and Support

One of the factors that make some problems more complex is the large number of people impacted by the problem and it's resolution. Identifying who "owns" and who is affected by the problem is critical if we are to deliver high payoff results.[6] The person tasked with managing the problem solving process will have to gain agreement on the formulation of the problem (steps 1 and 2).

This will require an influence plan to achieve shared meaning. Without a shared perception of the problem, it is very difficult to complete the other steps in the process. Some questions to ask follow.

3 Build Consensus and Support

- Do the main partners in planning agree on the needs assessment data?
- Do the main partners agree on the desired state (future results)?
- Do the main partners agree on the priority given to the problem?
- What will you have to do to influence those with conflicting views?
- How many people have to agree on the problem formulation?
- What level of commitment is required?
- How will we inform people?
- Who might support or resist the formulation of the problem?
- Who are the sponsors of change (that is, who wants the problem solved and has the authority)?
- What other parts of the organization will be affected by solving the problem?
- What are the consequences of low support for the problem formulation?
- What clients are affected (internal/external)?
- Arrive ready to move forward.

Troubleshoot the Problem (Causal Analysis)

Depending on how the problem occurred (or appeared), there are two very different ways of identifying what are the likely causes of the problem.

The Troubleshooting Causal Analysis.[7] This approach is concerned with figuring out what has gone wrong in the existing system, the team, or the individual performer. There are a number of powerful causal analysis techniques, especially those developed by the advocates of human performance technology (HPT).[8] Gilbert (1978), for example, identified six factors influencing human performance: directional information, resources, rewards, competencies, capacity, and motives. At the level of the whole organization, the factors increase and a wider range of causes have to be explored. At the individual and team level, these factors can pinpoint the causes of performance gaps and suggest appropriate solutions.

Opportunity/Solution Engineering. This approach starts with an opportunity gap. The opportunity is to achieve a result that has never been achieved before using new approaches, new means and/or new technologies. The desired result is a significant paradigm shift. In other words, things are OK at present but if you challenge the status quo (existing paradigm) there is an opportunity to achieve what appeared impossible yesterday. Some troubleshooting questions follow:

4 Troubleshoot the Problem

- Should we bother to look for causes?
- Were things OK before?
- Is there an opportunity to shift paradigms?
- Did the problem "pop up" suddenly?

- When did things go wrong?
- What went wrong? What was the first sign?
- What further information or data do we want?
- What changed? What behaviors are the indicators?
- Does this change account for the problem?
- At what level is the problem, Mega, Macro, Micro? Are they linked?
- What values, beliefs, and biases do we bring to the problem formulation?
- What causal analysis method is best suited to the problem?
- What paradigms and mental models have we used in the past to deal with this type of problem?
- Should we change how we formulate or view the problem?

Select and Design a Solution

"We are getting better and better at doing that which should not be done at all."
—Drucker, 1993

Sometimes a direct cause cannot be found or the causes of problems cannot be corrected. In this step the problem solvers will start searching for solutions through trial and error. Sometimes the solution is available "off the shelf," and at other times you will have to design one. Rather than leaving it to chance, viable solutions should meet the performance requirements (that is, be capable of achieving the high payoff results required for success). If the current vision, mission, and goals are stated in fuzzy, vague, or non-measurable terms, a *performance requirements analysis* should be conducted to derive the results specifications that potential methods and means must be able to accomplish.

When performance requirements have been identified and potential processes and inputs identified as potential solutions, a methods-means analysis should follow. For simple problems, the solutions are often obvious and easy to apply. The decision can more often be quickly made for simple problems, whereas complex problems often take longer to consider the options available.

The Organizational Elements Model provides a tool for completing a system analysis (Kaufman, 2000). Methods-means analysis, a step in system analysis, develops and defines the various alternatives for solving the problem and compares them before selecting the best one(s) for achieving the results. A methods-means analysis is conducted at each level of system planning—Mega, Macro, and Micro—after needs at each level are identified and selected. Some possible questions follow:

5 Select the Solution

- Should we use solution generation techniques?
- What elements of the Ideal Vision should and will influence the solutions selected?
- How can we compare the alternatives?
- What are the advantages and disadvantages of each alternative?

- Should we conduct feasibility analysis?
- Are there any solutions available "off the shelf"?
- Are there any constraints on the solutions we can select?
- Could we brainstorm solutions?
- Do we have the skills to recognize the solution?
- Do we require help in selecting the solution?
- Who should be involved in selecting the solution?
- Is the objective we are trying to achieve possible within the present paradigm?
- Will we have to learn to do things differently?
- What solutions have worked or failed in the past?
- Are there ethical considerations in selecting the solution(s)?
- Who can approve the solution(s)?
- What are the risks for each solution?
- What are the probable consequences for each solution?
- Are the risks of any solution unacceptable?

Unfortunately, many of us have a very limited set of solutions we commonly include in the methods-means analysis. We often have to read outside of our field and leave our comfort zones behind in order to discover the alternative solution(s) that may achieve the desired results most effectively.

Define the Means of Change—Using Solutions

Complex solutions often require a number of methods, tasks, tactics, and means to achieve them. Solving complex problems also involves change. In this step we focus on defining *what* to change and *what* to maintain. This requires attention to detail and specific skills in the area to be changed. The following questions are helpful.

6 Define the Means

- What skills are required for this step?
- Who are the change agents?
- What technology is available?
- Should we reengineer a process?
- What types of interventions are suitable for this problem?
- What resources are required?
- What people are required?
- Who has to change roles?
- What cultural norms and practices have to be changed?
- What tactics have to change?
- Should we conduct a SWOT analysis?
- Should we conduct a cultural screen?
- What training is required?
- What performance improvement is required?

Agree on a Plan

A plan describes the desired results and defines the methods, tasks, and activities required to achieve the results and solve the problem. This step requires a point person to coordinate people, resources, and time. Some of the questions to ask follow:

---

7 Agree on a Plan

- Who is responsible for carrying out the plan?
- Who will do what?
- What coordination issues must be discussed?
- What detailed planning tools will be used?
- What are the critical stages and tasks?
- How will the plan be communicated?
- Who should be involved in the detailed planning?
- Who will authorize the plan?
- Who will "own" the plan?
- Who will check the plan?
- Are there any conflicts?
- How will the conflicts be resolved?
- Is there a requirement for a contingency plan?
- What are the risks?
- What could go wrong?

Reconcile Constraints and Restraints

Effective planners proactively define the potential barriers to implementing the plan. These become more obvious after the detailed plan has been drafted. Planners can scan the detailed steps, stages, and means to identify restraints on the whole plan and parts of it. A *constraint* exists when no methods-means exist for meeting the need (that is, for closing the gap in results). A *restraint* is a condition/Input that provides barriers to progress and success. Some questions for this process follow:

---

8 Reconcile Constraints and Restraints

- What are our restraints (paradigms, policy, politics, personalities)?
- What are the things we can't (yet) do?
- Who says what we can and cannot do?
- Are the restraints physical or psychological?
- What are our assumptions and can they be successfully challenged?
- What are we overlooking?
- What are the internal barriers? External barriers?

- What has to give? What has to change?
- Who will resist and why?
- What are the resource limitations?
- What prevailing paradigms limit our options?
- What must we comply with?
- What are the risks?
- What government laws and legislation create barriers?
- What policies create barriers?

Prepare Plans and Schedules

This step documents the judgments made in steps 6, 7, and 8. This is primarily a documentation step to ensure the details are recorded to help all those involved in implementing the plan. Some of the questions follow:

9 Prepare Plans and Schedules

- What is the time frame for action?
- How urgent—the priority based on the costs to meet it versus the costs to ignore it—is the need?
- What planning tools are suitable?
- Who will document the plan?
- How will the plan be distributed?
- How will people be informed of changes to the plans and schedules?
- How will progress be recorded?
- What backup and support are required?
- Who will assess progress?

Implement the Plan

This step proves the worth of the previous steps. In complex problems you may have spent months—even years—getting to this step. So you have to revisit steps 1 and 2 to ensure the problem has not changed. Questions to ask follow:

10 Implement the Solution

- Is the problem still the same?
- Are the priorities still the same?
- Are we ready to do it?
- Are there any major barriers to action at this point?
- Do we still have the sponsors' full support?
- What is our level of commitment at this point?
- Do we still have the authority to act?
- What is the first practical step?
- Must the start be public?
- Are we progressing appropriately?

Assess Impacts and Consequences

The moment we start solving complex problems, we are usually initiating major change. Once we change one part of a system, every other part will change. Einstein famously called this the "*chuckle*" effect—if you tickle one part of a system, other parts will "chuckle." Unfortunately, solving one problem sometimes triggers other problems to appear. Some of these questions are listed below.

---

11 Assess Impacts and Consequences

- What happened once we started?
- How will we measure progress?
- What looks different? Have behaviors changed? Has performance improved?
- Is that what we wanted? Have the results improved?
- Have any problems emerged?
- Are the clients satisfied?
- Are we better off or worse off than before?
- Have we aligned people, performance, and payoffs?
- What are the payoffs?
- What did we learn? What did we do well?
- Has the need been eliminated or reduced or has it grown larger?
- Have results been eventuated at Mega, Macro, and Micro levels?
- What unanticipated externalities occurred as well?

Adjust and Revise as Required

Problems at all levels can (but do not always have to) take a long time to solve. The evaluation stage (step 11) will indicate changes and revisions to the original plans. Strategic thinking is a dynamic process of continuous adjustment to the accelerated rate of change in both the internal and external environment of the organization. To be strategic it must be Mega focused. Emerging gaps in results can occur any time, so flexible and dynamic planning is required. Important gaps become problems, and planners are faced with juggling multiple problems in any year, month, or week. Agile leaders are able to make rapid adjustments and revisions on an ongoing basis by asking questions similar to these:

---

12 Adjust and Revise

- What didn't work and what shall we do?
- What steps in the process should we revisit?
- What should we continue? Stop? Revise?
- What could we improve?
- Who requires feedback?
- Should our plans and schedules be revised?
- What time targets require adjustments?

- What people must be replaced? Retrained? Re-skilled?
- Can we trust the data?
- Who should change their behavior? Their performance?
- What assumptions must we change?
- Must we revisit/redefine the need (results-gaps problem formulation)?
- Do we require more resources, more money?

Solving Complex Problems

Use the checklist in Table 6.3 to assess how well you are dealing with the need and whether you have achieved the results.

Table 6.3. Assessment Checklist.

	Assessment Question	Yes	Unsure	No
1	Is the problem stated as a gap in (Mega, Macro, Micro) results?			
2	Is the desired state formulated in measurable (ratio or interval) terms?			
3	Is the problem worth fixing?			
4	Do the owners (internal and external) of the problem all agree on its formulation?			
5	Can alternative formulations of the problem be considered?			
6	Is there a high level of commitment to solving the problem?			
7	Is it worthwhile troubleshooting the problem?			
8	Is it worthwhile analyzing the causes of the problem?			
9	Do the problem solvers agree on the appropriate cause analysis method?			
10	Has the cost of ignoring the problem been compared to the cost of fixing the problem?			
11	Have a number of alternatives solutions been developed?			
12	Have the risks of each alternative solution been calculated?			

Table 6.3. (*Continued*)

	Assessment Question	Yes	Unsure	No
13	Have the probable consequences of each alternative been defined and compared?			
14	Has the level of uncertainty for each alternative been defined and agreed?			
15	Have the obviously poor alternatives been rejected?			
16	Is more information required to compare the alternatives?			
17	Are the decision makers' risk tolerance levels defined and recognized?			
18	Have the right people been involved in selecting the solutions?			
19	Does the solution(s) require significant change in behaviors and processes?			
20	Do the solutions involve ethical and moral decisions?			
21	Has the alternative, which involves unacceptable risk, been rejected?			
22	Have the tactics and methods to implement the solution(s) been developed and agreed?			
23	Have all the significant coordination issues been discussed by the planners?			
24	Have tactics and methods been communicated to the right people?			
25	Have conflicts about methods and means been resolved?			
26	Is there a requirement for contingency plans?			
27	Have the "what could go wrong" scenarios been worked through?			
28	Have the plans and schedules been documented?			

(*Continued*)

Table 6.3. Assessment Checklist. (*Continued*)

	Assessment Question	*Yes*	*Unsure*	*No*
29	Have roles and accountabilities been defined and negotiated?			
30	Has the detailed course of action (action plan) been agreed and approved?			
31	Have the major barriers been identified (constraints/restraints)?			
32	Have the methods for overcoming the barriers been included in the plan?			
33	Have the detailed plans and schedules been distributed to the right people?			
34	Has the start time been agreed?			
35	Has anything changed significantly since the problem was formulated?			
36	Are you ready to start?			
37	Are you on track?			
38	Have any unplanned consequences occurred?			
39	Have you appropriately dealt with unplanned effects and consequences?			
40	Have you achieved the desired result(s)?			
41	Have you made adjustments and revisions where required?			
42	Have you linked results and consequences to Mega, Macro, and Micro?			

Notes

1. Kaufman (2000, p. 47) makes the distinction between problems derived from gaps in results versus gaps in processes and inputs. He calls these latter ones "quasi-needs."

2. The concept of dialogue is about skilled discussions in which the participants agree to withhold judgment and explore mental models, memes, paradigms, and underlying assumptions. Dialogue can be defined as a sustained collective inquiry

into everyday experience. The objective of dialogue is to open new ground for inquiry. It is a setting in which people can become aware of and share their world, their experience, the processes of thought and feeling that created that experience. It is not the same as debate or advocacy for one point of view. It can be a solution to problems where the causes are due to low levels of interpersonal skills and clashes of paradigms. Dialogue can generate shared meaning and extra choices for resolving important strategic problems.

3. Although Deming was a statistician and developed quality management principles around statistical controls, the rigorous statistics are often overlooked by organizations that want to focus only on the "soft skill" components related to quality management, since they are commonly less threatening.

4. There are many ways to generate ideas and solutions to performance problems. Van Gundy (1988, pp. 76–79) identified over thirty individual idea generation techniques and thirty plus group idea generation techniques. If you think brainstorming is the only technique, you have limited your options. Examples are analogies, biomics, metaphors, relational algorithms, story writing, problem inventory analysis, storyboards, and synetics.

5. Kaufman (1992, 1998, 2000) has offered the six-step problem solving model in his books on strategic thinking and planning. In this book we expand on this model for complex problems. There is no contradiction—just more detail on those steps requiring a high level of participation in the problem solving process. It is seldom if ever possible to solve complex problems by oneself because complex strategic problems by definition have consequences for many, and therefore should involve many in their solution.

6. Kaufman (2000, pp. 55–59) emphasizes the requirement to identify the correct planning partners to guide the process and to "own" it when it is completed. An otherwise good plan might fail because those affected were not involved in the proposed change (solution), no matter how logical the process was.

7. Cause analysis follows on from Needs Assessment. Terms such as front end analysis (FEA), performance analysis, and needs analysis all involve some form of defining the problem and its causes. We believe that the original work of Gilbert on the six factors that influence human performance provides a sound foundation for diagnosing the causes of gaps in results (needs). Gilbert (1978, p. 88) offers an outline for skilled diagnosis of performance deficiencies for individual performance. Other practitioners such as Mager and Pipe and Rummler and Brache have expanded on Gilbert's model and added further value by providing practical diagnostic tools for analyzing the causes. The cause analysis adds further to the Needs Assessment because it points to the type of solutions, interventions, and methods that are best suited to eliminate the problem. Oakley-Browne has also developed a card based expert system, *The Needs Assessment Blueprint,* which provides a tool for conducting a thorough cause analysis at the individual and team performance level.

8. *The Handbook of Human Performance Technology* (2nd ed.) from Stolovitch and Keeps provides a wide range of articles on HPT. Chapters Three and Eight are good summaries of the HPT approach to cause analysis. However, we make a distinction between Needs Assessment and cause analysis or needs analysis, as it is often called. You first should assess the need before analyzing the causes. Needs Assessments define the critical problems worth fixing; cause analysis identifies the causes for the problems so that the right solutions can be selected and implemented.

CHAPTER SEVEN

Developing Smarter Objectives

Thinking Audaciously, Being Audacious,
Delivering High Payoff Results

CHAPTER GOALS

After completing this chapter you will be able to answer the following
questions.

❑ Why develop objectives?

❑ What are the myths about objectives?

❑ Why do objectives work?

❑ How can you categorize objectives?

❑ What is a *Smarter* objective?

❑ What are the common important/key result areas?

❑ What is a performance indicator?

❑ What is a *mission objective*?

❑ What is the *primary mission objective*?

WHY OBJECTIVES?

"Whatever you can do or dream you can, begin it. Boldness has genius, power and magic in it."
—Goethe, 2001

Through the history of human performance, many people have suggested the basic idea of setting objectives for desired results. Tom Peters, noted management consultant, has influenced many organizations and business leaders in recent years. In *Thriving on Chaos* he says:

> "The prime objective of goal-setting should be to turn 90 percent of people in your firm into confident winners who will take the new and always greater risks required by the chaotic times we live in." (Peters, 1987)

The Skill Gap

The reasons for setting objectives might appear self-evident to some. Yet, despite their use by people (especially leaders) over the centuries, we still find many examples to indicate that we still are not highly skillful at using them to define worthwhile, measurable results at individual, organizational, and societal levels. Politicians, executives, and team leaders still appear to be immersed in what George Odiorne called the *activity trap*—a singular focus on means and not ends.

There are many reasons for setting objectives, some more important than others. We will summarize these reasons and describe the critical ones in detail in this chapter.

Reasons for Setting Objectives

The following are the most frequently cited reasons for setting objectives:

❑ They describe a desired future. They give clear direction.

❑ They can improve performance.

❑ They provide measurability to a desired future.

❑ They are a communication tool; they provide a vehicle for developing shared meaning about where the group, organization, or community commits to head.

❑ They define success and satisfaction in measurable terms.

❑ They provide a justifiable foundation for allocating financial resources.

❑ They can motivate people.

❑ They provide a basis for measuring success or failure.

❑ They clarify expectations on what results are expected of a specific role in an organization.

❑ They provide an opportunity for positive reinforcement when achieved—they act as an incentive.

❑ They are the first step in effective planning for results.

❑ They define accountability and responsibility in measurable terms.

❑ They give an individual or team control over their lives.

❑ They convert espoused or implicit values into action and measurable results. They allow Mega, Macro, and Micro to "come alive."

❑ They are the basis for performance review, appraisal, and performance improvement.

Quick Assessment

Check those reasons from the above list that your organization espouses as the logic for using objectives. Share your assessment with one or more colleagues and decide whether both of you agree. If not, work with your colleagues to establish shared reasons for developing objectives for high payoff results linking the levels.

We are drawn into the future by an anticipation of positive reinforcement based on successful accomplishment of objectives. This triggers positive expectations because objectives define a desired future that is rewarding to achieve. You should spend time with your colleagues reflecting on why you should develop objectives. This is a fundamental leadership question for all organizations. We suggest that preparing measurable objectives—valid ones—is vital to any high payoff results effort. After all, as Mager (1997) points out, "If you don't know where you are going you may end up someplace else."[1]

Individual Accomplishment and Team Accomplishment

The weight of research on objectives has focused on individuals—where accountability for the accomplishment is clearly delegated to a single person. However, a single person cannot achieve objectives written for teams, units, organizations, and communities. Teams can often envision more *audacious* objectives than individual team members are capable of achieving. On the other hand, individuals can break the status quo and habits of "group think," thus achieving even the most seemingly difficult of objectives. So what is the real nature of objectives for the individual?

Myths and Misconceptions

A common myth about objectives is that they alone improve performance. Research, however, does not support this belief. In a study comparing financial reinforcers and objective setting, Huber (1985) concluded that:

> "The setting of goals regardless of the method does not evoke greater learning than that achieved when trainees are offered only a base salary."

Gilbert (1978) identified six factors that influence individual human performance, shown in Table 7.1.[2]

Table 7.1. Gilbert's Six Factors of Performance.

Directional Information 1	Resources 2	Rewards and Incentives 3
Competencies (Knowledge and Skill) 4	Capacity 5	Motive 6

The first *"window"* includes "directional information" . . . objectives. But the other five factors must be managed for objectives to have an influence. From our own experience, we know that setting objectives is insufficient to guarantee accomplishment. When the other factors are managed and objective setting is used appropriately, then results can be improved significantly.

Some other myths about performance objectives for individuals include:

1. We should eliminate objectives. Although the late W. Edwards Deming encouraged management to eliminate objectives, his criticism was aimed at *how* objectives were often focused only on financial goals and used to create fear (of repercussions for not achieving an objective). Objectives can be useful if written for the full range of key result areas for an individual's role and not used for blaming.

2. Impose "impossible" objectives to push people to accomplish more than they may initially believe possible. The concept of "impossible" is a tricky one. People thought, initially, that landing on the moon was impossible. Other old paradigm thinking and conventional wisdom turned out to be false, such as the 1899 statement by the then U.S. director of the Patent Office declaring that everything that could be invented had been invented! In reality, what we are coming to recognize is that it is impossibility itself that has been invented. In the never-ending marathon of contemporary life, impossibility is *uninvented* on a daily basis.

   We should push the envelope—push it continually toward the accomplishment of Mega level Outcomes. What some think is impossible is possible if we only set out there and continuously improve toward that destination. Walt Disney once noted, "If you can dream it you can do it" and overcame all of the naysayers to create one of the most revered entertainment industries in the world. If he listened to others about "impossibility," he would never have started out. Mega is an idealistic concept, and some might complain that it is impossible. It might not be achieved in our lifetime or even our children's . . . but if we don't set out to get there, where do we head? As President John F. Kennedy noted in his inaugural address, "If not us, who? If not now, when?" We suggest the time is now and it is up to us.

Even when they have a relatively convincing name such as "Smarter objectives," good objectives should specify *what* is to be accomplished, not *how* results should be gotten. Complaining about "impossibility" usually comes from fear; fear coming from past attempts to deliver high payoff results, only to be punished for shortfalls, and from being chastised by associates. We must push the envelope if we are to deliver high payoff results . . . if we only select objectives that can assuredly be achieved, we will stay mired in yesterday. We should set objectives that push us to achieve ideal objectives for the long-term, with intermediate milestone objectives leading us toward success.

"Audacious" means setting objectives that might be well beyond our current capability . . . or what at first blanch we might think is impossible.

3. Set common objectives for everyone. This myth ignores individual skills readiness and motivation, not to mention access to adequate resources. As Daniels (1994) says in his book *Bringing Out the Best in People,* "If we ask for a 10 percent improvement in productivity from everybody, it will generally be too difficult for the lowest performers, somewhat challenging for the average performers, and too easy for the best performers."[3]

Across-the-board changes or fixes without tying them to higher-level payoffs is blind management. Rather than "blanket objectives," the objectives for individuals and small groups should be derived (rolled down) from the Mega and Macro objectives so that everyone can make a unique contribution to the collective destination and success. So individual objectives might differ, but they all should be aligned to add value within and external to the organization. In addition to the ability to contextualize one's role, taking responsibility for personal objectives creates an authentic opportunity to demonstrate one's trustworthiness. This, in turn, can be a powerful drive for followership.

4. It is often good for low performing individuals or teams to initially focus on incremental gains with small achievable objectives. These "small wins" increase confidence in their ability to improve and keep their focus on how the results are linked to ideal long-term results at the Mega level.

What Makes Objectives Work

The rules for using objectives apply primarily to individual objectives (Micro results), but some apply equally well to team objectives, organizational objectives, and societal objectives:

1. Objectives are triggers for performance; they are antecedents because they come before the activities and establish expectations for performance. If well-written they also define measurable standards. The accomplishment of objectives is an opportunity for reinforcement, for appropriately tying incentives to results. If objectives are not paired with reinforcement, they will not likely produce consistent or exemplary performance in either the short or long term.

2. Objectives must be "owned." The ownership can be self-initiated, as with high achievers, or negotiated between managers and direct reports or between team members. The best objectives are commonly those willingly developed by the individual or the team through a relating and negotiation process. They all should link to Mega and Macro objectives.

3. Attainable objectives are those for which success is highly probable. The more achievable the objective, the more likely performers will reach it. Overly easy objectives might also be an "excuse" to not push one's self or the team. Trivial results will not deliver high payoff results. If objectives are paired with positive reinforcement, successful performers will want to develop higher objectives. Thus, you should set both audacious long-term objectives and short-term objectives that are clearly linked to the achievement of long-term success.

4. For team objectives, each team member must have an opportunity to influence the objectives. In addition, each team member must be asked to make a public commitment to the objective(s). But objectives should not be imposed either. Imposition doesn't work, since commitment to objectives is a uniquely personal matter. If representatives from a broad cross section of the organization—from top management to internal associates and external partners—derive and decide on the objectives, the probability of success is likely to be very high.

CATEGORIES OF OBJECTIVES

Objectives can be categorized in a number of ways:

From Vague and "Fuzzy" to Specific and Measurable. Goals are usually broad and measurable in nominal or ordinal scales (see Table 7.5), while objectives are written in interval or ratio scales of measurement (see Kaufman, 1998, 2000; Kaufman, Leigh, & Watkins, 2001). Some sample goals include:

- Improve performance.
- Increase fitness.
- Build better towns.
- Achieve excellence.

From Short Term to Long Term. Performance standards are an example of short-term objectives, whereas self-sufficiency of clients and neighbors may not be achieved in our lifetime, yet is only achievable if we start moving toward it now. If we don't set out to achieve perfection, what will we settle for? When is "good enough" good enough? What level below perfection would you settle for in a brain surgeon who is operating on you in the morning? The pilot flying the plane as you read this book? Your dentist? Your grocer's food inspector?

By Owner or Those Responsible. Objectives can be categorized according to who is accountable and responsible for their achievement. This category also includes defining who is the beneficiary (primary client) of successful achievement of the objective.

In this book we are concerned with measurable objectives at three levels of planning for organizational success:

1. *Mega Results.* These objectives are developed to describe the results that will be achieved to add value for society as the client.
2. *Macro Results.* These objectives are formulated to define the desired quality of the results delivered to external clients and stakeholders.
3. *Micro Results.* These objectives are formulated for individuals and teams inside the organization. They describe measurable results for the quality of products delivered to internal clients.

It is vital to align these three levels of results. Without the alignment, high payoff results will not be achieved.

Proactive Planning

Planning can be aimed at several levels. At all levels the purpose of planning is to create worthwhile results now and in the future and to continue to deliver results that have a positive impact on individuals and the whole of society. There are three types of results for which we can develop objectives. All three types of results apply to all organizations. They are shown in Table 7.2.

Table 7.2. Three Types of Results.

Result Type	Definition	Examples
Outcomes (MEGA)	These are the added value to society of the Outputs. These are the payoffs to society.	Profits over time (not just one shot). Self-sufficient citizens Zero disabilities from accidents Zero starvation
Outputs (MACRO)	These are the results delivered to external clients.	Delivered vehicle Discharged patient Competent graduate Dividend Unpolluted exhaust
Products (MICRO)	These are results delivered to internal clients by individuals and teams.	Delivered technical advice DVD Curriculum Component

Proactive planners recognize the relationships among these three types of results, and thereby set out to achieve high payoff results that have positive consequences at the Mega level. When you link all three levels of results, you are recognizing that strategic planning is concerned with the linkages and alignments. This type of planning can also be called holistic or system planning because it recognizes the relationships among all the elements of an organization, especially the linkage between the three levels of results.

"SMARTER" CRITERIA FOR HIGH IMPACT OBJECTIVES

Leaders Focus on Results

Effective leaders begin planning by first defining the results they want to achieve. This focus on results rather than activities is a key rule of accountability. This section describes the criteria for a Smarter objective. Smarter is an acronym for the characteristics of a well-written and useful objective, as shown in Table 7.3.

Table 7.3. SMARTER Objectives.

S	This means the objective is written for a *specific* result, a single topic or area of performance.
M	Each objective must be observable and therefore assessable. This means the objective includes a *measurable* component stated in interval or ratio terms. The objective must answer these questions: How much? or How successful? How many? or How audacious? How well? or How proactive?
A	If the objective aims at significant change, this criteria is about paradigm shifts and challenges to the status quo. We call these *audacious* objectives because they challenge individuals, teams, and the organization to stretch their horizons and exceed the present level of results.
R	Each objective must define the *results* to be achieved and excludes the methods and means to achieve the result. In other words, the objective is written for a key result area (key accountability), not for an increase in activity. The key result areas are at three levels—Mega, Macro, and Micro.
T	This means each objective must have a target time for completion (i.e., it must be *time bound* or refined).
E	The sum total of the objectives are *encompassing* (that is, they are aligned and supportive of each other—inclusive and linked).
R	Objectives should be evaluated and *reviewed* to check relevance and progress towards the results.

Specific

These criteria recognize that there are many opportunities for formulating objectives. Specificity allows you to focus on a clearly defined area of performance and define your desired result. Specificity helps you to set priorities from among many potential result areas. Key result areas are at three levels—Mega, Macro, and Micro.

The specificity rule also deals with goals that are often stated as vague, nonmeasurable statements such as *"improve our competitiveness."* We can, and should, develop Smarter objectives rather than vague general goals. This chapter will help you with this task. Some examples of specificity are given in Table 7.4.

Table 7.4. Specificity Examples.

Non-Example	Example
Increase sales	Increase product X sales by at least 25 percent.
Get healthy	Reduce the ratio of "bad" cholesterol to calories to no more than 1:3.
Reduce crime	Reduce rapes to zero.
Improve safety	Reduce road accidents due to alcohol to zero.

A problem with non-specific goals is that they are open to misinterpretation and cause confusion. With general goals we may end up somewhere we didn't want to be. In addition, general vague goals make it difficult to assess the intended results (ends) in measurable terms. In other words, how can you define success in precise measurable terms if the objectives are vague and non-specific? Specificity forces you to pinpoint the important result areas that are worth improving.

Measurable

The objective describes a specific desired result. To determine when or whether that result was achieved, you require some kind of measurement to assess success.[4] There are four scales of measurement, shown in Table 7.5.

Table 7.5. Four Scales of Measurement.

There are four scales of measurement. For rigorous Smarter objectives, develop performance indicators at the interval or ratio scale. There are statistical tools for all of these scales.		
1. Nominal (Least reliable; vague and might be confused)	Naming something (for example, excellence, beauty, cool, hot, guru)	Goals
2. Ordinal (Vague and fuzzy but more reliable than nominal)	Defining things as greater than or less than other things (for example, this team is better than that team)	Goals
3. Interval (More reliable, precise)	Relating items along a scale with equal intervals that has an arbitrary zero point (for example, degrees Celsius).	Objectives
4. Ratio (Most reliable, precise)	Relating items along a scale at a known zero point with equal intervals (for example, weight, distance, revenue)	Objectives

For each objective, you must select the most relevant (ratio) scale to indicate successful achievement of the objective. Goals are usually expressed on a nominal or ordinal scale while objectives are expressed on interval or ratio scales. Some examples are provided in Table 7.6.

Table 7.6. Examples of Goals and Objectives.

Examples of Goals	Examples of Objectives
Create safer beaches	Reduce accidents due to beach pollution and hazards to zero.
Increase sales of product X	Increase sales on product X by at least 25 percent.
Build a beautiful house	Complete the house to specifications (refer detailed specs) within the $250,000 budget by forty-eight weeks from today. The house will be awarded a local realtor's association Home Beautiful Award within five years.
Set up effective government for Developing Nation Q	Establish a government policy that meets all the democratic principles stated in the draft national constitution by 2044.

All the examples in the right-hand column are either ratio or interval measures. The last example on Nation Q is a qualitative measure because it refers to a set of specific criteria against which a judgment can be made with reasonable accuracy.

This criterion is the one most open to interpretation. Because objectives can be developed at four levels, the term can have different interpretations depending on the level.

Audacious

"The dreamers of the day are dangerous people, for they may act their dream with open eyes and make it possible."
—Lawrence of Arabia

Individual achievement is often taken in small steps—small steps toward large results and high payoffs. The specificity of these building-block objectives is vital, and all objectives must be linked to a larger set of purposes and payoffs.

The other three levels of potentially audacious results are team, organizational, and community and society.

Each is influenced by the ability of leaders to achieve shared meaning and commitment. The degree of complexity of communities makes it more difficult to gain acceptance to *audacious objectives.* A number of techniques are emerging on large-scale change. (These are well-described in the book *Real Time Strategic Change* by Robert W. Jacobs).

The *audacious* criterion must balance the paradox of challenge versus realism. Significant change occurs through challenging the status quo and shifting our orientations, views, and standard operating procedures to create a better world.

On the other hand, setting objectives, which some believe are not attainable within the time frame, may result in low commitment and low performance unless we can recruit them to see the folly of naysaying and not moving. As Tom Peters (1997) notes, "It is easier to kill an organization than it is to change it." If members of an organization want to commit organizational suicide, this is a good cue to help them find someplace where they are more comfortable. Why let the few who are frightened (and usually verbal) destroy the organization?

If people are involved in the objective setting process and can see opportunities for positive reinforcement, and if the objectives are achieved, they are more likely to set audacious objectives that shift the present performance paradigms from short-term comfort to longer-term satisfaction and survival. What is important is for all to understand that short-term objectives can and must build the pathway to high payoff results. Some people see the future, and others only see the stoplights along the way. Some audacious examples are listed in Table 7.7.

Table 7.7. Some Audacious Examples.

Audacious Examples	
Individual (Roger Bannister)	First broke the four-minute barrier for the mile.
Individual (Barry Bonds)	Broke baseball home run season record.
Team (NASA)	Put a man on the moon.
Team (Medical Breakthrough)	Eradication of smallpox worldwide.
Community Achievement	Formation of successful self-rule in Northern Ireland.

As with planning for your financial portfolio, your objectives portfolio should exemplify the amount of risk you and your organization are willing (and able) to take. Also, as with financial planning, high risk commonly goes with large reward. You should assess the risk level of the objective at the time you write it. One scale you could use is as follows:

Low Risk. This indicates there is a low level of perceived risk attached to committing to pursue the objective. This implies that the objective adds value to the organization but does not represent an orientation shift in performance levels. It can mean "more of the same" or simply maintaining the present levels of results. The objective will still require attention but will not require extraordinary effort to achieve it, unless there is a major crisis. The objective will be achieved without extra effort or resource allocation. It is still important, and these must make contributions to higher-level results.

Medium Risk. There is a perceived and real risk to committing to achievement. The objective requires a significant improvement in performance level over past benchmarks. Accomplishment will require additional effort, additional resources, creativity, innovation, and continuous improvement. Provided there are no major barriers, the objective is achievable in a short time frame.

High Risk. There is a high level of perceived and real risk in committing to attainment of the objective. The objective is a *paradigm shift* requiring significant changes in orientation, processes, practices, and convictions to achieve the objective. Full achievement may not be achieved in fewer than five years and may only be fully achievable in the future generations. The objective is complex, involving many interrelated systems and processes. A degree of uncertainty is implicit in the objective. However, an even higher risk is not to achieve these objectives. Note that many former Fortune 500 companies are gone from the list today—many because they did not link risk with gains at the Mega level but simply tried to do what they were already doing, but better. They did not keep focused on the new paradigm and high payoff results.

It is helpful to rate each objective as you develop them. Discuss them with colleagues and all those directly affected by them before final commitment and selection of methods and means.

Written for Results

Each objective must describe the results to be achieved, rather than the method or means to achieve the results. The results desired will be determined by whether they are personal objectives unrelated to the organization you work for, or results at one or more of the levels already described.

Activities are tasks or behaviors; they are what we do, not what we achieve. They, however, result in performance and consequences (accomplishments). Results are what are left behind after the activity is finished, the behavior is demonstrated, or the tasks are completed. Objectives are what Gilbert (1978) referred to as *accomplishments*.[5] Because there are so many potential areas for achieving results, we require some filters to identify priorities, and these we call *key result areas,* which will be explained in more detail later in this chapter.

Time Bound

The T component of a Smarter objective is a responsive criterion. It depends on the level of results with which you are dealing. At the Micro level you may have time frames from days to six months to two or three years. At the Macro level of results time frame could be anything from one year to ten years, whereas at the Mega level of results, the time frame could vary from ten to thirty plus years. Based on data and the Ideal Vision, it is up to the management and team to determine the time frame for achieving the results.

Typically, the lower the level you are in the organization the shorter the time frame of planning you engage in on a daily basis. At the executive level of an organization the managers should be capable of envisioning time frames of ten years and beyond. The longer the time frame you have, and with the ability and freedom (authority) to plan, the more proactive you can be. Again, all criteria should link all three levels of results. If not, there will be "disconnects" and time, resources, and efforts will be wasted.[6]

Expansive[7]

This refers to the linkages and relationships among Mega, Macro, and Micro objectives and whether they truly support the espoused or implicit values of the organization. *Expansive* is concerned with system and systemic thinking, which means objectives cannot be developed in isolation from each other. Further, it implies coordination and answering the following questions:

- Why am I (or are we) doing this?
- What are the implications of achieving this objective for other objectives (priorities)?
- Am I concerned about the impact of these Micro objectives on the quality of the Macro objectives?

- Am I concerned about the impact of my Macro objectives on the whole of society? (Mega)
- Am I concerned about my grandchildren's future? The future of tomorrow's child?
- What are the consequences of all our objectives?
- Have we placed too much emphasis on any one problem or opportunity?
- Have we addressed all the priority needs?
- Have objectives been developed for all the agreed key result areas?
- Have we identified all those who will be affected by these objectives?
- Are the methods and means relevant to the objectives?
- Are our objectives aligned and congruent with our Ideal Vision and organizational purpose?

Objectives at each level in the organization are written for all the key result areas. Strategic planning should be built on sound Needs Assessment, which documents the priority needs for the key result areas at all levels. Expansive is a criterion for assessing whether you have all the objectives to be doing all the right things at Mega, Macro, and Micro levels of results. Proactive planning is expansive because it accomplishes high payoff results.

Review and Evaluate

Results-based evaluation is a process that focuses on the measurable results accomplished by a program or project. Reviewing and evaluating on a regular basis is useful in determining success in accomplishing program objectives, as well as identifying strengths and weaknesses in program processes so that adjustments and/or improvements can be made. The marriage of evaluation and continuous improvement can also be helpful for identifying differential effects within specific stakeholder subgroups and determining whether a program's results meet the requirements of the organization for which it was designed.

Such an approach to evaluation might rightly be considered goal-driven. Goal-driven evaluation focuses on the goals and objectives of a program and its relationship to the goals and objectives of the organization that is to benefit from the program.

A detailed Smarter assessment checklist is provided in Table 7.8. Use this to check whether your Smarter objectives are well-formulated.

Table 7.8. Indicators of Well-Stated, Measurable Results.

	No	Yes
1. Is the objective written for a specific area of performance (for example, a key results area at Mega, Macro, or Micro)?	☐	☐
2. Does the objective appear to extend or challenge the individual (even shift paradigm)? Is it audacious?	☐	☐
3. Does the objective include a measurable standard in ratio or interval terms?	☐	☐
4. Is the objective apparently impossible on first observation?	☐	☐
5. Is the objective achievable in the defined time frame?	☐	☐
6. Is the objective written for a result rather than an activity?	☐	☐
7. Is the objective time bound (does it include a time target)?	☐	☐
8. Does the objective support your long-term strategic objectives and strategies (expansive)?	☐	☐
9. Is the objective stated in positive terms (that is, moving toward rather than away from something)?	☐	☐
10. Will achievement of this objective add value to your team's performance—Micro results (expansive)?	☐	☐
11. Will achievement of this objective add value to the customer/client? Will it improve a major process? Will it add value to society?	☐	☐
12. Does this objective support your perceptions and beliefs?	☐	☐
13. Is this objective one which will gain you an exemplary assessment if you accomplish it in the time frame?	☐	☐
14. Is this objective a definite opportunity to be rewarded if you accomplish it?	☐	☐
15. Does the group of objectives make up at least 75 percent of your work effort for the year?	☐	☐
16. Is there an evaluation/assessment in place?	☐	☐

IDENTIFY KEY RESULT AREAS

What's Important?

One of the most critical steps in writing Smarter objectives is to decide what performance areas will add the most value to the clients: aligning people, performance, and payoffs. Because there are three levels of clients for any organization, we require a way to define those areas that have the critical performance gaps or the greatest performance improvement opportunities. Again, we suggest that the most practical and pragmatic selection is to deliver high payoff results—to move ever closer to Mega.

There are many things you are influenced by day-by-day, week-by-week, and year-by-year. Some are attractive wants, some are hopeful wishes, and some will lead to useful results. We require a filter to screen out the unimportant from the important. Key result areas provide a tool for sorting out those performance areas that will add the most value if a result is achieved. Key result areas, or accountability areas, as they are often called, have traditionally been applied to management roles. In this book we apply it to all roles and also to teams, organizations, and communities.

What Are Key Result Areas?

Simply stated, key result areas are those selective performance areas of a role—the role of a manager, an organization, a community, or nation—in which a high level of results must be delivered to add value. They are usually the necessary results upon which all other results depend.

A key result area is not an objective; it is an area that merits the development of an objective. Some key result areas are unique to a role, unit, or community. Others are common across roles, organizations, and communities.

What Is Their Utility?

The most obvious reason for key result areas is that they help planners direct their limited time, capital, people, plant equipment, and information to the most important areas of performance where the return for effort will add the most value. In focusing on key result areas, planners take the first step to avoid the *activity trap* where activities become the dominant thought patterns and the end result is forgotten or assumed.[8]

The more expensive the activity, the more likely it will dominate the discussions; and often activity replaces results as the critical issue in decision making. Distinguishing activities from results requires a substantial shift in thinking. Defining key result areas forces planners to first think about the desired results before selecting the methods and means to achieve them.

Another reason for key result areas is that they define accountability at the individual role level very clearly. Key result areas clearly defined send a clear message that activities, qualifications, and good looks are not enough.

A final use of key result areas is to define uniqueness. Individual roles should contribute something unique, teams should differ by the unique results they contribute, and organizations will survive if they can continue to provide a unique contribution to society.[9]

Common Key Result Areas

There are some key result areas that occur frequently across all organizations, communities, and cultures. These can be classified by level, as shown in Table 7.9. These key result areas should be immediate candidates for objectives to be developed. We believe that best practices used by effective organizations provide evidence that these areas are important.

Table 7.9. Key Result Classifications.

Result Level	*Common Key Result Areas*
MEGA (Outcomes) Across most cultures, organizations should contribute to one or more of these global key result areas.	Societal Impact Areas • Security and safety • Health and well-being • Quality of life • Self-sufficiency • Murder-free • Poverty-free • Safety and well-being • Incapacitating accident-free
MACRO (Outputs) These are the four most common areas for the organization to deliver results.	Organizational Impact Areas • Employee satisfaction • Customer satisfaction • Organizational capital/capability • Investor profits
MICRO (Products) These key result areas define those areas in which leaders and individuals are expected to achieve measurable results.	Individual/Leadership Roles • Team performance • Team member performance • Information management • Innovative item • Performance improvement • Colleague support • Special projects • Effective police

Smarter objectives written for these common performance areas consistently make a difference. This is a more holistic approach than the *Balanced Scorecard* of Kaplan and Norton (1992, 1996a, 1996b) because it links result areas at three levels of results. Market-driven is not good enough if the focus is short term and the consequences for our grandchildren and tomorrow's citizens are ignored. The Mega level of results influences us to decide on a future we want to create with our clients (which includes making a future market). We should invent audacious ideas that will create a better world. Why not a planet free of war, rape, and disease, with healthy communities, long-term profit, and sustainability? What new markets would exist in this world?

To overcome these shortcomings, add Mega to a *Balanced Scorecard* and use a *Balance Scorecard Plus.*[10]

Each one of the key result areas shown in Table 7.9 can have one or more Smarter objectives developed for it.

Needs Assessment

Needs Assessment, as we noted earlier, is a process for identifying gaps in results and then placing the needs in priority order on the basis of the costs to meet the need as compared to the costs to ignore it. The key result areas isolate those areas that should be the focus of Needs Assessment. Needs Assessment takes each key result area at each planning level—Mega, Macro, and Micro—and gathers data about performance in that area to decide whether improvement efforts are justified. Needs Assessment is the foundation for developing Smarter objectives to address priority gaps or opportunities for performance improvement. (A need, again, is defined as a gap in results at the Mega, Macro, or Micro level, not as a gap in methods or means.) Table 7.10 lays this notion out.

Gaps in results become candidates for developing Smarter objectives and the later selection of appropriate methods and means to achieve them. Often there are no measurable statements of desired results when discussing methods-means; this is where Smarter objectives are developed.

In the absence of Smarter objectives, it is difficult to assess whether there is a performance improvement opportunity. Similarly, in the absence of clearly defined results, we revert to endless debates about methods and means that appear important but are not connected to worthwhile results. Without objectives, it is impossible to assess or evaluate the various alternatives proposed.

Table 7.10. Checking Your Key Results.

Key Result Area	What Is?	What Should Be?
Defines the area and scope of assessment	What are the measurable results now?	What are the desired or required results in the future?

What frequently happens is that planners and decision makers get involved in lengthy feasibility studies about complex methods and means in the absence of clearly defined and agreed objectives.

Strategic thinkers should have an obsession with results, as should leaders. Results oriented leaders continually ask, "What is the desired result in measurable terms?" before they decide how to get there.

Complete the exercise in Table 7.11 to identify the key result areas for your role and those that your organization contributes to society. You are asked to

Table 7.11. Rating Your Key Result Areas.

Code	Key Result Areas by Level	Not Addressed	Low Importance	We Have Smarter Objectives
1	MICRO LEVEL—LEADERSHIP ROLE			
1.1	Team performance			
1.2	Team member performance			
1.3	Information managed			
1.4	Innovative item			
1.5	Performance improvement			
1.6	Colleague support			
1.7	Special projects			
1.8	Self-development			
1.9	Internal customer satisfaction			
2	MICRO LEVEL—TECHNICAL ROLE			
2.1	Technical results			
2.2	Colleague support			
2.3	Innovative item			
2.4	Delivered technical advice			
2.5	Self-development			
2.6	Performance improvement			
2.7	Employee satisfaction			
2.8	Skills transfer (coach others)			
3	MACRO LEVEL—ORGANIZATION			
3.1	Customer satisfaction			
3.2	Organizational image			
3.3	Organizational growth			
3.4	Current investor satisfaction			
3.5	Economic Value Added (EVA)			

Table 7.11. (*Continued*)

Code	Key Result Areas by Level	Not Addressed	Low Importance	We Have Smarter Objectives
4	MEGA LEVEL—SOCIETY			
4.1	Health and well-being			
4.2	Security and safety			
4.3	Financial independence—economic survival			
4.4	Quality of life			
4.5	Self-sufficiency			

rate the key results area at one of three levels by checking one of the three right-hand columns.

SELECT PERFORMANCE INDICATORS

Sources of Objectives

Objectives can be derived and developed in a number of ways. Objectives can emerge from a number of sources. They do not, however, always occur through a systematic rational process. Here are some of the sources of objectives:

- *Needs Assessment.* This can and should be done at each of the three levels of results. Objectives can be developed to reduce or eliminate the gaps identified by the Needs Assessment data.

- *SWOT Analysis.* A SWOT analysis can identify gaps in results and opportunities for performance improvement.

- *Intuition.* Some managers set broad objectives based on a feeling for the future of the business. These broad goals may (and must) then be converted into Smarter objectives.

- *Crisis.* Often the trigger for objectives is a crisis in the organization. The crisis prompts managers to set objectives to deal with the crisis.

- *Key Result Areas.* If a key result area has been defined, agreed on, and performance assessed, then this is a sound foundation for deriving objectives.

- *Mission Analysis.* System analysis relies on the clear definition of results expected from the system. Often a broad mission has been developed, but it does not state in measurable terms the high payoff results intended. We can start with a broad mission and convert it into a cluster of Smarter objectives. Move from goal to an objective.

- *Problems.* A problem is defined as a gap in results selected for elimination or reduction. Problems can occur at all three levels of results: Mega, Macro, and Micro. Only a problem at the Mega level is strategic. Strategic thinking can be applied any day of the week; you don't have to wait for the annual organizational retreat to set objectives for identifying and solving strategic problems.[11]

Irrespective of the source of objectives, there is a systematic process for developing objectives to ensure they add value to major processes and define in measurable terms what is to be accomplished.

The Process

The process for systematically deriving objectives is depicted in Figure 7.1.

In this section we will amplify step 2 and practice selecting relevant performance indicators.

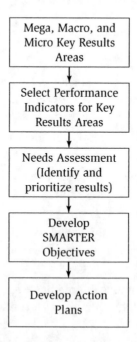

Figure 7.1. Process for Deriving Objectives.

Defining Performance Indicators

A performance indicator is simply the measurable criteria by which a key result area will be measured. It indicates how you will measure the result. Performance indicators can be described in three ways:

1. *Count.* This is the most direct measure for some key result areas. Level of profit, number of sales, years gained, diseases eradicated, and lives saved are examples.

2. *Ratio.* When a straight count is not relevant or meaningful, you may be able to use an index or ratio. Most key result areas can be converted into a ratio if data exists to compare and convert into a percentage.

3. *Interval.* Where direct counts are not suitable you can establish descriptive criteria and if relevant convert these into a scale of measurement. Some objectives are not suitable to measurement by number only; objectives that deal with service or product quality fit into this category. For example, you could build a house so that it fits the budget only, but most people have an additional set of criteria they desire their house to meet. These criteria are often lengthy, in which case they can be referred to in the objective as quality criteria.

Table 7.12 provides examples of performance indicators for various levels of results.

Each key result area can have a number of performance indicators. You should develop several before selecting the most appropriate ones to convert into Smarter objectives. Note that the performance indicators are for measuring the results, not for measuring the process. The important decision is to select indicators (measures) that contribute the greatest utility for the key result area being considered.

Advantages of Quantifiable Objectives

Performance indicators help to quantify and measure our desired results. There are five major advantages in measuring results precisely:

1. Relevant indicators bring *clarity* to our desired results. "To improve morale" is a vague, fuzzy platitude and a verbalized expectancy—but "To reduce employee grievances from ten to two by next year" is a specific target at the Micro level.

2. *Performance indicators* introduce a built-in measure of effectiveness. The measurement of progress toward an end result is difficult, if not impossible, with vague goals. Using a measurement to describe a future result provides a way of assessing the methods and means (activities) that will make it happen. Leaders can further see the relationship among information, resources, and skills required to deal with different objectives for different key result areas and needs.

Table 7.12. Performance Indicators by Level of Result.

Code	Key Result Areas	Performance Indicators
	MEGA Level	
1	Security	Percentage reduction in • Murders • Injuries due to war • Injuries due to riots • Elimination of major crime resulting in losses
2	Environmental quality	Reduction in incapacity to work Deaths due to air pollution Deaths due to unclean water
3	Health	Reduction in death due to substance abuse Reduction in teenage suicides Increase in longevity Reductions in deaths due to starvation
	MACRO Level	
1	Customer satisfaction	Increased ratings in survey Increase in value of shares
2	Organizational contributions	Increase in sales Increase in market share
3	Investor satisfaction	Increase value of shares Increased dividends
4	Product sales	Number of cars produced per quarter Number of patients discharged per month
	MICRO Level	
1	Team performance	Increase in sales Increase in market share
2	Information management	Reduction in complaints Reduction in access time Cost reduction to access
3	Personal development	Number of skills gained Qualifications gained Papers published

3. Performance indicators can help us perceive the *level of risk* and *audaciousness* inherent in the potential objective. Because a performance indicator is not yet converted into your benchmarks, you can have discussions about "how" to measure the key result area before rushing to an unrealistic standard.

4. Keep *unknowns* and *uncertainties* at an acceptable level. The performance indicators help you to visualize and assess the effects and consequences for other performance areas. It is better to know what you don't know (and seek to find out) than it is to be surprised later.

5. They allow you to assess the potential *payoffs* of various objectives written for one key result area.

Turning Performance Indicators into Smarter Objectives

The detailed chart that follows provides examples of how to convert key result areas into objectives. After selecting the performance indicator, you must look at the Needs Assessment data and identify the present result and then decide the desired result in the specified time frame for planning.

At the individual level of performance, you will set objectives for those key result areas for which you are accountable. You will also identify areas that you are not accountable for but may want to influence.

At the organizational level, a senior team will develop objectives at the Macro level for all those areas that add value to external clients and investors. The senior team will also link the Macro level objectives to the Ideal Vision that is the Mega level of planning. For each level of results, you will develop relevant performance indicators by which success will be evaluated, as seen in Table 7.13.

Difficult to Measure Areas

For each key result area you must select the best measure to tell you whether you have achieved the desired result. This is not always easy. A rigorous yet simple measure may not always be apparent. If you select a key result area for which no data has ever been obtained on performance, then it may take many months to gather the data. In this case you have to weigh the consequences of time and cost and decide the added value of rigorous measurement.

One way to deal with these tough-to-measure results areas is to develop *indicators*. Indicators are criteria that key players agree will "stand for" the actual results, and are close enough proxies for calibrating results.[12]

Some key result areas have traditionally been seen as "soft" and difficult to measure. Leadership is a good example. Too often managers made gut feeling judgments about leader performance based on no accurate evidence. We, however, do know more about leadership, customer service, and employee satisfaction—and have valid and reliable measures for each.

Table 7.13. Matching Key Results with SMARTER Objectives.

Code	Key Result Area	Performance Indicators	Smarter Objective
1	Team performance (sales team)	Increase in sales of cars	Increase sales on European cars by at least 25 percent by December 2004.
2	Team performance (car delivery team)	Reduction in costs	Reduce cost to deliver unit by at least 15 percent by June 2004.
3	Market growth	Margin growth/ Sales growth	Increase market growth by at least 2 percent in three years.
4	Customer satisfaction	Customer survey rating (10 point scale)	Increase the customer survey ratings by at least three points to five points overall during 2002.
5	Leadership performance	360-degree leadership survey results	All managers to gain at least five points on the 360-degree competency assessment by December 1, 2010.
6	Community security	Reduction in home invasions	Reduce home invasions to zero by December 1, 2008.
7	Revenue	Increase ROI	Achieve at least a 15 percent ROI within four operational quarters.
8	Employee satisfaction (global corporation)	Reduction in employee complaints	Reduce the number of complaints due to cultural discrimination by at least 75 percent over the next three years.
9	Family health	Reduction in child abuse	Reduce the incidence of child abuse in the community to zero by 2050.
10	Community health (developing Nation Q)	Reduction in starvation	Reduce the incidence of starvation in the community to 5 percent by 2005 and to zero by 2010.

Note: Some complex key result areas may require multiple performance indicators because no single indicator is adequate to measure the range of performance.

DETECTING NON-SMARTER OBJECTIVES

How to Sort Fuzzy Goals from Measurable Results

This chapter has focused on the process of developing Smarter objectives for results at the various levels of organizational performance. You will now be given the opportunity to detect poorly written objectives. If you cannot detect poor objectives, it will be more difficult to develop Smarter ones that add value to your organization. This skill will allow you to berate politicians, challenge educators, detect charlatans, and sort gloss from substance in your local community. The objectives in Table 7.14 are a mixed bunch, including results at the Mega, Macro, and Micro levels. Some are OK (Smarter); others are not.

EXERCISE—DETECT THE NON-SMARTER OBJECTIVES

Assume that each objective in Table 7.14 is owned by an individual or group in an organization. Read each objective and assess it against the Smarter criteria. You may not be able to judge whether it is audacious because that criteria is so contextual. However, you can note an opinion.

When you have completed the exercise, check your answers against the feedback sheet in Table 7.15.

Table 7.14. Detecting Non-SMARTER Objectives.

	Candidate Smarter Objective	Your Assessment and Why
1	Improve leadership skills.	
2	Implement an effective performance management process by December 2008.	
3	Promote physical, social, and emotional health through awareness programs and good health practices.	
4	Employ highly qualified teachers to conduct effective learning processes for students.	

(Continued)

Table 7.14. Detecting Non-SMARTER Objectives. (*Continued*)

	Candidate Smarter Objective	*Your Assessment and Why*
5	Reduce pollution levels in the city so that respiratory problems linked to pollution are reduced by at least 75 percent by 2008.	
6	Achieve an 8 point rating on the customer satisfaction survey throughout 2008.	
7	Reduce cultural discrimination incidents that result in hiring less qualified individuals.	
8	Become an agile organization by introducing a range of transformational leadership programs.	
9	Improve the strategic planning process through an integrated systemic approach by 2050.	
10	Perpetuate concern for social illnesses such as alcoholism, other substance abuse, and divorce through policies, practices, and treatment.	
11	Reduce teenage suicides in the community to zero by 2020.	
12	Eliminate the incidence of substance abuse in all schools by 2020.	

Table 7.14. (*Continued*)

	Candidate Smarter Objective	Your Assessment and Why
13	Reduce deaths on the road due to alcohol from fifty in 2000 to no more than ten by 2010.	
14	Establish a moon base by the year 2015 such that it can sustain human life for periods in excess of twelve months and within a budget of X billion.	
15	Increase the profit generated by eCommerce by 25 percent by 2008.	

Table 7.15. Feedback Sheet.

Code	Candidate Smarter	Your Assessment and Why
1	Improve leadership skills.	Missing a measurable standard—too vague. How many? and by when? A Micro level intention at best. NOT SMARTER
2	Implement an effective performance management process by December 2008.	A process objective because it hasn't answered the result question "why?" No measurable standards. Performance measurement should achieve a result of improved performance in measurable terms. This is a means not a result. NOT SMARTER
3	Promote physical, social, and emotional health through awareness programs and good health practices.	A vague wish that includes methods and means but no measurable result. No time target. No measurable standards. NOT SMARTER

(*Continued*)

Table 7.15. Feedback Sheet. (*Continued*)

Code	Candidate Smarter	Your Assessment and Why
4	Employ highly qualified teachers to conduct effective learning processes for students.	A general goal for a process. No intended result in measurable terms. No time target. NOT SMARTER
5	Reduce pollution levels in the city so that respiratory problems linked to pollution are reduced by at least 75 percent by 2008.	OK (that is, SMARTER)
6	Achieve an eight-point rating on the customer satisfaction survey throughout 2008.	OK (SMARTER)
7	Reduce cultural discrimination incidents that result in hiring less qualified individuals.	Includes no measurable standard or time target. We could only assume that it is aligned with a key result area and the intent is at the Macro or Mega level. NOT SMARTER
8	Become an agile organization by introducing a range of transformational leadership programs.	A vague general goal. No measurable standards. Includes methods and has no time target. NOT SMARTER
9	Improve the strategic planning process through an integrated systemic approach by 2008.	An important general wish with reference to some vague measure based on qualitative criteria. Not really written for a result. WHY improve this process? What is the desired result? NOT SMARTER

Table 7.15. (*Continued*)

Code	Candidate Smarter	Your Assessment and Why
10	Perpetuate concern for social ill-nesses such as alcoholism, other substance abuse, and divorce through policies, practices, and treatment.	A general goal. NOT SMARTER
11	Reduce teenage suicides in the community to zero by 2020.	OK. Some communities would consider this AUDACIOUS. And if we don't intend for this, what do we have in mind?
12	Eliminate the incidence of substance abuse in all schools by 2020.	OK (SMARTER)
13	Reduce deaths on the road due to alcohol from fifty in 2000 to no more than ten by 2005.	OK (SMARTER)
14	Establish a moon base by the year 2015 such that it can sustain human life for periods in excess of twelve months and within a budget of X billion.	OK (SMARTER)
15	Increase the profit generated by eCommerce by 25 percent by 2008.	OK (SMARTER)

DEVELOP MISSION OBJECTIVES

The Ideal Vision

An Ideal Vision is the only truly strategic level of creating and planning for a better world for today's citizens and tomorrow's child. It provides the primary evidence of long-term strategic thinking and planning. It is planning at the Mega level of results because it is concerned with a practical, useful, and measurable dream of the world you want to create for tomorrow's child.

A basic Ideal Vision describes in rigorous measurable terms the desired world you would like to create. This Mega level "practical dream" (Outcome) provides the meaning for planning at the Macro and Micro levels because the Products (Micro) and Outputs (Macro) can be linked to an overarching and higher level result, which is concerned with added value for society and the sustainability of the planet. The Ideal Vision is a group of Smarter objectives written at the Mega level of results, as shown in Figure 7.2.

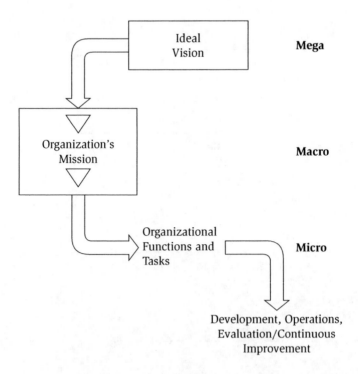

Figure 7.2. Relating and Rolling Down Needs from Mega to Macro to Micro.

Source: From Kaufman, 1998, 2000.

The Organization's Primary Mission

Each organization decides what unique contribution it can make to the Ideal Vision in measurable terms. This contribution is the organization's *Mission Objective.* An organization selects that "slice" of the Ideal Vision it will contribute. This organizational purpose will move it ever closer toward the Ideal Vision.

The Ideal Vision is practical evidence of the principles and values of those who are involved in planning the future. An Ideal Vision is more rigorous, practical, and measurable than the traditional list of organizational "beliefs and values" hanging on the receptionist's wall.[13]

Mission Objective

The mission objective is a summary of all the Macro level objectives that the organization contributes to immediate clients. For each key result area at the Macro level, the organization should develop Smarter objectives. These Smarter objectives are the organization's contribution to the Ideal Vision. These Smarter objectives if achieved will move the organization ever closer to the Ideal Vision. If the organization is truly committed to continuous improvement, then what are they moving toward as they get better? The Ideal Vision is a desired result committed to by the planning partners but seldom ever achievable in one planner's life span.

Mission Objective Criteria

The Mission Objective can be written in extended narrative form or as a series of coded Smarter objectives for each key result area. However you choose to write it, the criteria listed below apply:

1. All elements of the mission objective are written for results.
2. All the critical key result areas are covered (and related) and they have supporting Smarter objectives.
3. All objectives are measurable in either interval or ratio terms.
4. A time frame is stated.
5. No method or means are included in the mission statements.
6. Objectives at the Micro and Macro level should be linked through a chain of results to the Ideal Vision (Mega).
7. Accountability for all objectives making up the Mission Objective is clearly defined.

Key Result Areas

The Ideal Vision is concerned with the whole of society not just immediate customers. There are specific elements or key results areas that make up an

Ideal Vision. These key result areas appeal to all cultures and can be considered common elements that are shared by most communities. The key result areas shown in Table 7.16 are minimum elements of an Ideal Vision, in that each can be converted into a Smarter objective at the Mega level of results.[14]

Table 7.16. **Key Results and SMARTER Objectives.**

Key Result Area	Smarter Objective
1. Economic Effectiveness	Zero poverty. All citizens achieve self-sufficiency such that every man/woman earns as much as it costs to live. Stock/share value is sustained or increased in the long term.
2. Health	Achieve zero deaths from pollution. Reduce starvation malnutrition to zero by the year 2100. Reduce the incidence of deaths due to substance abuse to zero. Reduce death due to disease to zero.
3. Security	Reduce deaths due to war/riot to zero. Reduce deaths attributable to child abuse to zero. Reduce deaths due to partner/spouse abuse to zero. Reduce deaths due to rape, violence, or property destruction to zero.
4. Safety	Reduce deaths due to occupational accidents to zero. Reduce transport related deaths due to alcohol to zero.
5. Expansive	Achieve the survival of all living species required for human survival.
6. Cultural Safety	No person to be discriminated against on irrelevant variables such as color, race, culture, creed, age, sex, religion, and location as indicated by levels of survival, self-sufficiency, and quality of life.
7. Self-Sufficiency	No adult will be under the care, custody, or control of another person, agency, or substance. All adult citizens will be self-reliant and self-sufficient, as minimally indicated by their consumption being equal or less than their production.

Consequences

If any citizen or organization or community subtracts value from any of the key result areas for the Ideal Vision, what should happen? If society truly values the Ideal Vision and desires it for tomorrow's children, then there should be accountability when individuals, organizations, and communities subtract value from the desired results. To know whether we are adding or subtracting value, we must have valid and responsive objectives that calibrate high payoff results. A recent example of an organization subtracting value from the Ideal Vision is tobacco companies. They are slowly being litigated out of existence for pursuing one bottom line (profit) while ignoring societal consequences.

On the other hand, organizations that add measurable value to society will achieve long-term funding and long-term profit. This means they will still be around in one hundred years.[15]

SUMMARY

Smarter objectives can be created and developed at multiple levels. The planners decide what Smarter objectives to create by examining the key result areas at each level of planning. The key result areas define those performance areas that add the most value at each level of planning.

The key result areas also define those areas worth measuring and are the foundation for a balanced scorecard plus, because the Ideal Vision identifies those opportunities for societal impact.

Notes

1. There are some who feel that developing objectives is harmful—perhaps even "evil"—because it imposes someone else's agenda or purposes on someone else. Those who call themselves "constructivists" sometimes offer this view. Those objecting to the setting of objectives may feel that "exploring one's environment and discovering their own reality" is more humane and humanistic. While such makes for interesting coffee discussions, we feel that the arguments fail to pass muster for a number of reasons, including: (1) no one really accepts another's objectives; if one doesn't like the objectives, they have, from time immemorial, found ways to avoid them (such as walking out of classes, switching of teachers, and so forth) and if someone accepts an objective it is of his or her own volition; (2) providing objectives as a roadmap provides others the opportunity to accept, reject, or negotiate new destinations; (3) discovering new realities and new information is always a human option, even on the way to preexisting objectives; (4) there is "life after objectives"; many objectives specify milestone results, rather than final destinations; and (5) not setting objectives is setting objectives. Societal results.

A full discussion of the issues involved here are easily found in the literature, including: C. D. Gruender (1996, May/June), "Constructivism and Learning: A Philosophical Appraisal." *Educational Technology, 36*(3), 21–29.

2. Gilbert (1978, p. 88) has clarified why objectives are necessary but insufficient to achieve audacious results. The six-factor model he developed shows the systemic nature of human performance. The relationship between the six factors must be managed to achieve worthy results in individual and team performance.

3. Aubrey Daniels has done a lot to bring some sound behavioral science into the reason for writing objectives. Objectives describe the desired results; behavior is the key to the results. We agree with Daniels that both results and behaviors must be pinpointed. Managing the relationship between desired results and the critical behaviors that achieve them is the major challenge of leadership.

4. The original work of Mager and Pipe (1997) on writing objectives was focused on producing precise measurable objectives for the training and instructional environment. The structure of the objectives was built around the performance of a task or the demonstration of a skill. These objectives were process objectives because they were clear descriptions of (1) the desired behavior; (2) the conditions under which the desired behavior was to be performed; and (3) the standards (criteria) required to be a competent performer.

   In a sense they were written for a result—the result or end point of the instruction. They were not intended to describe the cumulative results as proposed by the Mega, Macro, Micro model. The Mager-type objectives are best suited for the instructional and training environment and for describing the standards expected when performing a key task. They were never intended to be management or strategic planning objectives. This book uses the Smarter model for developing strategic, operational, and tactical objectives because they reflect a long-term result that is the cumulative product, output, or outcome of collective effort. Mager objectives are about individual performance on specific tasks.

5. Gilbert (1978, p. 19) explains the distinction between behavior and accomplishment. Accomplishment implies competence. The competency approach defines a competency as those underlying characteristics of a person that consistently produce superior results. Results and accomplishments are what we leave behind after the competencies (behavior patterns) have been applied. Both behaviors (competencies) and results are inseparable when you want to improve performance. It is all in the relationship between behavior and results that audacious performance will emerge.

6. There may be other considerations for an objective: "All men seek one goal; success or happiness. The only way to achieve true success is to express yourself completely in service to society. First, have a definite clear practical ideal—a goal, an objective. Second, have the necessary means to achieve your ends—wisdom, money, materials and methods. Third, adjust your means to the end." (Aristotle)

7. This book emphasizes getting the right relationships between the desired results at Mega, Macro, and Micro levels and choosing the right means to achieve the results. The Ideal Vision sets the expansive context for all present and future action.

8. A focus only on means and resources and not on results and consequences.

9. Herb Simon, a professor of management and decision making, won the Nobel Prize in economics for developing the concept of "satisficing." This theory suggests that, in many cases, when faced with decisions or choices people do not (or should not) attempt to achieve the optimal or best solution but a minimally acceptable one. Satisficing involves recognizing that some results are more important than others, and that in some cases a minimum standard of achievement may be sufficient in the short run. Key result areas help the decision makers and planners to isolate those areas of performance where minimum performance is OK (for the time being) from those areas where maximum performance must be achieved. Again, if everyone is not contributing to Mega are they required?

10. We build on Kaplan and Norton's score card by adding the requirement for adding value to society. We propose a *Balanced Scorecard Plus*—the plus is the Mega level of results.

11. Recall that problems at the Macro level are "tactical" problems, and those at the Micro level are "operational" problems.

12. An example, the temperature we note on television news: when it says it is 91 degrees (F) on the screen that means that is the airport temperature and it might be different from where you live. But it is close enough—an indicator—of the general outside temperature for your use.

13. Ever notice that virtually every organization's statements are identical?

14. For examples of a basic Ideal Vision refer to Kaufman (1998, 2000).

15. One hundred years? Do you expect your organization, your country, and your world to exist then? If so, why not plan for that now?

CHAPTER EIGHT

Creating Change

Making Sure the Change Effort Really Brought About Change

CHAPTER GOALS

By working though this chapter, you will be able to answer the following questions:

❏ What is the big mistake in creating change?

❏ What are the three levels of change (only one of which is strategic)?

❏ When is change considered strategic?

❏ Why is pain usually the antecedent for change?

❏ What are the key roles in successful change?

❏ What are the requirements for a successful sponsor?

❏ How can you assess the sponsor's commitment?

❏ What are the six critical success factors for effective change?

❏ How can you prepare change agents and advocates?

❏ How can resistance be managed?

❏ What is a "force field analysis"?

❏ What are the key points to check in managing the change process?

CREATING AND MANAGING THE CHANGE FROM PRESENT RESULTS TO DESIRED RESULTS

Imagine the organization has completed the following steps to create and plan for an Ideal Vision:

- Developed an agreed on Ideal Vision (Mega level results).
- Developed mission objectives for desired results to be delivered to its external customers (Macro level results)
- Conducted a Needs Assessment to identify the priority gaps in performance between current results and desired/required results (that is, problems selected for fixing).
- Developed improvement plans to bridge the gaps in performance (using selected methods and means).
- Assessed the risks and implications of making (and not making) the changes (costs-consequence analysis).

Accomplished all of these? There is still something missing at this stage: the organization has not developed a plan to create and manage the change. This chapter will provide you guidance and tools on how to create and manage change in an organization where change is profound.

The Big Mistake

Based on our experience, the biggest single mistake in managing and creating strategic change is to attempt to implement the improvement process too quickly and without buy-in from the organizational partners and without integrating the change with everything else going on in the organization without changing the incentive. Effective planning coordinates the change and resources required with other activities going on within the organization. Many organizations tend to overcommit to change efforts. It is probably better to be conservative during the first initiation, rather than be too aggressive. The target should always be defining and achieving high payoff results and align the payoffs to these.

Many organizations today already feel they are working over their capacity. When the improvement process starts, there is an increase in workload, and because most people are learning to do things differently, there can be significant productivity drops. To offset this downturn, consultants and temporary employees may be used to supplement the staff. In some cases there is a reason to have some teams maintaining the present production and operational requirements while a "believable" team plans for the new processes and operational systems. The change management plan is the key to achieving strategic improvement. This plan provides a structured, disciplined, and coordinated blueprint for managing and implementing the change.

Change Is a Process

Change is a process and not an event.[1] The creation of strategic change is by definition a shift in paradigms, which involves changes in all the following:

- Values and paradigms.[2]
- Norms and practices.
- Expectations and feelings.
- Thoughts and beliefs.
- Sudden events.
- Behaviors and competencies.
- Paradigms.

To make this change in mind-sets even more daunting, the change will likely impact people who are already overwhelmed with the increasing acceleration of change in their professional and personal lives. Therefore, all organizational members must recognize that organizational change can and must be focused on useful results aligned at all three organziational elements levels (Mega, Macro, and Micro). Change must be perceived as a useful process, which it is most often if identified in the context of adding measurable value at all levels.

TRANSITION MANAGEMENT PLAN

"Instead of viewing change as a mysterious event, we approach it as an understandable process that can be managed."
—Connor, 1992

Changing from the present state to the desired state within any organization typically involves a transition from dissatisfaction with the pain of "the old" to the remedy implicit in "the new." Another way to depict this process using parts of the Organizational Elements Model is shown in Figure 8.1.

Current State

The current state refers to the established culture. Organizational culture can be considered as patterns of expectations and the normal routine people are

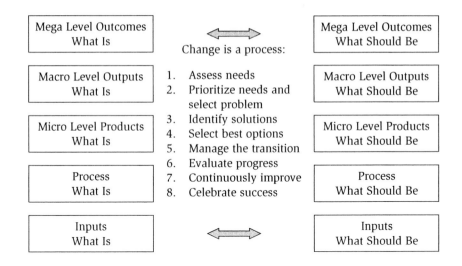

Figure 8.1. The Change Process.

following before the change effort. This state also refers to the present results at the Mega, Macro, and Micro levels. In this state, the organization is locked into the paradigm that has been successful in the past and is likely to bring disaster in the future: tomorrow is not a linear projection of yesterday or today.

Transition State

The transition state is the point in the change process where people break away from the status quo and start to work with the new paradigm. They no longer behave as they have done in the past, yet they still have not established the new processes of operating. They may not yet have internalized the importance of Mega.

The transition state begins when the improvement plan solutions disrupt individuals' expectations and they must start to change the way they work. Under extreme conditions, people become dysfunctional. Also realize that the same reward structure is in place—one based on previous goals and objectives and not responsive to the new direction and the new realities. (Many change efforts fall short because the incentives are not realigned with the new objectives. What gets rewarded gets continued, and without a change in the reward system to align with the new objectives, failure is probable.)

Desired State

The desired state at the Macro and Micro levels of results is the point where the change initiatives are implemented and integrated with the new organziational behavior patterns, including resources, that are required by the change. Performance improvement has occurred, and expectations and the culture have changed and high payoff results are being accomplished.

The Mega level of results may not be achieved completely in our lifetime; however, we can move ever closer to the Ideal Vision in our lifetime (and that is a start that is well worth our efforts) . . . and if we are not going there, where are we headed?

The Three Levels of Change

Change is possible at three levels, all of which must add value at the Mega level. Only strategic change adds value at the societal/Mega level. It is vital that change at any level provide measurable payoffs at the Mega level. Here are the three levels for change:

Mega Level. Strategic change at this level has a longer horizon as it includes future generations and their survival, self-sufficiency, and quality of life. The Mega results (Outcomes) are described in an Ideal Vision. Change at this level should be the preferred approach for all organizations because it moves us ever closer to a better world that we can create for our grandchildren and other citizens of the future. This provides a higher meaning for our lives and the lives of our organziations through the accomplishment of high payoff results.

Change at this level is profound because it deals with a wider range of relationships in the various subsystems we can influence. We potentially touch more people, more living things, more matter through planning change at this level. This is the road less traveled. It is holistic, profound, and deep change. It is *the* basic orientation for useful strategic planning, thinking, and doing. In the final analysis, this is the most practical and pragmatic starting point for useful change, for defining and delivering useful results; aligning people, performance,and payoffs.

Starting here aligns what any organization uses, does, produces, and delivers with adding value to external clients and society.

Macro Level. Planning change at this level is concerned with changing the results (Outputs) delivered to external clients and the intended consequences for the various stakeholders as a result of the changes. The intent—target—for Macro level results (Outputs) are the elements of Mega that the organization has commited to deliver and move ever-closer toward. If change is planned at this level, then the plan will be rolled down to implement changes at the Micro level.

Micro Level. Planning change at this level is concerned with changing the key results achieved by individuals, teams, and processes within the organization so the quality of Products delivered to internal clients is improved. Any change at this level will influence change at the Macro (Outputs) and Mega (Outcomes), even if it is not managed.

Strategic Change

Change can be considered strategic when it meets the following criteria:

- When it requires significant shifts in the methods, means, processes, and behaviors required to achieve the basic and key results at the three levels: Mega, Macro, and Micro.
- When it involves a different response to the new realities from the response you used (unsuccessfully) yesterday.
- When it involves significant changes in the various relationships between individuals, teams, and various elements of the organization.
- When all elements of the Organizational Elements Model are taken into account when planning the future (especially their relationships to each other in causing worthwhile results).
- When two bottom lines are considered and planned for: (1) societal results and (2) organizational survival and profits.

The common and conventional—but now old paradigm—"bottom line" is this second one: organizational success. However, for an organization to be successful over time it must add value to all stakeholders, including society, and this means that the most basic and important bottom line is the first one: societal value added. This bottom line is achieved when:

- All partners participate in developing (or ratifying) the Ideal Vision and when all partners are given the opportunity to influence the creation of the high impact results and payoffs.
- Methods and means to achieve change are selected only after shared meaning on results desired at the Mega, Macro, and Micro levels are agreed by the planners.
- The overriding concern is with the health, safety, and welfare of today's and tomorrow's citizens.
- The cost of ignoring a problem or opportunity is unacceptable to the various partners (including society).
- The consequences of failure to achieve the change involve high cost and unacceptable risk to the community and society.

EXERCISE—ASSESS PRESENT INITIATIVES IN YOUR COMMUNITY

In the exercise in Table 8.1 you are given the opportunity to select a number of initiatives in your community, town, or city (for example, beautification efforts, road expansion, and so forth). They are considered strategic if they gain a check mark (✓) on at least eleven of the items while also having a check mark on at least one of the first three items.

Table 8.1. Assessing Community Initiatives.

Code	Strategic Criteria / Describe Initiative	Initiative 1	Initiative 2	Initiative 3
1	Linked clearly to results at Mega level (Outcomes)			
2	Linked clearly to measurable results at Macro level (Outputs)			
3	Linked clearly to measurable results at the Micro level (Products)			
4	It requires a significant change in the way people behave; they have to develop new competencies and skills			
5	It requires a significant change in the methods and means to achieve the results			
6	It requires a significant allocation of resources to achieve the results			
7	It requires a high commitment by those involved to achieve the results			
8	It requires a significantly different response to the problem or opportunity in order to fix it			

Table 8.1. (*Continued*)

Code	Describe Initiative / Strategic Criteria	Initiative 1	Initiative 2	Initiative 3
9	It involves significant changes in the relationship between the elements of the organization or unit			
10	It requires all elements of the organizational model to be considered			
11	It affects both bottom lines now, and especially in the future			
12	It should involve all the customers—internal and external—in influencing the desired results			
13	It concerns the health, safety, and welfare of today's and tomorrow's citizens			
14	The cost of ignoring the problem or opportunity is unacceptable			
15	The consequences of failure to implement the initiative are unacceptable to the community			

THE PARADOX OF BUILDING COMMITMENT THROUGH PAIN

One of the common pitfalls in change creation and management is the failure to build the resolve and commitment necessary to achieve long-term useful change. There are many examples of change initiatives that floundered from lack of resolve to sustain a project through to completion.

Achieving informed commitment at the beginning of a project is one of the key issues in any change project.

Creating Acceptance of the Need—Gaps in Results—Through Pain

A basic formula can be applied that addresses the perceived cost of change versus the perceived cost of maintaining the present paradigm and status quo. As long as people perceive the change—and consequences—as being more costly (including emotionally) than maintaining the status quo, it is unlikely that the resolve to sustain the change process has been built. The initiator of the change must move to increase people's perceptions of the high cost of maintaining the status quo and decrease their perception of the cost of the change so that people recognize that even though the change may be expensive and frightening, maintaining the status quo is no longer viable and is in fact more costly.[3]

Pain Management[4]

Pain management is the process of consciously surfacing, orchestrating, and communicating specific information in order to generate the appropriate awareness of the pain associated with maintaining the status quo compared to the pain resulting from implementing the change. The pain we refer to is not physical pain, but the level of dissatisfaction a person experiences when his or her objectives are not being met or are not expected to be met because of the status quo. This pain occurs when people are paying or will pay the price for an unresolved problem or for missing a key opportunity. Change related pain can fall into two categories: *current* pain or *anticipated* pain.

Current Pain. Current pain revolves around an organization's reaction to an immediate crisis or opportunity. It is short-term and has high visibility. We see it all of the time when there are changes in rules, policies, organization, or competitive challenges.

Anticipated Pain. Anticipated pain refers to looking into the future and predicting possible problems or opportunities. There are two popular techniques for identifying probable situations in the future:

1. *Scenario Planning.* This concept was popularized by Royal Dutch/Shell as a planning tool. A series of plausible and well-focused stories are imagined in the future so as to better prepare the organization for any external eventualities. These scenarios can be used to identify potential obstacles to growth. However, by working with scenarioes, planning can, without realizing it, limit itself to the known and not "stretch" or envision new and different realities and consequences. Beware of this possible limitation. When using scenarios, be sure to envision new and perhaps audacious possibilities and consequences.

2. *Environmental Scanning.* This technique has been around for the last twenty plus years. Data is gathered about the trends and demands in the external environment. Data generated can help decision makers recognize opportunities and threats.

Create a Critical Mass with Shared Needs

You frequently have to raise the heat if you want to get the attention of those you want to change. This rule of thumb is a way of calculating change success. See the formula below:

$$C = A \times B \times D \times X \times Y$$

Where C = the probability of change being successful; A = dissatisfaction with the status quo (based on needs assessment data); B = a clear statement of the desired results; preferably at the Mega, Macro, and Micro levels; D = specific first steps toward the objectives; X = the cost-consequences of change; and Y = the cost-consequences not to change. The concept is summarized in Table 8.2.

Tichy (2001) maintains that waking the organization to the requirements for change is the "most emotionally wrenching and terrifying aspect" of any major organizational change. What makes this step in the change process so wrenching and terrifying is the extreme intensity of feeling that people must experience before they are prepared to change. If you want people to change, you often don't want to give them a choice; you want them to understand that there are no alternatives for their safety and survival. You have to raise the temperature—set the

Table 8.2. Critical Mass.

A	If you want people to change, you have to convince them that they should change—you must show them that the perceived threat of the new realities is not as bad as the pain of the status quo. This is the most important step. This involves Needs Assessment data.
B	Provide an Ideal Vision of a better world and show how their lives and others' will be better if they change.
D	Demonstrate that you know what you are doing by providing successes early in the change process.
X	Calculate the true costs of change and tell the targets of change the costs. True winners do this despite the risk. This sorts out those with the resolve to change from those who will fall out.
Y	Then consider the costs to ignore the need.

once comfortable platform of the status quo on fire—if you want them to jump into the cold, dark, scary sea of change. At least 75 percent of your team and virtually all your top executives plus most of your employees must be convinced that change is essential if you are to achieve major change.

The Joy of Change

Another reason to change is because we have imagined a better and more joyful state of being. Our dreams can be powerful triggers for change. Anticipating a pleasant, joyful future can be a powerful way to move toward a better future.

DEFINE KEY ROLES FOR CHANGE

There are a number of key roles in the change process.[5] These roles must be clearly defined and managed if the change program is to be successful. These roles can be named as follows: initiating sponsor, sustaining sponsors, change agent, change target, and change advocate.

Identifying the members of an organization who must fulfill these roles and then orchestrating them during the change process is a "best practice" organizations can use to increase the likelihood of sucess of any major change project.

Initiating Sponsor. The initiating sponsor is the individual or group with the power and authority to legitimize the change for all the affected people in the organization.

Sustaining Sponsor. A sustaining sponsor is the individual or group with the political, logistic, and economic proximity to the people who actually have to change. Sponsors don't necessarily have to be senior or middle management. A sustaining sponsor can be someone who has no real line power but has significant influence power as a result of his or her relationship with people influenced by the change or credibility based on past successes. Sustaining sponsors must continually reinforce the positive steps in change.

Change Agent. A change agent is the individual or group with responsibility for implementing the change. They are given this responsibility by the sponsors. Agents do not have the power to legitimize change. They do not have the power to motivate the organization to change, but they certainly have the responsibility for implementing the change. They must depend on and use the power and influence of their sponsor(s) to make the change happen.

Change Target. The targets of change are those who must change their norms, practices, and behaviors as a result of the change. In strategic and tactical change, the sponsors can also be the targets of change. When the paradigm shifts from the status quo, everyone can go back to zero on competencies in some performance areas. This means everyone has to learn new ways of doing things at times.

Change Advocate. The change advocate is the group or individual who wants to achieve change but who lacks sponsorship. Their role is to advise, influence, and lobby support for change.

Role Relationships

"None of us exists independent of our relationships with others."
—Wheatley, 1992

These roles can be depicted in various relationships depending on the culture of the organization. They can be *linear, triangular,* or *square,* as shown in Figure 8.2.

The process of change is driven by relationships. The glue that holds the organization together or what allows it to become dysfunctional is the quality of the relationships between the different roles. One aspect of change is learning how to learn. The quality of the relationships between the various roles in change will influence whether the organization learns and adapts to the new realities to create long-term success. Some possible relationships are shown in Figures 8.3, 8.4, and 8.5.

Linear relationships are the simplest to understand. A sponsor delegated implementation responsibility to a change agent who implements down to the

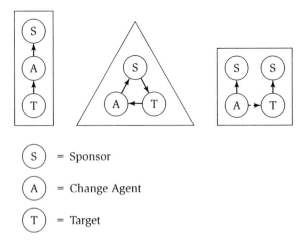

Figure 8.2. Relationships Among Sponsor, Change Agent, and Target.

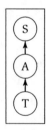

Figure 8.3. Linear Relationship.

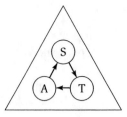

Figure 8.4. Triangular Relationship.

Figure 8.5. Square Relationship.

target. Triangular relationships are more complex because the change agent and targets report to the same sponsor, but the target does not report to the change agent. What tends to happen is the change agent uses his or her legitimate power to implement change. The target knows who the boss is, so the sponsor/change agent relationship must be clarified. The square can be dysfunctional. Problems occur when a sponsor or change agent tries to implement a change on a second sponsor's employees/targets. What sponsor number 1 is usually unaware of is that these targets will rarely respond to change directives unless those directives are received by those who control the consequences. The solution is for sponsor number 1 to become an advocate to sponsor number 2 in order to bring him or her on board with the change initiative. If this fails, appealing to a higher authority to intercede may be necessary.

EXERCISE—IDENTIFY THE ROLES

In the exercise in Table 8.3, you select an existing major change project or you can imagine one in your organization and name the people filling the roles described. You can also comment on whether they recognize their role. Check your answers with a colleague.

Table 8.3. Identifying Roles.

Code	Role	Comments
1	Who is the initiating sponsor?	
2	Who are the sustaining sponsors?	
3	Who are the change agents?	
4	Who are the advocates?	
5	Who are the targets of change?	

Sponsor Requirements

Strong sponsors recognize that personal, political, or organizational costs always occur with major change, and they are willing to pay the price. A committed sponsor can delay the gratification of other opportunities if they pose a risk to the original objectives. So what are the requirements for an effective sponsor?

The following are potential criteria:

Power	The sponsor must have the *authority* power to legitimize the change for the targets.
Evidence	Needs Assessment data must generate sufficient pain or anticipated joy to make the status quo and present paradigm unacceptable and the desired state more attractive.
Results Orientation	Objectives at the Mega, Macro, and Micro levels of results create a measurable vision of a better future. The sponsor must create direction and indicators of success in measurable terms.
Resources	The sponsor must recognize the resource requirements to support the change. Resources must be linked to the intended results.
Implications and Consequences	The results desired at the various levels will have implications and consequences for customers, partners in the change, and society. The sponsor must be a systematic thinker who understands the relationships among all elements of the organization.
Empathy	The sponsor must have the leadership competency of "empathy." Change is a human process involving the whole person. The sponsor must be able to recognize and respond to the emotions change will elicit.
Customers	Profound change has impact on all the customers: internally, externally, and in society. The sponsor must plan the impact to achieve worthwhile results at the Mega, Macro, and Micro levels.
A Public Role	Effective sponsors demonstrate high public support for the change. They publicly recognize and reward strong commitment to the change.
A Private Role	In addition to a highly visible role, the sponsor has a wide range of influence strategies and methods to impact privately on key individuals or groups to communicate strong support for the change.
Performance Management	The sponsor implements effective performance management to translate the change objectives into measurable changes in behavior. Desired performance is rewarded; poor performance is punished.

Evaluation Tactics and Plans	Effective sponsors evaluate progress and plan feedback mechanisms to measure progress and celebrate successes.
The Motivation to Sacrifice and Delay Gratification	Effective sponsors are there for the long haul; they recognize the price and costs of change and demonstrate the competency of "resilience."

Sponsor Commitment Assessment

On Table 8.4 you are given the opportunity to assess the commitment of your sponsor to the change project. If you are a change agent, this helps you to predict the probability of success or failure and then take appropriate action. The sponsor requirements for successful change are listed. Check (✓) the column that best describes the sponsor. Use a different mark (code) for each one assessed.

Table 8.4. Sponsor Commitment Assessment.

Code	Sponsor Requirement	Relative Weakness	Average	Relative Strength
1	Positional power			
2	Needs assessment evidence			
3	Results orientation			
4	Resources available and committed			
5	Implications and consequences recognized			
6	Empathy			
7	Customer recognition of number affected			
8	Sponsor's public role			
9	Sponsor's private role			
10	Performance management			
11	Evaluation strategies and plans			
12	Motivation to sacrifice			
13	Persistence—(stickability)			
			Total	

Effective change will occur if the sponsors of the change show a high level of support for the project. If you are a change agent, you should identify your sponsor(s) and assess their level of commitment. The assessment allows you to make some predictions about the probability of achieving successful change. The range of responses is laid out in Table 8.5.

Use this assessment to discuss with your sponsor(s) the implications of failure. As a change agent you will often be required to coach, educate, and support your sponsor(s) to be effective in their role.

Table 8.5. Range of Responses.

Code	Range	Response
1	Relative strength score 10 plus	1. Likely success 2. Give sponsors feedback 3. Develop actions to lift low scores
2	Relative strength score 6 to 9	1. Uncertainty of success 2. May change for the worse suddenly 3. Commit more time to educate sponsor 4. Develop strategies to influence sponsor(s)
3	Relative strength score 5 or less	1. High probability of failure 2. Prepare for failure 3. Give feedback and influence action

DEVELOP SPONSORSHIP

A common barrier to managing change among the sponsor group is an assumption that once the decision has been made and communicated as a detailed action plan, no further involvement by them is required. Top management sometimes tends to ignore the importance of the other key roles, relying instead on employee compliance with orders from senior management. The education of sponsors is often required to avoid the cost of failure. This process is called the building of *"cascading sponsorship."*

Black Holes

Daryl Conner, in his book *Managing at the Speed of Change* (1992), talks of *"cascading sponsorship"* as a method for eliminating the organizational "black hole." *Black holes* are those places in an organization where change decisions enter but are never heard from again.

These typically occur when there is a manager who does not sponsor the change, and therefore the targets beneath that person do not adopt the change. There is little initiating sponsors can do to maintain the change at lower levels because they do not have the logistical, economical, or political proximity to the targets of change. The result is that change cannot succeed if there is not a network of sustaining sponsorship that maintains the integrity of the implementation as it moves down through all levels of the organization—therefore *cascading sponsorship.*

How Cascading Sponsorship Works

Cascading sponsorship works by starting with the initiating sponsor and working down through the different levels specific to any improvement project. Sponsors prepare the change agents to fulfill their roles, giving them the required competencies to manage not only the technical aspects of the project but the people aspects as well. The success of any major improvement project usually starts at the top in traditional organizations and ultimately rests on the shoulders of the sponsors at all levels. Sponsorship is the most critical risk factor in any change project.

To have an effective network of sponsors, organizations implementing major change should apply these critical rules:

1. Sponsorship is critical to major change, so all sponsors must demonstrate high commitment, both publicly and privately.
2. Weak sponsors must be educated or replaced.
3. Sponsorship cannot be delegated to change agents.
4. Initiating and sustaining sponsors must never attempt to fulfill each other's roles. Initiating sponsors are the only ones who can start the

change process, and sustaining sponsors are the only ones who can sustain it.

5. Cascading sponsorship must be established and maintained.

6. It is essential that the sponsors develop measurable objectives for the desired results of change at the Mega, Macro, and Micro levels. Linking these results and then choosing the best methods to achieve them is the blueprint for effective change.

Sponsors must communicate the implications of the change to people at all levels, especially the impact on the personal lives of the change targets. In addition to allocating resources, sponsors must also be prepared to pay the price of success. Finally, sponsors must develop rewards for those who facilitate the implementation process and discourage those who attempt to inhibit the acceptance of change.

Critical Factors for Organizational Change

The sponsors of change will increase the probability of success if they recognize the critical organizational change factors in managing change.

Change Sponsors. For major change to occur, you require an initiating sponsor and a network of sustaining sponsors. These sponsors must demonstrate a high level of public commitment.

Shared Desire for Change. Profound change addresses significant gaps in organizational results. Needs Assessment is the data-generating process for identifying, justifying, and prioritizing the gaps in results at the Mega, Macro, and Micro levels. The Needs Assessment data must create enough expected pain or joy so that the status quo is no longer an option for the sponsors so that, despite the uncertainty of a new paradigm, the organization must leap into the future.

Ideal Vision—Statement of Success. Strategic thinking and planning efforts will develop an (or ratify an existing) Ideal Vision that is a measurable statement of the desired results for future citizens—for tomorrow's child. This Ideal Vision will provide a guiding star for the chain of results linked in the Organizational Elements Model. The vision of success must be stated in measurable terms at the Mega, Macro, and Micro levels of results.

Mobilizing Commitment. This factor refers to the management of the key roles in change, specifically: change sponsors, change agents, change advocates, and change targets of great importance to provide valued incentives for the desired change.

Process Improvement. The Needs Assessment data in profound change projects frequently requires process improvement or redesign if change is to occur. Successful change is built on clearly defined high payoff results followed by process improvement or redesign.

Progress Evaluation. Effective sponsors determine how progress will be measured on the journey toward the results. Tracking progress ensures the change is heading in the right direction. Feedback on progress keeps all the partners in change informed on *"how it's going."* Such feedback is often called *formative evaluation,* for it tracks en-route performance and allows for revision at any time.

Making It Stick. Organizational change, if it is not trivial, always involves culture change and personal shifts. Aspirations and dreams often fail, not on their relative merits, but on how well we are able to manage resistance. Effective sponsors use the power of resistance to build support for change. The larger the change, the stronger the resistance commonly is. The voice of resistance can keep us from taking untimely or foolish actions.

Effective sponsors listen to the fears and concerns of others and use the energy of resistance to improve the change process.

There are seven essential elements for managing change successfully. They are listed in Table 8.6. Rate your organizations by placing a check (✓) in the column that represents how well your organization is demonstrating the factor.

Compare your answers with those of a colleague, and if you are a sponsor, develop actions to deal with any factor that rates less than a relative strength.

You may want to ask a sample of people in your organization to complete the questionnaire and then analyze the results to decide what action should be taken to increase the probability of managing the change successfully.

Table 8.6. Assessing Capacity to Change.

Code	Essential Element	Relative Weakness	Average	Relative Strength
1	Highly committed change sponsors—an initiating sponsor supported by a network of sustaining sponsors is clearly defined.			
2	Requirements for change are clearly defined and shared by sponsors and other partners based on sound Needs Assessment data.			

(Continued)

Table 8.6. Assessing Capacity to Change. (*Continued*)

Code	Essential Element	Relative Weakness	Average	Relative Strength
3	Vision of success—measurable results agreed at the Mega, Macro, and Micro levels.			
4	Commitment. High levels of commitment from sponsors, change agents, change targets, and other key partners in change.			
5	Process improvement. The implications of change for all elements of the organization, including people, have been identified. Major Process improvement has been identified and initiated.			
6	Progress evaluation procedures have been designed; feedback mechanisms for all roles in the change are included.			
7	Resistance is recognized as part of the change and it is managed effectively.			

PREPARING CHANGE AGENTS AND ADVOCATES

The Rate of Change

We are living in a turbulent environment where change is accelerating dramatically in three ways:

- *Volume.* The amount of disruption to people's lives is reported as increasing annually.
- *Speed.* Organizations expect change to be implemented quicker and people are given less time to respond.
- *Complexity.* New technology has made change more complex. We are also learning to recognize complexity.

This means that we can no longer manage as we have in the past. A potential barrier in this area is that sponsors often incorrectly assume that those identified as change agents and advocates possess the skills necessary to deal successfully with the human and technical implementation problems. You must challenge this assumption or face the possibility of failure due to knowledge and competency gaps. A work environment that has increasing volume, momentum, and complexity of change is termed *turbulent.* As the world becomes more uncertain, employees often start to feel out of control because of this turbulence.

Change agents have traditionally dealt with the technical aspect of change while frequently ignoring the human aspects. Yet today, effective change agents are expected to consider and plan to influence both the technical and *soft processes,* including performance management, leadership, team effectiveness, compensation and rewards, selection interviews, and performance review. Some of the *competencies*[6] that will be expected of the change agent in the future follow: influence, coaching, empathy, active listening, self-confidence, self-control, self-insight, customer service orientation, teamwork and collaboration, analytical thinking, conceptual thinking, initiative, strategic (Mega) thinking, assertiveness, technical skills, ability to manage resistance, achievement orientation, optimism, and a results and payoffs orientation.

This set of competencies increases the probability that the desired results of change will occur. However, even the highly skilled change agent cannot successfully implement major change by him- or herself. The *advocate* role must also have a similar range of competencies.

Preparing Advocates

Advocates must first of all identify and influence a sponsor. Successful advocates influence the sponsor(s) to recognize the requirement(s) for change and help them to identify the benefits of the change versus the pain of continuing the status quo and they seek the approval of those in power and avoid at all cost wasting time/energy with people who cannot say "yes."

Effective advocates are results-oriented and are willing to accept nothing less than successful change. They are unwilling to simply adjust to the unacceptable status quo.

Advocates must be ready to challenge and confront poor or decreasing sponsorship. They must either educate the sponsor, replace the sponsor, or ultimately prepare to miss deadlines and projected budgets. The advocate should follow the following five basic steps to be successful:

1. Define the desired results of change at the Mega, Macro, and Micro levels in measurable terms and include a time target.

2. Identify the key targets that must accommodate the change.

3. For each key target or target group identified, determine the initiating and sustaining sponsor(s) that must support the change.

4. Evaluate the correct level of sponsor commitment.

5. Develop *"pain management"* strategies to gain and increase the appropriate sponsor commitment level.

When all roles are clearly defined and the role holders have the requisite competencies, then the probability of successful change is increased and the risk of failure decreased. A quick assessment of change agent and advocate competency is provided in Table 8.7. This tool will help you to identify any competency gaps and help you to assesses the probability of success or the risk of failure for the change program.

Table 8.7. Competency Assessment for Change Agents and Advocates.

	Competency	*Often Displays*	*Sometimes Displays*	*Rarely Displays*
1	Influence—ability to skillfully influence			
2	Coaching/mentoring—able to coach others			
3	Empathy—recognizes other's view			
4	Active listening—listens to content and feelings			
5	Self-confidence—presents well			
6	Self-control—can control emotions			
7	Self-insight—knows own weaknesses			
8	Customer service orientation			
9	Teamwork—good team player			
10	Analytical thinker—breaks things into parts			
11	Conceptual thinker—can perceive relationships			
12	Initiative—takes action to fix problems			

Table 8.7. (*Continued*)

	Competency	Often Displays	Sometimes Displays	Rarely Displays
13	Strategic thinking—defines results at Mega, Macro, Micro			
14	Assertiveness			
15	Technical skills			
16	Manage resistance to change			
17	Achievement orientation—wants to do better			
18	Optimism—proactive expectations			
19	Results and payoffs orientation			

MANAGING RESISTANCE EFFECTIVELY

Resistance can destroy a change program. New ideas often fail, not on their relative merits but on how effectively we are able to manage resistance. The human cost of failed change efforts is high. Trust is lost, people blame each other, and any further attempts at change experience increased resistance. We must recognize that change (especially strategic change) means managing resistance as well.

What Is Resistance?

Change that threatens no one must be very trivial. Resistance is a force field that prevents movement toward a new paradigm, especially strategic change. It is also a natural and expected part of change. As much as you might want otherwise, progress without resistance is impossible. Resistance creates energy and is a paradox, because it can preserve us from harm and also create a barrier to essential change.

Resistance is a reaction to an emotional process taking place in the resister. It is seldom a reflection of a rational or logical thought process. In summary, resistance is any opposition to a shift in the status quo. The amount of resistance generated will vary from person to person or group to group because each individual or group has its own unique frame of reference that influences how people view the change. Much resistance is directly traceable to fear—fear of not being in control and fear of not knowing how to cope with new requirements.

How to Recognize Resistance

It is important to recognize the indicators of resistance so you can avoid being a victim of the resistance energy. Here are some indicators:

- *Confusion.* People hear at different times and in different ways. Often the new information and skills required for change create *"information anxiety."* Even if you have explained the new paradigm a number of times people will ask:

> "Why are we doing this?"
> "How will it affect me?"
> "What will it cost?"
> "What is my new role?"

Other frightening responses include:

> "We already tried that."
> "It won't work here."
> "I don't understand your words."
> "I don't like the words you use."

When the change requires new skills, you can always expect some level of confusion. The change sponsors and change agents must plan to repeat the information again and again and display patience.

- *Immediate Criticism.* Before all the details are explained, some people will express their disapproval. When individuals or groups criticize too quickly, it is probably because they have been burned before and have developed a shell of resistance to avoid potential pain.
- *Denial.* Some people deny there is requirement to change. They screen out the data on needs or deny that it is as bad as indicated.
- *Malicious Compliance.* Some people agree to go along with the change in public but walk out of the public room and immediately start to drag their feet or do the bare minimum to avoid punishment.
- *Sabotage.* Outright sabotage is easy to spot. People take strong action to purposefully stop the change. The positive side to sabotage is that there is no doubt that someone is opposed to your plans for change.
- *Too Easy Agreement.* People agree without much challenge or criticism in the early stages of the change. Later when they realize the full implications they start to express resistance.

- *Silence.* The plan is presented and no one expresses thoughts and feelings openly. Sometimes silence can indicate support, but how do you know? Don't assume silence means acceptance. Probe behind the silence.

- *Aggressive Criticism.* These people are "in your face" critics who aggressively challenge and criticize. Often they may be saying what others are too timid to express. Listen actively and resist the feeling to attack back.

Why People Resist Change

One obvious reason people do not accept a change is because they do not view it as positive. They see less security, less money, less challenge, loss of status, loss of autonomy, loss of authority, less social contact, or being incompentent at a new process. However, there are other reasons, which we have classified into six categories:

1. *Peceived Negative Results.* This is where the individual or group that must change will be negatively affected by the change—or at least think they will be.

2. *Fear of More Work.* Employees perceive that the change will result in having more work to do and less opportunity for rewards. This category involves questions such as:

   "How hard will I really have to work?"
   "What recognition and/or financial reward will I get for my efforts?"
   "Are the rewards worth it?"

3. *Habits Must Be Broken.* Strategic change requires everyone to shift paradigms and break longstanding habits and install new habits. This is not easy. There must be more pain associated with the old pattern than with the new pattern of behavior for change to happen.

4. *Lack of Communication.* The organization does not effectively communicate what they want, why, how, and by when. Unless the objectives, standards, and expectations of new behaviors are communicated clearly, people will keep performing to the old standards. Here are some questions that the change targets expect answers to:

   "What will this mean to me?"
   "What will it mean to my friends?"
   "What will it mean to the organization?"
   "What other options exist?"

"Are there better options?"
"Can I do what is expected?"
"How will I get the new skills?"
"Will I have to make sacrifices?"
"Is this really necessary?"
"Will I look stupid?"
"Will I get fired?"
"Will we perform better?"
"Can I really do it"

5. *Poor Strategic Alignment.* Strategic changes require the alignment of two streams of behavior, strategy and culture. You can't change one stream and ignore the other; both have to be aligned and managed.

6. *Employee Resistance.* Those who resist change often do so because they feel it is being forced on them. People probably don't resist change so much as they resist being changed. Threats and coercion are not good tactics for lasting change.

FORCE FIELD ANALYSIS

A fundamental flaw in many change management programs is that they focus only on the innovation tactics and ignore how the organization will resist the change. There is a failure to take into account the "corporate culture" and what is rewarded currently, and how that current reward scheme can limit innovation and useful change. In managing profound change, we are faced with managing the learning of individuals, teams, and the whole organization. The alignment model introduced in this chapter emphasizes the requirement to plan the change of the obvious elements such as objectives, tactics, processes, and structures, but also one must manage the less obvious yet more difficult elements such as values, norms, beliefs, and habits. It is these hidden drivers of behavior that influence why people do what they do and what results they accomplish. Effective leaders identify these hidden limits to change, growth, and long-term success. One way to surface these resisting forces is to conduct a *force field analysis*.

The *force field analysis* model was advanced by Lewin (1936) as a framework for problem solving and for effecting planned change. Lewin identified pressures or forces in an organization that either strongly support the change or strongly resist it. The simplest presentation of the model is depicted in Figure 8.6 as *driving* forces arrayed against the *resisting* forces within the force field of a living system, the organization, as it tries to achieve its results.

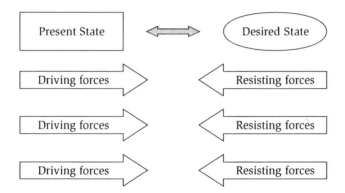

Figure 8.6. Force Field Analysis.

Common Resisting Forces

"Everybody wants to go to heaven, but nobody wants to die" could be used to describe people who want all of the advantages of change without the commitment and pain that might go with it. When initiating strategic change at the Mega, Macro, and Micro levels, some frequently recurring challenges and resisting forces occur at different stages in the change process:

1. *Not Enough Time.* Those who are expected to be involved in the new initiatives lose their feeling of control over their priorities. To use the metaphor of the "full bucket," they perceive their bucket to be already full with existing priorities. How can they fit more into their bucket? What can they pour out and what will be the new priorities? People should be given discretionary time to reflect and problem solve. New priorities should be negotiated so that people have some flexibility in how they manage their time.

2. *Lack of Performance Support.* Without performance support, performance deteriorates. Challenges like a lack of skills coaching, lack of information in the form of standards and specific feedback, as well as inadequate resources and incentives are common limits to effective change.

3. *Lack of Needs Assessment Data.* In the absence of strong evidence for change, people will legitimately ask about the relevance of the change. If the change initiative is not clearly linked to measurable results at the Mega, Macro, and Micro levels, then there is no real case for learning new skills and abilities.

4. *Poor Leadership and Sponsorship.* The leaders and sponsors at all levels must provide the example and display the new behavior patterns,

norms, and practices. When leaders espouse new values but continue to practice old patterns of behavior, the credibility of the change initiative is undermined. Leaders must invite and seek feedback. Those who have the courage to talk about the "*untalkable*" must be rewarded. Often issues that are avoided are the greatest barriers to moving forward. Harmony is not helpful when it means that open dialogue about difficult issues is avoided or punished.

5. *Fear and Anxiety.* Once the change has been initiated successfully, there is a requirement to sustain the change and overcome fear and anxiety. The more complex the change, the greater the demand on people at all levels to learn new competencies and skills. The related fear and anxiety are expressed in many ways. Fear and anxiety are natural responses to the perceived risk and uncertainty of learning new behaviors and skills. Leaders must create a supportive environment for learning new norms and practices.

6. *This Stuff Isn't Working.* When you walk on the "flat earth,"[7] you measure success by the rules of a flat earth paradigm. When you move to the round earth paradigm, the rules and ways of measuring success change. The challenge of a new paradigm involves basic issues of measurement and assessment. How will people judge performance in the new paradigm? When learning new ways there is always some drop in productivity. Improvements sometimes lag behind expectations. Interventions are often piloted with low skill levels. When it doesn't work, people tend to first blame the program. Sponsors must initiate new measurement processes and ensure people are trained in their use.

7. *We Have the Magic Elixir.* Effective change agents have great focus and energy to support their belief on the "rightness" of the change program. The downside of overuse of change management competencies can be perceived as misguided fanaticism by some. The critical mass of believers often run so far ahead of the others that they get isolated. This isolation takes many forms. Here are some examples of what people may think:

> "The organization is neglecting us!"
> "Why don't the others understand us?"
> "What a bunch of zealots!"
> "What's this new jargon they are confusing us with?"
> "I can't understand anything these project people are doing!"
> "This is the only way to move on this!"

The change agents and sponsors must be competent and open to feedback so they can avoid the barrier of the "true believers" versus the nonbelievers.

8. *Who's the Emperor?* This potential barrier is concerned with issues of governance and control. Questions which arise in this area are:

> "How much autonomy does the change agent have?"
> "How much freedom does the pilot group have?"
> "What decisions will the sponsor let the change agent make?"
> "How will the pilot group deal with conflict with other groups?"
> "Will results be used for blaming (or for improving)?"
> "How will the interdependencies with other units be managed?"
> "Who will manage at the boundaries?"
> "What are the rules and regulations during change?"
> "How will accountability be defined?"
> "Who owns the critical key result areas?"

9. *Reinventing the Wheel.* This challenge is about transferring innovative practices and early successes across the organization. This is the issue of diffusion of new knowledge and practices. The silo mentality of traditional organizations creates resistance to new ideas that are "not invented here." Members from one unit hear about an innovation in another unit and dismiss it for no rational reason. Good ideas do spread, however. The sponsors of change must reward behavior and practices that transfer good practices across functional boundaries. This is the thrust of the *learning organization* paradigm.[8]

10. *Unclear Strategic or Tactical Direction.* The issue of strategic or tactical direction can become a major hurdle if the planners have rushed to change without an adequate needs assessment, without the valid data about the gaps between current and required results and consequences. Objectives linked to high payoff results are the fundamental foundation for successful change. In the absence of clear strategic direction based on measurable results the following questions will be raised frequently:

> "Why are we changing?"
> "Where are we heading?"
> "Who will benefit?"
> "Will performance improve?"
> "What are we trying to create?"
> "Will this benefit me?"
> "Will this benefit my grandchildren?"
> "What is our purpose?"
> "Do we have shared language about the future?"
> "Who should be involved in conversations about their future?"
> "Will I be safe?"

There are many potential resisting forces to change. Each organization will have its own unique mix. The ten outlined above are frequent because they occur at some time in most organizations managing profound change. They must be recognized and dealt with.

Conducting a Force Field Analysis

To wind up this section you get the opportunity to conduct a force field analysis on your own organization or unit. A tool for identifying and managing the resisting forces is presented in Table 8.8. First read the following instructions.

Instructions. Think about your own organization or unit. If it is undergoing major change, you can complete this analysis on that unit or division you are part of. Otherwise imagine your organization is about to embark on major changes.

Step 1. Identify from the Needs Assessment section the gaps in results that are driving change in your organization. Note them down on the *Driving Forces* side of Table 8.8.

Step 2. Identify the *Restraining Forces* by referring to the ten frequent restraining forces described in the previous pages. Note down those that are most obvious to you. You can design a rating system to weight the resisting forces. For example: 1 = major impact on success of change; 2 = medium impact on success of change; and 3 = minimum impact on success of change.

When you have completed the analysis, develop tactics to manage and deal with each resisting force. As a rule of thumb limit yourself to ten each of driving and resisting forces.

Table 8.8. Force Field Analysis Form.

Unit/Organization: _____

Analyst Name: _____ Date: _____

Driving Forces (Needs as Gaps in Results)	Weight	Restraining Forces	Weight
1. _____ _____		1. _____ _____	
2. _____ _____		2. _____ _____	
3. _____ _____		3. _____ _____	

Table 8.8. (*Continued*)

Driving Forces (Needs as Gaps in Results)	Weight	Restraining Forces	Weight
4. _____		4. _____	
5. _____		5. _____	
6. _____		6. _____	
7. _____		7. _____	
8. _____		8. _____	
9. _____		9. _____	
10. _____		10. _____	

Notes

1. We draw on the ideas of Daryl Conner (1992, p. 10) who explains that change is a process, not discrete events that occur through purely linear progression.

2. Values are usually unchallenged and unexamined predispositions to act and respond to certain situations. We suggest that working with an Ideal Vision as a referent allows people to examine their values in a context about the importance of adding value to everyone.

3. The worldwide experiences of terrorism in the 1990s and the next decade show-cases the costs and consequences of not dealing early and directly with reality. As the late Australian management consultant Phil Hanford noted, "What's real is real." Indeed.

4. Pain may not be the only reason why people choose to change. Conners empha-sises orchestrating information to help people understand the high price they will pay if the status quo is left in place (see Conner, 1998, p. 119). People may change

because of the anticipated joy of a future state. The mere process of designing a better world in some way may be sufficient to initiate profound change. Our dreams and imaginings allow us to construct reality twice—once in our consciousness then out there for others to see, touch, and enjoy.

5. See Conner (1992; 1998) for ideas on roles in change. For these roles to be successful, we must first have created the descriptions of the desired results at Mega, Macro, and Micro levels. Change creation must precede change management. Kaufman (2000, p. 142) makes this distinction.

6. We define competencies as those underlying characteristics of a person in a role that allow them to perform at exemplary levels more often than not. Competencies are those differences we can prove distinguish between the "best performers" and the merely average. Competencies are those patterns of behavior, thoughts, and feelings that produce consistently better accomplishments. In Gilbert's (1978) terms—competencies allow the performer to get better results more often in more situations than those without them. A summary of the scientific research on competencies over the last thirty years can be found in Spencer and Spencer (1993).

7. We use "flat earth" to highlight the fact that many people will deny reality even when provided convincing data to the contrary. We are reminded of people, then and now, who are convinced that the earth is flat. Old paradigm thinking.

8. Senge's (1990) *The Fifth Discipline* has popularized the concept of the learning organization. We caution the readers to first create the desired results in measurable terms before selecting the mix of methods to help the organization learn to change and achieve the desired results.

CHAPTER NINE

Scoping and Scanning the Organization

What Means Will Achieve the High Payoff Results

CHAPTER GOALS

After completing this chapter, you will be able to answer the following questions:

- ❑ What is the purpose of scoping and scanning?
- ❑ What are the three scoping and scanning tools?
- ❑ What are the advantages and disadvantages of the three scoping and SWOT tools?
- ❑ What is a SWOT analysis and how can you record it?
- ❑ How can you do a quick analysis of your process strengths and weaknesses?
- ❑ What is a cost-consequences analysis?
- ❑ How can you rate the importance of the SWOT data?
- ❑ What are the key questions to ask about strengths and weaknesses?
- ❑ What are the key questions to ask about opportunities and threats?
- ❑ What is the purpose of a business logic analysis and what are its five elements?

❑ What is the purpose of a cultural screen and what are its key elements?

❑ What Products should you provide for implementing continuous improvement?

❑ How can you align your methods and means with your Smarter objectives?

SCOPING AND SCANNING

At this stage in the strategic thinking and planning process, you have completed a Needs Assessment. You should have identified desired results, problems to overcome, and the implications and consequences of ignoring the needs. The strategic planners can now start generating responsive methods, means, and tactics required to achieve the desired high payoff results; aligning people, performance, and payoffs. The three scoping[1] and scanning methods described in this chapter are helpful tools for analyzing the present methods and means and for selecting the best means to achieve the required results.

We can scope and scan the organization at two levels:

1. *Results.* Scoping at this level is concerned with deciding to use the Mega planning paradigm.

   • How will Mega, Macro, and Micro be linked?
   • Will all six critical success factors be used?
   • What are the relationships among all the organizational elements?
   • Will planning start with a rigorous Needs Assessment?
   • How can ends and means be aligned?

2. *Means and Methods.* Scoping and scanning at this level is concerned with analyzing and defining the present range of methods, solutions, tools, models, and processes used to achieve the results.

   • What tactics (means) are used at present?
   • What cultural norms and practices influence the present methods and means?
   • What is the "business logic"?
   • What are the strengths and weaknesses, opportunities and threats?
   • What are your responses to the new realities?
   • What are the trends in the external environment?

This chapter will provide you with three major tools for scoping and scanning the organization as well as its internal and external environment.

Scoping/Scanning Proposal(s)

Needs Assessments are a methodical way of scoping and scanning the organization by analyzing and defining the gaps in results at three levels of results, then placing the needs in priority order on the basis of the costs to meet the needs as compared to the costs of ignoring them. "Scoping" in this chapter is analyzing and defining the various means used at present to achieve the results. Scoping can be used to select better methods and means and to ensure that the strategies and tactics are aligned with the three levels of results. Scoping the means ensures the relationships between ends and means are efficient, effective, and aligned.

Three Scoping Tools

The three scoping and scanning tools described in this chapter are:

1. *SWOT Analysis.* The *s*trengths, *w*eaknesses, *o*pportunities, *t*hreats analysis.
2. *Business Logic.* A technique for analyzing the drivers of an organization's present methods and means of achieving results.[2]
3. *Cultural Screen.* A technique to identify the major cultural elements that must be managed for profound and major change to occur.

Each of the three has advantages and disadvantages. Each can provide a structure for accelerating the process of finding out what appears to be going on in "the mess" (Ackoff, 1981) at the moment.[3] Table 9.1 compares the three tools.

SWOT ANALYSIS

The acronym SWOT refers to a method for analyzing four aspects of an organization and is a way of conducting a performance audit on methods and means and their effectiveness. The letters stand for:

- *Strengths.* Analyze those strengths that will allow future strategies and tactics to be implemented successfully.
- *Weaknesses.* Analyze those internal processes, resources, and cultural elements that will be barriers to achieving objectives.
- *Opportunities.* Analyze those external demands and influences in the environment that could be used in the future to develop better methods and means.
- *Threats.* Analyze those external demands and influences in the environment that could be barriers to future results.

Table 9.1. Comparison of Scoping and Scanning Methods.

Characteristics	SWOT Analysis	Cultural Screen	Business Logic Analysis
Purpose: All three methods can be used to generate methods and means to achieve strategic results at the Mega, Macro, and Micro levels.	To identify internal strengths and weaknesses of the organization, unit, or team. To identify the external opportunities and threats faced by the organization unit or team. To scan the environment and identify trends and new realities. To identify methods and means to achieve results. To identify barriers to achieving the results at all levels: Mega, Macro, and Micro.	To identify strategies and tactics. To identify the major elements of an organizational culture. To analyze what to unlearn in managing profound change. To analyze and plan what cultural elements must be changed in shifting the cultural paradigm of an organization. To align tactics and culture with the results at Mega, Macro, Micro levels. To identify the methods and means for achieving the strategic (Mega) results. To identify gaps in "soft" processes. To identify problem causes.	To analyze the present business logic. To link and align business logic with objectives at the Mega, Macro, and Micro levels. To identify changes required in methods and means. To identify paradigms that are not working. To challenge the status quo. To generate solutions to problems selected for fixing (based on needs).
Focus	Gathers data about external and internal elements.	Gathers data primarily about internal norms, practices, behaviors/ accomplishments, processes, policy, and procedures.	Gathers data primarily about internal tactics (method-means, processes, activities).

Table 9.1. (*Continued*)

Characteristics	SWOT Analysis	Cultural Screen	Business Logic Analysis
Data	Unless highly structured and well-planned, tends to elicit soft, unverifiable data. Can generate too much data unless well-planned. Participants often mix internal data with external data. Can waste time and achieve "paralysis by analysis." Can produce good hard and soft data about issues external to the organization.	If well-planned can gather both soft and hard data. Produces mostly opinions unless well-planned and structured. Identifies data related to hard-to-change organizational culture elements.	Can produce verifiable hard data if well-planned. Reduces data gathering to the important methods and means.
Disadvantages	Can generate too much data and not enough information. Can generate "wheel spinning" and "paralysis by analysis" unless well-structured and linked to results. Can generate too much soft data and not enough hard data.	Inward focus can lose sight of results and get bogged down in activity.	Can have limited time horizon and be concerned with short-term market driven tactics.

Usually the SWOT[4] method has been an essential step in strategic planning; however, it can be applied to any organizational unit, team, or individual. A SWOT analysis is often part of a performance audit that seeks to establish how well the organization is performing in response to external and internal demands and influences. The SWOT analysis often includes a range of data gathering methods, such as stakeholder analysis, issues analysis, competitor analysis, environmental scanning, and scenario analysis.

Whatever mix of methods is used, the purpose is for the planners to develop a shared perspective on the capabilities of the organization to achieve its desired objectives at the Mega, Macro, and Micro levels. Needs Assessments identify gaps in results. A SWOT analysis identifies the factors that can influence the results.

Benefits of SWOT Analysis

The benefits of a rigorous SWOT analysis are as follows:

1. The planners gain a shared perspective on the state of the organization and the risks to be managed to achieve business (or organizational) continuity.

2. The major barriers to achieving the strategic objectives are identified and responses developed.

3. The present methods and means are audited to establish their effectiveness, and new solutions identified.

4. New methods and means are generated to achieve required results and overcome barriers and problems.

5. Hard and soft data are generated to assist planners in making reasoned decisions about strategies and tactics based on sound evidence.

6. The relationships between internal issues and external issues can be identified and proactively dealt with.

7. SWOT analysis helps to identify the major influences on behavior and results in the organization.

Criteria for an Effective SWOT Analysis

A poorly organized or conceived SWOT analysis can lead to a lot of "wheel spinning" and "paralysis by analysis." One way to avoid these downsides is to have a method for keeping track of the strengths and weaknesses data and the opportunities and threats data. In addition, the analysts and planners can agree to discriminate between "soft" and "hard" data.[5] The final criterion for an effective SWOT analysis is to have a process for identifying the relationships between the internal data and the external data.

In summary, here are the criteria for an effective SWOT analysis:

1. Keep the purpose of the SWOT clear—to help generate data for developing strategies and tactics to achieve the required results. Be sure one does not do the SWOT analysis as an end in itself. Take it only as far as required to get the answers you must have.

2. Develop a classification system for the data to be collected internally and externally. Rate the data for importance.

3. Discriminate between soft and hard data and ensure recording documents reflect the difference.

4. Identify the relationships between internal strengths and weaknesses, and external opportunities and threats so that strategies and tactics can be developed to achieve the required results.

5. Allow sufficient time for the data to be collected, preferably well before the planners meet to plan.

6. Involve as many representative planning partners as possible in data generation.

Here are some of the key questions that should be answered to identify internal strengths and weaknesses.

Key Questions

- What are you good at?
- What major processes give you a competitive edge?
- What methods and means appear to be working well or limiting performance?
- What are your distinctive core competencies?
- What can you do that others cannot?
- What allows you to repeat high performance?
- What makes you unique?
- Why do your customers value your products and services?
- Will your present strengths continue to make you successful?
- What positive impact do you make on society?

Your paradigm of an organization will determine the way you perceive and understand what is going on in the organization, which is a system, driven by a set of Processes that interact and relate to produce results at all three levels of results. So what are some of the major Processes?

The organization is driven by a set of interrelated Processes and value-added streams. The following are common to many organizations:

- *Strategic Thinking.* The formal process of strategic planning that uses Mega as the starting referent, this is a process for predicting the future we want and then designing and delivering required changes in the external environment.

- *Cultural Leadership.* The formal and informal leadership processes for influencing the norms, beliefs, and behaviors of the people who make up the organization.

- *Process Management.* The policies, procedures, and processes for mapping and managing the major processes (capabilities) of an organization.

- *Performance Management.* Performance management is much more than traditional performance appraisal. The process translates the tactical decisions into daily and weekly behavior and operational results.

- *Financial Management.* The financial management process should be clearly related to the strategic planning and performance management processes.

- *Structure.* The organizational structure is a means for achieving tactical objectives.

- *Marketing and Sales.* Your marketing and sales processes put your products and services in the customers' hands, minds, and hearts. Drucker notes that you "sell" when no one can use what you have, and you "market" when there is a relationship between what you can deliver and what the client can actually use.

- *Information Management.* Your processes for managing information can have a direct influence on performance.

- *Research and Development (R&D).* Even organizations that don't have R&D processes should at least have processes for identifying technology applications. New technology provides opportunities for performance improvement.

- *Supplier Processes.* The inputs to your processes are influenced by the quality of your suppliers. How strong are your supplier relationships?

Focusing on the strengths and weaknesses of these organizational processes will provide a classification system—a way of "keeping score" or tracking useful data. The processes listed are common to most organizations, but you will have to identify additional processes unique to your business, such as manufacturing processes.

Table 9.2 provides a quick process assessment. The following questions will also help you to decide whether your major processes are a relative strength, average, or a relative weakness:

1. Are your major processes documented (mapped)?
2. Does each major process have a sponsor or owner?
3. Are there excessive delays in delivering results?
4. Are there high levels of rework?
5. Does each process have audacious objectives that will deliver high payoff results?
6. Are you consistently delighting your customers?
7. Are you underachieving on your results at the Mega, Macro, and Micro levels?

Table 9.2. Quick Process Analysis.

Code	Process Title	Relative Weakness	Average	Relative Strength
1	Strategic thinking and planning			
2	Cultural leadership			
3	Process management			
4	Performance management			
5	Financial management			
6	Structure			
7	Marketing			
8	Sales			
9	Information management			
10	Research and development			
11	Supplier processes			
12	Manufacturing processes			
13	Administration			
14	Health and safety			
15	Human resource development			
16	Measurement and review			

8. Do you have agreed measures for process performance?

9. Do you have agreed measures for internal results, external results, and consequences?

Key Result Areas

In Chapter Seven we identified a set of common critical/key result areas that can apply to most organizations. In addition, every organization has a set of key result areas at the Macro level that reflect their unique outputs, as shown here.

Mega Key Result Contribution Areas

- Continuing profits
- Continuing customer satisfaction
- Societal value added
- Economic value added
- Continued share value
- Individual security

For each Mega level key result, contributions can be derived from the key Macro results, and Smarter objectives are developed. The planners can work backward from the objectives and ask the question: "What internal strengths and weaknesses contribute directly to accomplishing or failing to achieve our required results?"

This approach has the SWOT analysis conducted after the required objectives (results) have been developed. In other words, plan the required results and then analyze the present methods and means to determine whether they are the best to achieve the ends. This approach helps to link the key result areas with those processes that produce the required results. A SWOT analysis can identify those strengths and weaknesses in the major processes that contribute most directly to the objectives at all three levels of results.

For each major process, planners should develop a set of specific questions that help to identify the strengths and weaknesses of the process. In addition, questions can be developed for analyzing the core competencies of the organization and the competencies of key individuals and teams in the organization.

Process Improvement Is Not Enough

A word of caution, improving processes[6] alone will not achieve maximum levels of results. The desired purpose of any organization is to increase the value added at all levels of results. Breakthrough performance occurs through managing all the organizational elements, and addressing all levels of performance—individual, process, and organizational and socialtal.

The SWOT analysis should address these issues. Performance improvement is a balancing act between focusing on results and managing processes. (See Figure 9.1.) Rummler and Brache (1995) summarize this balancing act well:

> "The process level represents a wealth of largely untapped potential. We are learning that it is not enough to manage results. The way in which those results are achieved (process) is also important. If we are achieving the results we need to know why. If we are not achieving the results we need to know why."

A rigorous SWOT analysis can help the planners to answer the two key questions of "Why?" and "Why not?" and will then help them to build on the strengths and limit the weaknesses.

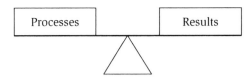

Figure 9.1. Balancing Processes and Results.

Documenting the SWOT

There are a variety of ways to document the SWOT analysis. The form in Table 9.3 is a simple way to show the relationships among data categories. Each item of SWOT evidence can also be rated. A sample rating code for each item is shown in Table 9.4.

Opportunities and Threats

External opportunities and threats are those influences and conditions outside the organization, the unit, the team, or the individual that can improve or hinder the achievement of results. These influences are never under the full control of the planners, but they can be responded to by proactive strategic planning and thinking. The SWOT analysis identifies these external conditions and influences, and as a result, the planners can develop responses to priority demands in the form of strategies and tactics. The key question to answer about opportunities and threats is "How important are they to the achievement of the required results?"

When analyzing the external opportunities and threats, use the following categories as a guide:

- Customers/consumers
- Competitors
- Economic trends

Table 9.3. Sample Recording Device for a SWOT Analysis.

Strengths	Rating	Opportunities	Rating
Weaknesses	Rating	Threats	Rating

Table 9.4. Sample Rating Code.

Strengths		Opportunities	
Use these rating rules to assess the impact of the strengths data and to establish priorities.	*Rating*	Use these rating rules to assess the impact of the opportunities data and to establish priorities.	*Rating*
A significant advantage; a perfect match between customers needs and societal needs, and our services/products and capabilities; defines uniqueness.	3	A must win opportunity; it has the greatest impact on the Ideal Vision and our primary mission objective.	3
Advantageous for us but insufficient by itself to be competing.	2	A key opportunity that should be pursued, but its loss would not be critical.	2
Offers us some advantages but can be copied by competitors.	1	An interesting opportunity that may evolve to be critical in the long term. More evidence required before response justified.	1
Weaknesses		Threats	
Use these rating rules to assess the impact of the weaknesses data and to establish priorities.	*Rating*	Use these rating rules to assess the impact of the threats data and to establish priorities.	*Rating*
A significant weakness; could be a fatal flaw; has obvious negative impact on results at Mega, Macro, and Micro levels. Customers badly affected. Directly impacts on results.	3	A significant threat. Major barrier to achieving results at Micro, Macro, and Mega levels. Major negative impact on service/ product quality. Demands strong action on our part.	3
An important weakness; could have serious implications if not fixed, but requires more evidence before action.	2	A serious threat that cannot be dismissed. Require more data before action.	2
An annoying weakness, but can be overcome. Concerned with adequacy of methods and means.	1	A remote threat; caution is necessary, but it is not a major worry. We could delay any action.	1

- Technology trends
- Socio-cultural trends
- Political climate
- Raw resources/physical factors
- Legislative demands
- Industry factors

Planners must sort the opportunities and threats generated by this list into priorities that are derived from rating the risk or impact on the desired results. In times of high uncertainty, each category will have a different influence. Historical influences are poor guides to future impact in an environment of high uncertainty and accelerated change, since tomorrow is not a linear projection of today (Kaufman, 2000).

Here are some key questions to ask to identify potential opportunities and threats:

Opportunities

- What new technologies are relevant to your organization, your clients, and the society you can or do have impact on?
- What changes in customer values, preferences, and desires could be an advantage for you?
- What are the possibilities of e-commerce for you?
- What new government legislation creates a potential advantage?
- What demographic shifts are occurring?
- What external opportunities can be linked directly to your internal strengths?
- What competitor weaknesses amplify your strengths?
- What long-term scenarios are advantageous to you?
- What are the possibilities in globalization?

Threats

- Who are your major competitors? Who could be?
- What changes in the market create major risks for you?
- How uncertain is the environment?
- What emerging customer requirements are you unable to meet?
- What economic issues create high risk for you?
- Is there any factor that could threaten your existence?
- What are the greatest external barriers to growth?

- What external demands have the greatest negative impact on your customers?

- How reliable are your key suppliers?

- What future scenarios scare you the most? Who or what could put you out of business?

- How easy is it for new players to enter the market?

- How organized are your suppliers? How strong is their bargaining power?

- How fierce is the competition?

- How likely is it that your customer product will be completely replaced with something new?

- What change in your product or environment could make you obsolete or put you out of business?

ANALYZING THE BUSINESS LOGIC

This technique is an adaptation of Albrecht's (1994) model described in his book *The Northbound Train*. We have added to the four business logics of Albrecht by including a planning logic. This fifth dimension adds a strategic perspective. The concept of business logic provides a framework for auditing and assessing the present strategies and tactics used by the organization and their relationship to desired results. This linking to Mega is unique in terms of most conventional business models and is what will define and deliver high payoff results.

The technique provides a business frame of reference by using the language and issues most business managers use in their everyday thinking and acting. This technique can be used in conjunction with a SWOT analysis or as an alternative to a SWOT analysis.

Purpose and When to Use

The purpose of the business logic analysis is to conduct a quick "scoping" of the business and how the various methods and means interact and relate to each other. The technique helps to generate and classify some preliminary data about the business as a foundation for a more rigorous and detailed SWOT analysis.

The business logic analysis can be used in a number of situations:

1. It could be used before a rigorous Needs Assessment to get a feel for the nature of the business through a manager's eyes, or used after a Needs Assessment to determine alignment.

2. It is best used before a rigorous SWOT analysis to quickly define the business issues and how the business operates at present, especially its primary strategies and tactics.

3. It also could be used as an alternative to a SWOT analysis where time is limited.

To be successful, the business logic analysis (like the SWOT analysis) must be aligned with other organizational efforts focused on achieving high payoff results.

The business logic provides a mental model for looking at the business and how it all hangs together from a manager's perspective. The six parts of the business logic are as follows:[7]

1. *Planning Logic.* How the organization plans and creates the future. Are they short-term "reactive" or long-term "proactive" planners?

2. *Customer Logic.* How the organization acquires and retains customers.

3. *Economic Logic.* How the organization creates economic value in terms of profit and economic value added (EVA) and long-term sustainability of share value.

4. *Product Logic.* How the organization's services and products attract and satisfy their customers; how the products and services are categorized and differentiated and what the customers value.

5. *Structural Logic.* This logic is concerned with how the organization organizes itself to do its work. This area includes what goes on in the "white space" of the organizational chart.[8]

6. *Societal Value Added Logic.* This unique frame assures that everything your organization uses, does, produces, and delivers adds value to all external clients and society. Without adding value to society, your organizational future is at risk. This element is almost always missing from conventional "business" and "strategic management" models.

Each of these logics can be broken down into the tactics and methods that are used to implement it.

Planning and Value Added Logics

The business logic is shown in the model in Figure 9.2 as the organizational responses to the external threats and opportunities.

As the external environment changes, the organization should be agile enough to change its business logic to continue to achieve high payoff results linking the Mega, Macro, and Micro levels. We will now examine four of these logics in more detail.

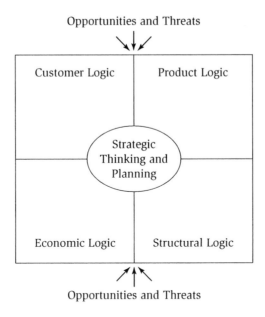

Figure 9.2. Responses to External Opportunities and Threats.

Planning Logic

All organizations are means to societal ends. Therefore, planning partners should have an obsession for high payoff results. The first step in creating a better world for tomorrow's citizens and our grandchildren is to develop an Ideal Vision. We can then plan to move ever closer to the Ideal Vision by our organizational contributions at the Macro and Micro levels.[9]

Strategic thinking and planning should be a rigorous process of adding measurable value to all our partners, clients, and society. We must produce good evidence that we are delivering the required results at all levels. When the planners have agreed on the desired results and the relationships and linkages among them, then the emphasis in planning can shift to the appropriate business logic required to achieve high payoff results.

Most so-called "organizational visions" are flawed and incomplete because of one or more of the following reasons:

1. Most are stated as one person's vision—organizations are communities and thus visions must be owned and believed by many.

2. Most are vague generalizations with no precise measurements of success.

3. Many include the means and methods without clearly defining the end result.

4. Most focus only on the organization, while ignoring the contributions and impact on society now and in the future.

5. Many include espoused values shared by other organizations so there is no uniqueness identified.

Here are some of the key questions for evaluating your present planning logic:

- Do your planners agree on the new realities?
- Do your planners agree on the logic for strategic thinking and planning?
- Are your planners reactive or proactive?
- What is the time horizon for your planning?
- Are your planners committed to making a measurable positive impact on society?
- At what level do you link your plans—Mega? Macro? Micro?
- Do you have a shared language for where you are heading?
- Are your planning decisions built on data from Needs Assessments?
- Do you have an explicit model for the strategic planning process?
- What is the level of participation in strategic thinking and planning?
- How rigorous is your database on results?
- Do you have agreement on a balanced scorecard plus (with Mega included)?
- Do your planners agree on the critical success factors for effective strategic thinking?

Changing Your Planning Logic

Too many organizations espouse social conscience but fail to match their espoused values with practical objectives (results) at the Mega level. Too often we see leaders talking about social impact, but the planning of results at the Mega level is left to chance. The move to a proactive strategic planning model, which includes all three levels of planning explicitly linked, gives us the greatest opportunity for creating a better world tomorrow and one hundred years in the future. Changing your planning logic will have an influence on the other business logics. The methods and means chosen to achieve the results can be clearly aligned and linked more directly to the required results.

Listed in Table 9.5 are the six critical success factors for proactive strategic thinking and planning (refer to Chapter Two). Use the table to evaluate your present planning logic and make notes against any of the critical success factors in terms of what you want to do differently.

Table 9.5. Changing Your Planning Logic.

Code	Critical Success Factors	Notes (Changes You Want to Make)
1	Bust your paradigms for strategic thinking—move out of your comfort zone.	
2	Distinguish between ends and means.	
3	Use all three levels of planning results, and link them (Mega, Macro, Micro).	
4	Use an Ideal Vision as the foundation for planning (Mega results).	
5	Develop measurable objectives at all planning levels.	
6	Define need as a gap in results, not as a gap in means and methods (quasi-needs).	

Customer Logic

Customer logic is the range and mix of means and methods that the organization employs to achieve its results, especially how it seeks to acquire and keep its customers or clients.

Customer logic can be classified into three groups of tactics:

Product/Service Tactics. These are concerned with how you satisfy customer needs and wants. Included in this should be helping customers to be successful and add value to their clients and society. Some examples of focus include:

Niche Focus	Wide Focus
Extreme adventure tours	Retail stores
Surfing equipment	Software
Sea kayaking tours	Household products
	General contractors

Market Tactics. These are concerned with how you divide up and segment the market, demographic groups, psychographic groups, how customers buy, how products are used. Here are some examples:

Tactic	Examples
Demographic groups	Teenagers
	Elderly
Psychographic	Gay and lesbian
How customers buy	Bulk purchase
	Organic food
How products are used	Commercial air transport
	Cooking utensils

Here are some examples of market segments you could be targeting:

Segment	Products
High net worth	Luxury resorts
	Luxury yachts
Senior citizens	Health services
	TV programs
Young people	Music CDs
	Clothing

Relationship Versus Transaction Tactics. These are concerned with whether you are building on a high volume of transactions or more on developing long-term relationships with customers. Are you focusing on developing a high volume of transactions or more on developing long-term relationships with customers? Here are some examples of tactics:

Tactic	Example
High transaction volume	Superstores
	Fast food
Relationship: frequent, ongoing contact	Fitness club
	Local grocery
Relationship: infrequent; sole source	General practitioners
	Investment advisors
	Major equipment vendors

Table 9.6 gives you an opportunity to assess your present customer logic and identify potential changes to your present tactics. The changes should be linked

Table 9.6. Customer Logic Assessment.

Code	Key Questions	Present Status	Potential Changes
1	Service/product tactics: How are you satisfying client/customer desires? Narrowly defined products/services Wide focus—wide range of products		
2	Market tactics: How are you dividing up the market? Which niches are you going after and why? • Age groups • Level of wealth • Special interest groups		
3	Relationship vs. transaction tactics: Are you concentrating on developing high volume of transactions or more on developing long term relationships with customers? Why?		

to your Smarter objectives. Assess your present customer logic and make notes on any changes required.

Economic Logic and Product Logics

For those organizations using a balanced scorecard plus (including Mega), the following performance areas will be measured and assessed on a regular basis—these are two possible balanced scorecard options:

Balanced Scorecard Plus

• Societal impact (Mega)	• Societal impact (Mega)
• Financial performance (Macro)	• Organizational deliverables (Macro)
• Product/service quality (Micro)	• Building block results (Micro)
• Customer satisfaction (Macro)	• Process efficiency
• Internal customer satisfaction(Micro)	• Resource availability and quality
• Employee satisfaction (Micro)	
• Process/team performance (Micro)	
• Supplier performance (Micro)	

or

Your economic and product logics are concerned with the tactics and strategies you select to achieve long-term profit and growth.

Your economic and product logics have three major categories of tactics: cost structure, pricing tactics, and growth tactics. Some categories of cost are shown below:

Cost	*Examples*
Fixed; costs that are always incurred regardless of what the business is doing.	Equipment Facilities Permanent staff Energy
Variable; costs that change with the volume of business.	Short-term rentals Raw materials Stationery Temporary staff
Organizations with high fixed costs plus relatively lower variable costs	Airlines Hospitals Refineries
Organizations that have high variable costs and relatively lower fixed costs.	Retail stores Small consulting firms General contractors

Check the following points for your organization:

1. Which is more of an issue for you—fixed or variable costs?
2. What are the key ones you focus on?
3. What are you doing to manage these key costs?

Note that in times of rapid change and turbulence these fixed costs can be an increased risk for an organization. Organizations can respond to this risk by switching fixed costs to variable ones. Examples include: downsizing, outsourcing, subcontracting, leasing, and partnering.

Check the following points about your pricing tactics:

1. How are you pricing your products/services?
2. Which end of the market are you targeting? Why?
3. What mix of prices do you use?

Here are some possible pricing tactics with examples:

Pricing Tactic	*Examples*
Top of the market: Charging highest prices and competing on prestige, uniqueness, and perceived quality.	Luxury cars Designer clothing Exclusive clubs Boutique; high-quality wine
Mid-range: Minimize focus on price by staying in the middle of the pack.	Taxi companies Most airlines
Low end of market: Competing to be the low cost provider.	Superstores Value airlines Buses

Check on your tactics for growth. How are you growing the organization? Here are a few examples of growth strategies:

1. *Acquisitions.* You could increase market share by buying a competitor or acquire intellectual capital, distribution channels, and/or distinctive competencies.
2. *Alliances.* You could expand business by joint ventures and strategic alliances to reduce risk.
3. *Internal Development.* You could add value to the business by hiring special people to expand capacity, developing/training expertise in-house, or building new facilities.

4. *Market Growth.* You could increase the sales force or expand to other locations.

5. *Vertical Integration.* You could add services you usually buy from a vendor.

6. *Price Dominance.*

7. *Cost Performance.*

To assess your economic logic, fill out Table 9.7. Consider your economic logic and assess the present status. Assess whether the economic logic is the best way to achieve your objectives. Note any potential changes needed.

Table 9.7. **Assessing Your Economic Logic.**

Code	Tactics	Status	Potential Changes
1	Cost structure • Fixed? • Variable?		
2	Pricing tactics • Top of market • Mid-range • Low end of market		
3	Growth tactics • Alliances • Acquisitions • Internal development • Market growth • Vertical integration • Price dominance • Cost performance		

Structural Logic

Before World War II there were not many alternatives for structuring the organization. The major organizations in the world, such as religious, military, medical, government, and large corporations all demonstrated the characteristics of bureaucratic hierarchies. There were few flat structures and the paradigm of a "networked structure" driven by computers didn't exist. Some now talk of "virtual" organizations and "paperless" factories. The traditional assumptions, principles, and practices of the industrial era are bankrupt. We require new structures to cope with the new realities.

Internal Structure

Structural logic is concerned with the means and methods used to structure the organization to achieve its desired results. Here are some of the key questions to answer when analyzing and assessing the structural logic of your organization:

Structural Logic Key Questions

- Are you a flat or tall structure organization?
- What happens in the white space of the organizational chart?
- Are you a networked structure?
- Do you have a system paradigm for the organization?
- Have you mapped your major processes?
- Are the three levels of performance (individual, Process, organizational) aligned with the results at Mega, Macro, and Micro levels?
- What is your formal structure?
    Profit centers
    Functional divisions
    Geographic divisions
    Producer divisions
    Self-contained profit centers
- Do you suffer from a "silo"* mentality?
- Are accountabilities clearly defined?
- What are the characteristics of your informal structure?
- Do you use cross-functional teams?

*Some people refer to these as "stovepipes."

These are just some of the questions related to structure. The process reengineering approach to organizational improvement is an example of a structural means to improve performance in organizations. Three aspects of the structure considered here are internal structure, human resource systems, and organizational culture. We will now look at these in more detail.

What does your organizational chart look like?[10] Why is it structured this way? What is happening in the "white space" between units and departments?[11] Here are some examples of formal structures:

Formal Structures

- Tall hierarchies
- Flat hierarchies
- Networks
- Profit centers
- Functional divisions
- Geographic divisions
- Product divisions
- Cross-functional teams
- Self-directed work teams

Your structure should help to achieve the desired results rather than hinder their accomplishment.

How does the organization acquire human capital? The following are options:

Skills/Knowledge Acquisition

- Purchase exemplary performers
- Purchase potential and develop
- Lease
- Develop

How do you develop the value of your human capital? Here are examples:

Develop Human Capital

- Retain with good reward and compensation system
- Replace
- Manage performance
- Develop
- Reconfigure—re-deploy
- Retrench
- Mentor
- Develop and train (utilize competency models)

Here are some key questions to address about organization culture:

Organizational Culture

- What mental models and paradigms drive the organization?
- What behaviors/accomplishments and practices are rewarded?
- What stories are told?
- What are the trust levels like?
- Who has the informal power?
- What are the survival skills required to get on in the organization?
- What would constitute "blasphemy" in this organization?

You can assess your present structural logic and identify potential changes by filling out Table 9.8.

Table 9.8. Assessing Structural Logic.

Code	Structural Logic	Present Status	Potential Changes
1	Internal Structure		
	• Are you tall or flat?		
	• Are you networked?		
	• Are you reliant on computer networks?		
	• Do you have a silo mentality?		
	• Are roles clearly defined?		
	• Are your processes mapped?		
2	Human Resources System		
	• Do you use competency models?		
	• Do you have an explicit performance management process?		
	• How effective are your training and development processes?		

(Continued)

Table 9.8. Assessing Structural Logic. (*Continued*)

Code	Structural Logic	Present Status	Potential Changes
3	Culture		
	• What are your paradigms?		
	• What is rewarded?		
	• What is talked about?		
	• What is espoused?		
	• What is practiced?		

THE RELATIONSHIPS AMONG THE BUSINESS LOGICS

Now that you have examined each of the business logics in isolation, it is time to link and align them. Five business logics identify the present means and methods you use to achieve results. However, Needs Assessments often identify that managers get results, but not the required or desired results. Here are some questions to answer to assess whether the business logics are aligned and related to the required results at Mega, Macro, and Micro levels:

Aligning Business Logics with Required Results

- Are the results at Mega level defined?
- Are the results at Macro level defined?
- Are the results at Micro level defined?
- Can the various logics be clearly linked to the results at Micro level?
- Can the various logics be linked to results at the Macro level?
- Can the various logics be linked to results at the Mega level?
- Do the logics have evidence to support their continuance?
- Are any of the logics contradictory with other logics?
- Do any logics contribute to meeting needs (selected problems) identified in the Needs Assessments?
- Do you have sufficient evidence that you have identified the business logics being used?
- Do the logics respond effectively to the new realities?

Assess and record the logic the business appears to be applying by filling out Table 9.9. Refer to the individual logic worksheets and summarize your

Table 9.9. Desired Changes to Business Logics.

Planning Logic	Customer Logic	Economic Logic	Product Logic	Structural Logic

findings in the columns, leaving room to write in any desired changes you want to make. After you have assessed the effectiveness of the alignment between desired results and the various business logics, identify the changes you intend to make or research further. Note these research areas or intended changes in each relevant column.

The model in Figure 9.3 depicts the relationships among the five business logics.

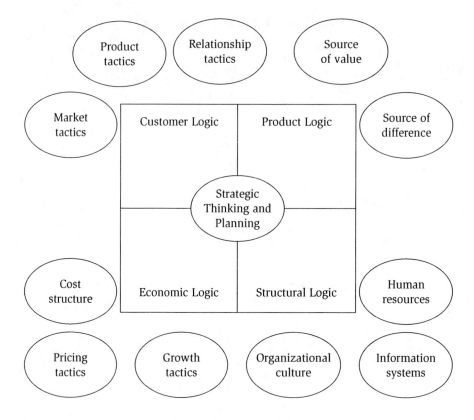

Figure 9.3. Relationships Among the Business Logics.

THE CULTURAL SCREEN

Organizational culture has become one of the more frequent topics for research and discussion over the last twenty years. Strategic thinking and planning is concerned with deep and profound change. Profound change only occurs when the present paradigms are challenged and new paradigms are applied to achieve measurable performance improvement. Strategic thinking requires changing the culture. However, the new realities demand that organizations change and that they change quickly (see Haeckel, 1999). The planners of change must answer the following questions to achieve deep cultural change in the organization:

1. What results at the Mega, Macro, and Micro levels do you commit to accomplish?

2. What is the Ideal Vision that all other results and means should be linked to?

3. What new results and new ways of performing (working) do you want to create, accomplish, and deliver?

4. Which characteristics of the culture, especially cultural assumptions, are most likely to hinder change?

5. Which characteristics of the culture are likely to help with change?

6. What behaviors, mental models, and paradigms have to be unlearned?

7. What new behaviors and paradigms have to be learned at all levels?

8. What antecedents and consequences have to change?

9. How big is the change for the average employee?

10. How big is the change for the average manager?

11. Are the sponsors of change skilled and willing to lead the change?

There is some general agreement on what an organizational culture is; yet different writers and researchers describe it in different ways. The definitions that follow are examples of how the concept can be summarized into a short definition—all have merit.

Corporate Culture

"A pervasive pattern of behaviors that are either reinforced or punished, by the company's systems and/or people over time" (Braksick, 1999).

The Culture of an Organization

"The culture of any group of people is that set of beliefs, customs, practices, and ways of thinking that they have come to share with each other through being and working together. It is a set of assumptions people simply accept without question as they interact with each other. At the visible level, the culture of a group of people takes the form of ritual behaviors, symbols, myths, stories, sounds, and artifacts" (Stacey, 1994).

Culture

"The way we do things around here" (Burke & Litwin, 1989).

Strategic Alignment

We have emphasized that strategic thinking starts with creating the required and desired results at three levels before selecting the methods and means to achieve them. Strategic alignment means coordinating all the various methods, means, and tactics to ensure they support and contribute to the desired high payoff results and consequences. Alignment ensures that strategies and tactics do not contradict each other (that is, sub-optimize at the subsystem level). Alignment is concerned with relationships between all the elements of an organization. *Alignment develops the relationship between the two paths to results:*

The Strategy Path. This path for implementation (which goes the opposite direction of the path for planning) is rational, logical, systematic, and systemic. It includes the logical linkages between the following overt steps. It is shown in Figure 9.4.

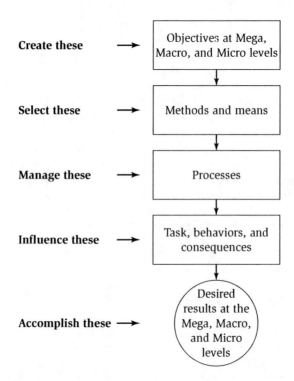

Figure 9.4. The Strategy/Tactics Path.

This path can be considered left-brained, rational, and "hard," which too often ignores the important "soft" data that drives performance, such as feelings, beliefs, and values.[12] This path is necessary but insufficient to guarantee best performance.

The Cultural Path. The culture drives how the strategy path is carried out in a specific organization. Culture makes the organization unique. Two organizations can follow the same strategy path, but their distinctive culture will influence how they apply the strategy path. This path is more covert, irrational, out of consciousness, and right-brained. See Figure 9.5 for this path.

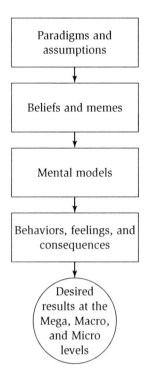

Figure 9.5. The Cultural Path.

Both paths must interact with each other, even if they are not managed. Proactive planners manage the relationship between the two. Our paradigms and assumptions will influence the results we choose to create and accomplish.

These two paths are embedded in each other. The relationship between the two paths creates a unique highway to the future if they are aligned and well-managed, as shown in Figure 9.6.

When the desired results have been defined, there is a requirement to identify how the corporate culture will support or hinder the required changes within the organization. The *cultural screen* is a tool for implementing the "right" changes in the culture to support the accomplishment of the results. It identifies the critical components of the culture that must change for the results to be achieved. The culture screen supports the development of appropriate means and tactics to achieve high payoff results. It indicates what to do to make the change stick.

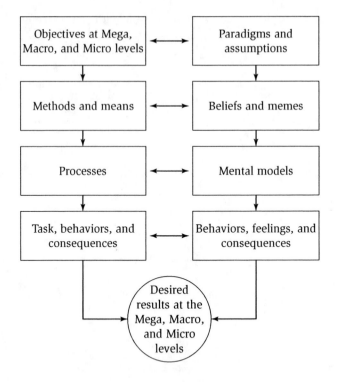

Figure 9.6. Intermingled Paths.

Proposed organizational changes can be checked through the culture screen. This process of screening identifies how best to implement and embed changes in the organizational culture. The following are the elements of the cultural screen:

1. Objectives, means, and tactics.
2. Rules and policies.
3. Behaviors and norms.
4. Ceremonies, rites, and events.
5. Performance management.
6. Communication and relating.
7. Physical environment.
8. Organizational structure.
9. Core competencies and capabilities (major processes).
10. Paradigms (mental models).
11. Leadership practices.

We now present a series of guidelines on what to change for each element.

Objectives, Means, and Tactics

Measure and assess your strategic thinking and planning approach. Review your objectives and create Smarter objectives at the Mega, Macro, and Micro levels. Create audacious objectives that bust your paradigms and challenge the status quo. Link methods and means with results at the three levels of results (and achieve alignment). Develop a measurement system that is a balanced score-card plus. Align your processes with your desired results and map them so they are obvious to those working in them. Then align the "hard stuff" of strategy with the "soft stuff" of culture.

Rules and Policies

Rules and policies can be changed with the stroke of a pen. They are *antecedents* to desired *behavior.* To gain the necessary behavior change in this category, you will have to provide positive *consequences* for the new rules and policies. Implementation is often complex. See Figure 9.7 for a visual reminder of this concept.

To change rules and policies, eliminate those that will hinder performance of new methods and procedures. Develop new rules and policies (antecedents) that describe in specific terms the desired behaviors and practices. Develop and document new standard operating procedures (SOPs). Use structured writing techniques to make documents friendly and accessible and design electronic performance support systems (EPSS) to make rules, policies, and procedures easily accessible and useable.

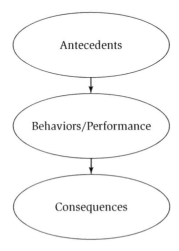

Figure 9.7. Rules and Policies.

Behaviors, Norms, and Memes

Behaviors[13] are those observable actions that are evidence of the culture in action. Norms are those patterns of behavior that determine the rules for behaving in specific situations. Memes are the basic units of cultural transmission or imitation. They are imbedded in organizational members' skills, knowledge, attitudes, and abilities that serve as the vehicles for "corporate memory."

Memes are spread from mind to mind in much the same way viruses are spread through proximity and contact. The memes are responsible for the continuation of an organizational culture. Change the memes, change the culture. Memes are the software for the mind; they program us to think and act in certain ways. Here are some guidelines:

1. Pinpoint and specify behaviors/accomplishments which support objectives at the Mega, Macro, and Micro levels.

2. Publish and reward desired behaviors/accomplishments, performances, and norms.

3. Extinguish undesired behaviors/accomplishments and norms.

4. Identify memes that are barriers to performance and extinguish them.

5. Discriminate between good memes and bad memes (viruses) and reinforce appropriately.

Ceremonies, Rites, and Events

Culture is expressed through various ceremonies, rites, and events, such as how new entrants are inducted or how significant accomplishments are celebrated and social events (for example, the Friday happy hour). Here are some guidelines for change:

1. Establish ceremonies and events to reinforce the new ways and the new results.

2. Conduct award ceremonies for teams that achieve or exceed their objectives.

3. Hold recognition events for employees and leaders who successfully implement changes.

4. Initiate watershed events that create moments of truth. Shape and structure rites of passage.

5. Redesign the induction process if it is not aligned with accomplishing desired results.

Performance Management

Performance management is usually thought of in a narrow way as the performance appraisal process. Performance management should be thought of as an integrated and systemic process for translating strategic objectives into daily, weekly, monthly, and annual performance. An effective performance management process should include at least the following critical steps:

1. Selection—getting the right people.
2. Role definition—defining expectations.
3. Competency modeling—setting standards.
4. Objective setting—defining desired results (Smarter—See Chapter Seven).
5. Definition of key tasks and behaviors—pinpointing.
6. Analysis of antecedents and consequences—getting the performance you require.
7. Detailed planning—defining who does what, when, and how much.
8. Assessment and review—assessing performance gaps and progress toward results.
9. Training development and coaching—filling the skill/competency gaps.
10. Reward and compensation—influencing repeat performance through positive reinforcement.

These steps must all be managed holistically to ensure that the desired and required results are achieved. Here are some guidelines for change:

1. Develop an explicit performance management process.
2. Develop clear role definitions for key roles and negotiate Smarter objectives.
3. Identify and eliminate major *demotivators* in the culture.
4. Develop a common language for performance management.
5. Introduce regular performance reviews that focus on results and value added.

Communicating and Relating

How people relate to each other, including how they give feedback, tells a lot about the culture. Effective communication is built on the ability to apply four steps of relating, shown in Figure 9.8:

1. Give your perspective.
2. Get the perspectives of others.

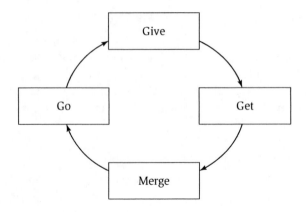

Figure 9.8. Communicating and Relating.

3. Merge perspectives.
4. Influence others to agree to action.

All purposeful one-on-one communication is built around these four steps. Here are some guidelines for improving the communication aspects of the future:

1. Improve relating skills at all levels.
2. Use multiple channels to communicate.
3. Seek feedback frequently.
4. Design and conduct meetings that work.
5. Select people with high levels of emotional intelligence.
6. Listen for feelings as well as facts.
7. Develop high levels of trust and openness.

Physical Environment

The physical design of the workplace is a reflection of the culture.[14] Here are some guidelines:

1. Design workplaces where people can think and work.
2. Co-locate people on the same team.
3. Reduce physical and mental interferences to work.

4. Improve physical factors such as lighting, furnishing, and equipment.

5. Reduce the sensory overload and boredom of routine work.

Organizational Structure

The design of the formal organizational structure is a means to achieving the objectives at all levels of results. Here are some guidelines:

1. Establish a structure that contributes to results (Mega, Macro, Micro).

2. Eliminate management layers that do not contribute to results in a measurable way.

3. Let the structure be driven by the major processes and core competencies linked to desired results at the Mega, Macro, and Micro levels.

4. Challenge the assumptions and beliefs on which the present structure is designed.

5. Define key roles clearly so that accountability for results is clearly defined.

Core Competencies[15] and Capabilities

Hamel and Prahalad (1990) suggested: "The most powerful way to prevail in global competition is still invisible to many companies."

They state that top executives should be judged on their ability to identify, develop, and exploit the core competencies as means to achieve desired and required results. A core competency[16] is a cluster of related specific competencies that relate to a key technology or are transferable across processes. Black and Decker, for example, developed core competencies in power tools. Microsoft changed its software development methods to use object-oriented techniques.

Core competencies drive the major processes (capabilities) that deliver high payoff results. Here are some guidelines for changing them:

1. Develop major processes aligned to create and deliver societal value.

2. Identify and develop core competencies to drive the major processes.

3. Develop competency models for key roles.

4. Convert the formal training process into a performance based approach, such as criterion referenced instruction (Mager, 1997).

5. Develop a performance support process to make sure training sticks.

6. Develop tactics to protect your core competencies and intellectual capital.

7. Apply human performance technology.

Human performance technology (HPT) is a scientific and results focused approach to developing and applying methods to improve human, and thus organizational performance, measurably. It includes proven methods to reproduce useful performance in individuals, teams, the organization, and society.

Mental Models and Paradigms

Our mental models, assumptions, beliefs, and memes are often deep-seated and outside of conscious awareness. These assumptions or "theories in action" are taken for granted and seldom examined or challenged. Often, these factors lead to organizational inertia and clinging to the status quo. Deep organizational change can only occur if these deep-seated models are surfaced and challenged. Below are some guidelines for making those changes:

1. Develop tactics to help the organization unlearn and learn.
2. Reflect on present assumptions and change them if there is no hard evidence to support them.
3. Stop taking for granted what is being taken for granted.
4. Develop know-how about the science of human performance.[17]
5. Recognize organizational defense patterns and "fancy footwork"[18] for what they are. Develop tactics for ensuring defensive mechanisms; don't form barriers to achieving desired and required results.
6. Identify contradictions between "espoused" values and "values in action."
7. Identify faulty logic unsupported by evidence and challenge it.

When a group of people shares a mental model, we can call it a "paradigm." A paradigm filters the world we experience and provides rules by which we comprehend reality.

Leadership Practices

The leadership practices of an organization contribute significantly to the culture of an organization. Leaders are often the most at risk when a new paradigm is introduced because they were the success evidence of the old paradigm. They often have the most to lose under the new paradigm. Here are some guidelines:

1. Develop competency models for all leadership roles.
2. Make the competency models accessible to all leaders.
3. Introduce regular performance reviews and opportunities for self and other assessment.

4. Provide challenging opportunities for practice and feedback, and install performance support systems and tools.

5. Require leaders to be sponsors of change.

6. The ABC model is a practical application of behavioral science. Students of Skinner such as Aubrey Daniels have refined and developed the model to apply to a wide range of performance areas. Originally the ABC model was most frequently applied to deviant behavior. Daniels' *Performance Management* (1989) book provides a wide range of practical guidance on the ABC model applied to the organizational performance arena. The ABC model is a powerful tool for execution after the desired results have been planned at the Ideal Vision levels. Linking the right behaviors to the right results is a primary leadership challenge.

7. Hold leaders accountable for linking their results at the Micro and Macro levels with societal value added objectives at the Mega level.

8. Assess all leaders on their commitment to innovation and self-development.

9. Coach all leaders to create Smarter objectives that are written for results linked at the Mega, Macro, and Micro levels.

10. Select and develop leaders who recognize and act on the basis that organizations survive and thrive in the long term to the extent that they add value to society now and in the future.

How to Use the Cultural Screen

When the Smarter objectives have been created and linked at the Mega, Macro, and Micro levels of results, check each element of the cultural screen and identify what changes will have to be made in the culture to manage the change. You may not have to change every element, but the relationship among them means that if you change any one part significantly, then every other part will change. Asking the systemic question, "If I change this element, what will be the implications for every other element" is a characteristic of strategic thinking.

Table 9.10 provides a cultural screen analysis. Start by accessing your Smarter objectives and then ask: "What parts of this cultural screen element will have to be managed or changed if the results are to be achieved?" Then read through each cultural screen element and note what parts you think should be changed and why.

Table 9.11 is a cultural screen checklist. Use it to help you identify the required changes in methods and tactics at the corporate culture level to achieve the desired and required results. Use this checklist to help you identify those elements of the cultural screen that should be addressed when creating cultural change.

Table 9.10. Cultural Screen Exercise.

Code	Element	Changes Required	Why
1	Objectives and tactics		
2	Rules and policies		
3	Behaviors/accomplishments and norms		
4	Rites, rituals, and events		
5	Performance management		

Table 9.10. (*Continued*)

Code	Element	Changes Required	Why
6	Communicating and relating		
7	Physical environment		
8	Structure		
9	Core competencies		
10	Assumptions, beliefs, mental models, and memes		
11	Leadership practices		

Table 9.11. Cultural Screen Checklist.

	Question	Unsure	No	Yes
1	*Objectives/Means/Tactics*			
1.1	Are your objectives linked to an Ideal Vision?			
1.2	Are objectives written for key result areas?			
1.3	Are all objectives Smarter?			
1.4	Are all means and tactics linked to Smarter objectives at Mega, Macro, and Micro levels?			
1.5	Do you have a balanced score card plus?			
1.6	Are all major processes aligned with your key result areas?			
1.7	Are all major processes mapped?			
1.8	Has the "hard" stuff of strategy been aligned with the "soft" stuff of culture?			
1.9	Are the major processes owned?			
2	*Rules and Policies*			
2.1	Have you identified and removed rules and policies that will hinder desired performance?			
2.2	Have you developed useful rules and policies to support desired behaviors/ accomplishments and results?			
2.3	Have you documented new and useful standard operating procedures?			
2.4	Are your documents useful and easily accessible to users?			
2.5	Have you developed useful electronic performance support systems (EPSS)?			

Table 9.11. (*Continued*)

		Question	Unsure	No	Yes
2.6		Have you reviewed all the key antecedents for desired behaviors/accomplishments and results?			
2.7		Have you reviewed your positive reinforcement processes (rewards and incentives)?			
3		*Behaviors/Norms/Memes*			
3.1		Have you pinpointed key behaviors/accomplishments that support results at the Mega, Macro, and Micro levels?			
3.2		Have you published desired behaviors/accomplishments and norms?			
3.3		Have you planned to extinguish undesired behaviors/accomplishments?			
3.4		Have you identified dysfunctional "memes" (viruses)?			
3.5		Have you identified key competencies for key roles?			
3.6		Have you linked behaviors/accomplishments, norms, and memes to results?			
4		*Ceremonies/Rites/Events*			
4.1		Do you have an explicit performance management process?			
4.2		Do you have a proven selection process?			
4.3		Do you have clear role definitions for key roles?			
4.4		Do you have competency models for key roles?			
4.5		Do you have a process for setting Smarter objectives?			

(*Continued*)

Table 9.11. Cultural Screen Checklist. (*Continued*)

		Question	*Unsure*	*No*	*Yes*
4.6		Do you have tasks lists for key tasks, including standards of performance?			
4.7		Do you have a process for detailed planning?			
4.8		Do you have a coordination process for planning?			
4.9		Do you have frequent performance reviews?			
4.10		Do you have a performance referenced training and development system?			
4.11		Do you have a shared common language for performance management?			
4.12		Do you know what the major demotivators in your organization are?			
5		*Communicating/Relating*			
5.1		Do your people have high levels of interpersonal skills?			
5.2		Do your people deal with conflict effectively?			
5.3		Is information useful and easily accessible?			
5.4		Do you measure the effectiveness of meetings?			
5.5		Are feelings a legitimate part of conversations?			
5.6		Do you have high levels of trust and openness?			
5.7		Do you recognize the implications of low levels of emotional intelligence?			

Table 9.11. (*Continued*)

	Question	Unsure	No	Yes
6	*Physical Environment*			
6.1	Do your work sites support working and thinking?			
6.2	Where possible do you co-locate people on the same team?			
6.3	Can you reduce physical and mental interferences to work?			
6.4	Can you improve physical factors such as lighting, furnishing, and equipment?			
6.5	Can you reduce the sensory overload and boredom of routine work?			
7	*Organizational Structure*			
7.1	Does the structure support achievement of results at Mega, Macro, and Micro levels?			
7.2	Can you eliminate any management layers and add value?			
7.3	Have you defined your core competencies and linked them to desired results?			
7.4	Have you mapped your major processes?			
7.5	Have you challenged the beliefs and assumptions on which the present structure is designed?			
7.6	Are there clear role definitions for key roles?			
7.7	Are role definitions clearly linked to accountability for results?			
8	*Paradigms/Mental Models*			
8.1	Does the organization put time aside for reflection on its mental models?			

(Continued)

Table 9.11. Cultural Screen Checklist. (*Continued*)

		Question	Unsure	No	Yes
	8.2	Do you challenge your espoused values against your values in action?			
	8.3	Do you challenge your shared paradigms for acting?			
	8.4	Do you have means to discover what you don't know you don't know?			
	8.5	Do you make assumptions explicit and challenge them as teams?			
	8.6	Do you have means to identify organizational defense mechanisms?			
	8.7	Do you have means to deal with defensive mechanisms so they don't impede achievement of results?			
	8.8	Is faulty logic challenged?			
	8.9	Do you use cost-consequences analysis to link results and means?			
	9	*Leadership Practices*			
	9.1	Do you have competency models for all leadership roles?			
	9.2	Are the competency models linked to results desired at the Mega, Macro, and Micro levels?			
	9.3	Are the competency models easily accessible to the users?			
	9.4	Do you have regular performance reviews?			
	9.5	Are leaders encouraged to self-initiate self and others assessment events?			
	9.6	Are leaders required to be the sponsors of change?			
	9.7	Are leaders required to develop Smarter objectives for their key result areas?			

Table 9.11. (Continued)

		Question	Unsure	No	Yes
9.8		Are leaders required to link their Smarter objectives (results) at Mega, Macro, and Micro levels?			
9.9		Are leaders assessed on their commitment to innovation and self-development?			
9.10		Are leaders provided challenges to take them out of their comfort zones?			
9.11		Are leaders provided support for their developmental challenges (before, during, after)?			

Notes

1. Kaufman (2000) defines scoping as defining who is to be the primary client and beneficiary of the strategic plan. He proposes three possible client groups that planners might select (while noting that the most practical one is Mega). In actuality, only Mega is true strategic planning.

2. "Business logic" is often used as a Macro focus because it targets the profits and well-being of the organization without formally linking those organizational results with value added for external clients and society. Beware of stopping at this level.

3. Ackoff (1981, p. 79) coined the term "the mess" to describe the complexity and chaos of complex organizations in his book *Creating the Corporate Future*. Ackoff identified the messiness of organizations before chaos theory popularized the discoveries of quantum mechanics and tried to apply them to understanding our social structures. Refer also to Wheatley (1992) for more insights into the chaotic mess and uncertainty of complex organizations.

4. Be sure that a SWOT analysis doesn't become an end in and of itself and just continue on and on. Stop when you get the data required to assure successful results.

5. Kaufman (2000, p. 62) makes a clear distinction between soft and hard data and the value of them both, especially their relationship to each other.

6. Some recent efforts have converted quality management and continuous improvement to "continuous process improvement." This is comfortable, but why would one want to improve a process unless it delivered measurably useful results? This "escape to means" can be seen in many areas and is symptomatic of fear or ignorance.

7. We have added the planning logic and societal impact to the idea.

8. Again, this points out an earlier observation that we made that conventional organizational charts are convenient fictions . . . line communications and reporting rarely work as documented in organizational charts.

9. Kaufman (2000) has formally addressed societal impact through the development of an Ideal Vision as the only truly and practical strategic perspective on long-term planning. If our plans are not formally linked to an Ideal Vision, are we not leaving the future to chance? The Ideal Vision is practical, measurable, and cross cultural; it avoids the vague "wishy-washy" platitudes of so many "visions" presented on reception room walls.

10. The traditional organizational chart with its structured boxes and lines told us very little about organizational performance. For instance, the most important stakeholder, the client, was never shown on the chart. The chart also hid the cobwebs and pattern of human influence networks that made things happen. Rummler and Brache (1995) make a valuable contribution to our understanding of human and organizational performance. We add a further level of performance to the Rummler-Brache model by emphasizing the performance of society (the community) as results of organizational performance. Managing the link between (Macro) results delivered to immediate clients and stakeholders and results delivered to the wider society (Mega) is the strategic paradigm of thinking, planning, and creating long-term futures.

11. In some cases, one of the authors has used a round organization chart with society and external clients in the center in order to assure this important focus and to keep operations from being rigid and hierarchical.

12. Again, beliefs and values almost always relate to means and resources rather than to results and value added at the Micro, Macro, and Mega levels. A focus on beliefs and values is popular, but we suggest that using an Ideal Vision replaces a means focus with a results focus. People confront their beliefs and values when they derive or approve an Ideal Vision (Kaufman, 1998, 2000).

13. Behaviors become important when the result is performance.

14. Refer to the book *Creating Workplaces Where People Can Think* by Smith and Kearney (1994) for more detail on the impact of physical space and design on human performance and to *Cultural Due Diligence: A Manager's Guide to Increasing the Success of Mergers and Acquisitions* by Lineberry and Carelton (2003).

15. Core competencies are not the same as individual competencies. Martin (1995, p. 306) defines a core competency as a technological or production skill at a point on a value stream, whereas a strategic capability is an entire value stream. Core competencies are groupings of individual competencies that establish uniqueness for an organization. The core competencies of today might be the burial competencies of tomorrow, so make certain that they can and will change with new realities.

16. A warning, however. Simply sticking to one's core competency might make it resistant to minor and major change. For example, what value are the core competencies of a typewriter manufacturing company in our computer world? Some transfer; some do not.

17. Thirty years plus of research on "best performers" in a wide range of roles and occupations is now available. We can detect the X factor that distinguishes high performers from average or mediocre. We are reasonable certain that there is no "one" factor. Gilbert (1978) helped our understanding of what influences peak performance with his six-factor model. The competency modeling methodology developed out of the work of David McClelland of Harvard and his colleagues Boyatzis, Spencer, and Spencer point to those distinguishing characteristics and skills that contribute to the X factor. The X factor should be thought of as "emergent," that is, it emerges out of the relationship between all the elements of the Gilbert six-box model. Competencies are important and necessary for high performance but insufficient by themselves. Competencies provide the measurable standards, but they are not the X factor—they contribute to the X factor. Combining the work of Gilbert and McClelland provides a sound approach to defining the patterns of behavior thought and feelings that contribute to superior results. Refer also to Spencer and Spencer (1993).

18. "Fancy foot work" is an apt description for the defensive mechanisms of senior managers threatened by new realities and paradigms. Argyris (1990) explains the term in his book *Overcoming Organizational Defenses.*

CHAPTER TEN

Delivering High Payoff Results

Throughout this book we have provided the concepts and tools (the *what's* and *how's*) for defining and delivering high payoff results for and through your organization. From the development of an Ideal Vision through the creation of significant change in your organization, the ingredients for the achievement of high payoff results have been detailed. In order to put the concepts and tools to work, in this chapter we show the order, steps, and flow of moving from strategic planning and thinking to the high payoff results and payoffs using the Organizational Elements Model (OEM) as the basis for effective and systematic implementation. Because all thinking, planning, and doing are based on adding value for external clients and society—Mega—it is a *system approach*.

High payoff results flow from the effective processes that define and justify what results should be delivered. Strategic planning and Needs Assessment are processes that begin at the Mega level. These two tools should be used to assure the accomplishment of useful results.

We have provided three templates that will better assure your success:

- The Organizational Elements Model (OEM) that identifies what every organization uses (Inputs), does (Processes), produces internally (Products), delivers outside of itself (Outputs), and the impact they have in and for external clients and society (Outcomes). Linking all of the organizational elements will provide the alignment for high payoff results that will add value—measurable value—for all stakeholders, as laid out in Figure 10.1.

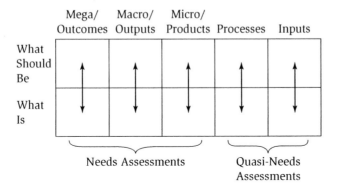

Figure 10.1. The OEM as a Framework for Needs Assessment.

Source: From Kaufman, 1992, 1998, 2000.

- Six critical success factors define the ground rules for assuring that results are correctly defined, related, and delivered. These are seen in Table 10.1.

Table 10.1. Six Critical Success Factors.

Critical Success Factor 1

Move out of your comfort zone—today's paradigms—and use new and wider boundaries for thinking, planning, doing, evaluating, and continuous improvement.

Critical Success Factor 2

Differentiate between ends (what) and means (how).

Critical Success Factor 3

Use all three levels of planning and results (Mega/Outcomes; Macro/Outputs; Micro/Products).

Critical Success Factor 4

Prepare all objectives—including the Ideal Vision and mission—to include precise statements of both where you are headed, as well as the criteria for measuring when you have arrived. Develop "Smarter" Objectives.

Critical Success Factor 5

Use an Ideal Vision (what kind of world, in measurable performance terms, we want for tomorrow's child) as the underlying basis for planning and continuous improvement.

Critical Success Factor 6

Defining "need" as a gap in results (not as insufficient levels of resources, means or methods).

- The six step problem solving model provides a guide for building the bridge between What Is and What Should Be for results. It is the basic guide for solving simple or complex problems. It always starts with the identification and verification of needs before defining, developing, and implementing any solution, as shown in Figure 10.2.

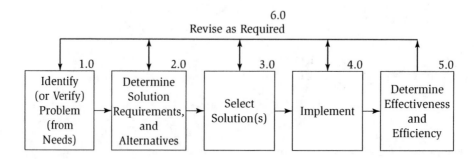

Figure 10.2. A Process for Identifying and Resolving Problems.

Source: From Kaufman, 1992, 1998, 2000.

Together these three guides, if used correctly and consistently, will deliver organizational and personal success. They must be used, however. Success is really quite straightforward if one uses the right tools with consistency.

HIGH PAYOFF RESULTS

Not all results deliver value added. Nor do all results have equal impact and contribution. In Chapter One we defined high payoff results as those that add value at all levels of the Organizational Elements Model (OEM): Mega, Macro, and Micro. *Low payoff results* are those that focus on individuals and small groups within one's organization, but do not necessarily add value to all.

For example, a low payoff result could be the development of a training program that merely meets design objectives for the population for which it is intended without also making a contribution to external clients. Such low payoff results rarely provide clear answers to questions like: Will meeting training objectives add value on the job, add value within the organization, and add value for external clients and society? In fact, training results seem to have a minimal impact, since there is little transfer (less than 10 percent) to use on the job (Clark & Estes, 2000, 2002; Stolovitch, 2000). While low payoff results may be better than nothing in some cases, with a little extra planning, most organizations can move toward the accomplishment of high payoff results.

The conventional auto mechanic turns and calibrates brakes. Few, however, formally realize that the quality of their work and the consequences of making them both meet factory specifications and safety requirements could have huge consequences for drivers using the brakes. High payoff results add value at all levels of the organization as well as to external clients and society. The individual tasks (turning and calibrating the brake disks) must yield safety for the driver and the vehicle. High payoff results focus on external health, safety, and well-being and the enormous importance of linking all levels. A hallmark of this approach is that internal results must add value to external clients and society. High payoff results are those that will add value for the entire "results chain" that flows from individual performance accomplishment to organizational and external/societal contributions, as shown in Figure 10.3.

The influence of high payoff results can be seen throughout an organization. High payoff Products (Micro level results) are the basis and the building blocks for organizational success. These results are the accomplishments of individuals and small groups (that is, Micro level results) and have significant impact on the achievement of organizational Outputs (Macro level results) as well as the results delivered to external clients (Mega level results). It is this linking of influence from accomplishments that makes for high impact payoffs. High impact

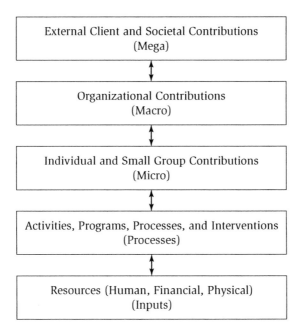

Figure 10.3. Aligning All Elements of an Organization.

Source: Based on Kaufman, 1998.

payoffs and results may be obtained by any organization that finds it important to do so and commits to deliver them. It is not the conventional approach (although it should be), and thus is not usually delivered. Why?

Most conventional approaches to strategic planning and needs assessment are systems models, and thus are restricted to limited definitions of "business needs."* This limitation ignores or assumes that business objectives are formally and measurably related to and deliver value added for both external clients and our shared society. Organizational success depends on meeting the requirements of clients. In addition, however, perspectives on success must also include significantly wider definitions of clients than are usually used today: society must be included and be top priority.

The direct clients (internal or external) to which you market products are only part of the picture. In competitive markets, successful organizations ensure that their products assist direct clients is serving their clients (and their client's clients) more effectively and efficiently. Actually, this enlarging perspective of clients quickly becomes synonymous with the local community and shared society. Thus, effective organizations are not only examining the requirements of the internal clients, but of a variety of external and linked clients as well. In other words, they add value to and for the external clients and partners, while at the same time ensuring that the internal clients and partners are also accomplishing the results required of them. The balance of this relationship is critical for success. This is shown graphically in Figure 10.4.

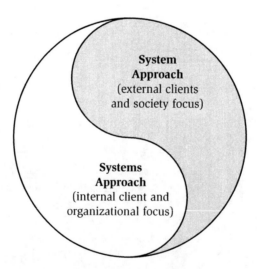

Figure 10.4. A Systems Approach vs. a System Approach.

---

*This term distorts the definition of "need" used in this book.

Achieving a balanced system approach to planning and assessment is not, however, the result of applying conventional models. There are many names for various planning approaches in use today. The labels include strategic planning, strategic management, business planning, corporate planning, tactical planning, and operational planning. Each can be a useful process if done correctly and if the understanding of what each does and does not deliver is clearly identified and understood by all partners. Unfortunately, there is much confusion concerning what each process provides. Table 10.2 compares each planning process with the others and with the Organizational Elements Model (OEM). The arrows note the primary flow direction.

Table 10.2. Frameworks for Plans in Common Use Today.

	MEGA/ Outcomes	MACRO/ Outputs	MICRO/ Products	PROCESSES	INPUTS
Strategic planning	-------▶	-------▶	-------▶	-------▶	-------▶
Strategic management			◀-------	◀-------	◀-------
Business planning			◀-------	◀-------	◀-------
Corporate planning		◀-------	◀-------	◀-------	◀-------
Tactical planning			-------▶	-------▶	-------▶
Operational planning				◀-------	◀-------

Direction of flow is a vital consideration for defining and achieving high payoff results. Notice that strategic planning (and thinking), as defined in this book, is proactive and starts from Mega. In addition, we have suggested that in order to be effective it "flows down" from Mega to link with all of the other Organizational Elements. Tactical planning also "flows down" from Micro to Processes to Inputs. Other planning processes are reactive and "flow up" from Inputs. Operational planning extends to Processes. Strategic management and business planning flow up from Inputs to Processes to Products. Corporate planning flows "upward" from Inputs to Processes, to Products, to Outputs.

The difference in upward and downward flowing of planning processes is as basic as the questions they ask. In upward flowing models (starting with Inputs and moving towards results), the planning questions are similar to these: If we have these resources, how are they being used? If we are conducting this activity, what results are we getting? However, when applying a downward flowing planning process (see Figure 10.5) questions are likely to include: We want to accomplish these results, what building block results must we first achieve to ensure our success? If we are going to achieve these results, what Processes will be most effective and efficient in doing so? The differences may appear subtle at first, but they are significant. The first questions are really those questions that we ask during an assessment (or evaluation) following the decision to purchase some resource or implement some Process. That is not, according to our definitions, strategic planning. The second questions are those that are most useful in setting direction and deriving a path for accomplishing required results.

Each of the planning processes identified in Table 10.2 can be useful if one considers the limitations and "reach" of each. Only strategic planning, however, links all levels of results and Processes and Inputs (and is thus holistic). Others, used alone, will only provide a partial picture of organizational impact and contributions. If useful performance is to be defined and achieved, Mega/ Outcomes must be part of all planning and subsequent design, development, implementation, and evaluation/continuous improvement.

The Organizational Elements Model (OEM) provides the conceptual framework to move from planning to the achievement of useful results. Using it, we can define the steps for moving from needs (gaps in results) to requirements, from requirements to identified alternative methods-means to meet those requirements, and then to the selection of those methods-means that are most effective and efficient at delivering the required, and specified, high payoff results.

In addition to providing a framework for Needs Assessment, the Organizational Elements Model (OEM) provides a structure for examining the implementation of high payoff planning and sensible assessment. This use of the OEM as the framework for linking strategic thinking to high payoff results offers organizational leaders—and those who would become leaders—the tools for ensuring that justifiable and measurable objectives at the Mega, Macro, and Micro levels provide the necessary direction for moving an organization from current (What Is) results to useful and required results. Figure 10.6 illustrates the steps for utilizing the OEM as this linkage element between planning and effective implementation.

Using the OEM as the framework, organizations can use the following questions to guide implementation. The first set of questions relates to planning and are each related to the steps in Figure 10.6 linked to What Should Be.

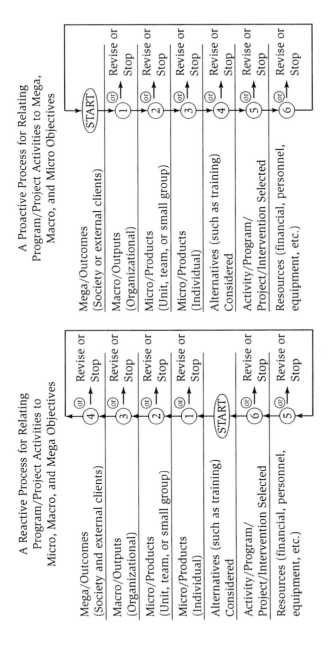

Figure 10.5. Upward/Reactive and Downward/Proactive Decision Processes.

Source: Kaufman, 2000.

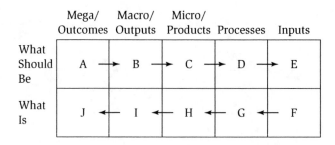

Figure 10.6. OEM Links from Planning to Results.

Proactive Planning Questions

In order to deliver results for external clients and society in *A*, what results must we obtain at the organizational level of *B*? In order to obtain useful organizational results in *B*, what building block results must we obtain in *C*? In order to obtain useful individual and small group results in *C*, what Processes in *D* must we obtain and use? In order to deliver useful processes in *D*, what resources (including human, capital, and financial) must we obtain in *E*?

At the same time in an interrelated process, organizations should assess their current performance at each level of the OEM. The questions related to this assessment are outlined in relation to the steps related to the What Is tier of the OEM.

Here are some questions that an assessment might ask and answer if one is starting from the "inside" to the "outside," or moving from What Is to What Should Be. Of course, starting at this inside level carries some risk, for it might lure people into assuming that the problem selected is the real and important one. Starting from the outside and moving in (from Mega, to Macro, to Micro, to Processes, to Inputs) will likely overcome pre-selected solutions in search of problems.

Assessment Questions

- If we currently have the resources in F, what processes do they enable us to implement in G?
- If we currently implement the processes in G, what results do they enable us to achieve at H?
- If we currently achieve the results in H, what results do they enable us to achieve at I?
- If we currently achieve the results in I, what results do they enable us to achieve at J?

In answering the planning and assessment questions above, organizations are better able to relate the information in a Needs Assessment. The Needs Assessment identifies and prioritizes the gaps between the What Should Be and What Is for the three levels of results. Cooperatively, the Quasi-Needs Assessment identifies and priorities the gaps in Processes and Inputs. Only together does an organization have an effective framework for achieving high payoff results.

What are the implications for doing an assessment from inside out (starting with Inputs and rolling up through the Organizational Elements to Outcomes), as opposed to starting from the outside in (starting with Mega and rolling down through the Organizational Elements to Processes and Inputs)? What do you and your organization gain from the outside-in approach?

Needs Assessment Questions

- Does A = J? If not, based on the costs to meet the need versus the cost of not meeting the need, what should be the priority order?

- Does B = I? If not, based on the costs to meet the need versus the cost of not meeting the need, what should be the priority order?

- Does C = H? If not, based on the costs to meet the need versus the cost of not meeting the need, what should be the priority order?

Quasi-Needs Assessment Questions

- Does D = G? If not, based on the costs to meet the quasi-need versus the cost of not meeting the quasi-need, what should be the priority order?

- Does E = F? If not, based on the costs to meet the quasi-need versus the cost of not meeting the quasi-need, what should be the priority order?

What are the advantages and disadvantages of defining needs in this manner? What are the risks for not progressing as described above?

Causal Analysis (or Needs Analysis) Questions

- If A ≠ J, why and what can be improved?
- If B ≠ I, why and what can be improved?
- If C ≠ H, why and what can be improved?

The Quasi-Needs Assessment should follow the completion of the Needs Assessment in order to maintain the correct results focus throughout the initiative.

Needs Assessment vs. Needs Analysis

Needs analysis (the breaking down of identified needs to determine root causes and identifying, but not selecting, the possible methods and means to close the gaps in results), by logic then, follows Needs Assessment and Quasi-Needs Assessment. The Needs Assessment and Quasi-Needs Assessment relationships were illustrated in Figure 10.1.

Based on the needs and quasi-needs identified and prioritized during the Needs Assessment, change requirements can then be identified. Change requirements are derived from a combination of analyzing performance requirements as well as possible causes. Performance requirements analysis provides decision makers with the specific criteria that must be met for a potential intervention (or combination of interventions) to be considered adequate in meeting the defined need (gap between What Should Be and What Is). When strategic planning includes the writing of measurable objectives—as it must—the standards set in performance requirements analysis are easily derived from those objectives. However, if strategic plans are left as obscure or indistinct statements of general goals, then a *performance requirements analysis* will be required to determine the criteria for selecting among possible interventions (Kaufman, Watkins, & Leigh, 2001).

The second analysis used in determining change requirements is a causal analysis (Kaufman, Watkins, & Leigh, 2001). Causal analysis examines the gaps in ends (Mega, Macro, and Micro) as well as means (Process and Inputs) to derive likely casual relationships for current levels (What Is) not meeting the desired standards (What Should Be). Without this additional examination of likely causes, decision makers are rarely able to determine which intervention (or combination of interventions) addresses the actual causes of needs—the identified gaps in results[1]—rather than merely the symptoms. By using both types of analysis, change requirements can be identified for each level of the OEM.

Following the specification of change requirements, it is now time for potential interventions (solutions, activities, training, and so forth) to be systemically[2] and rigorously examined. Up to this point, no single intervention has been selected or even given priority. Rather, all possible interventions—no matter how much anyone wants them—should have been kept separate from the planning and assessment processes in order to reduce bias. However, now that we have identified likely causes as well as performance criteria that adequate interventions must meet in order to close the gaps in results (needs) we have identified, potential interventions can be systematically examined based on their ability to achieve the required results.

Costs-consequences analysis (see Kaufman 1998, 2000; Kaufman, Watkins, & Leigh, 2001) provides a useful tool for estimating the ability of interventions to meet these requirements. By examining the cost relationships of meeting the need (closing the gap in results) versus not meeting the need for each intervention, costs-consequences analysis provides decision makers with necessary data for making difficult decisions. Based on the data substantiating an intervention's ability to adequately achieve required results as well as address likely causes of the need in a cost-effective and efficient manner, decision makers can again use the OEM framework to identify possible interventions and select interventions for implementation.

FOURTEEN STEPS TO USEFUL RESULTS AND PERFORMANCE

The concepts and tools provided above for defining and delivering high payoff results should be integrated into an implementation and continuous improvement plan. The basis for this can be the fourteen-step model shown in Figure 10.7. The fourteen steps represent the essential decision point in implementing and continuously improving initiatives designed to generate high payoff results. The key to success is being proactive, using societal value added as the focus, being results driven, and using performance data to continuously improve.

In applying each of the fourteen steps, organizational leaders should use the many tools provided throughout this book in order to ensure the consistency in purpose (the Ideal Vision and Mission Objective), the results focus (Mega, Macro, and Micro), and the emphasis on systemic change management and creation. When applied in an organization, the OEM framework can ensure a holistic (Outcome-based), comprehensive (Output-based), and inclusive (Product-based) planning and assessment process that leads to high payoff results and societal value added.

1. Decide to Create a Better Future

Strategic planning and thinking are the result of a desire for the future to be in some way improved from the current. When the decision has been made that current accomplishments and contributions at the Mega, Macro, and Micro levels are not meeting the requirements of changing perspectives or requirements, then it is time to begin a process for positive change creation and the accomplishment of high payoff results.

Useful resources for the implementation of step 1 include:

- *Mega Planning* by Kaufman (2000)
- *Post-Capitalist Society* by Drucker (1993)
- *The Business of Paradigms: Discovering the Future* by Barker (1989)
- *The Popcorn Report* by Popcorn (1991)

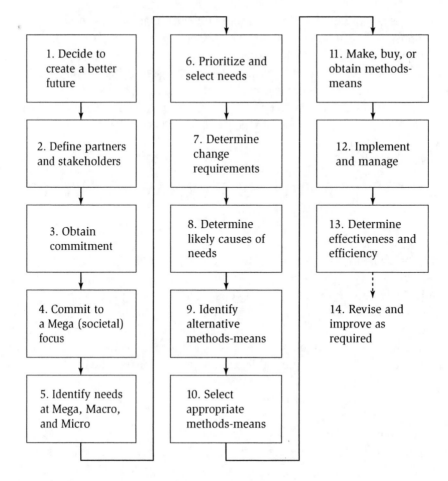

Figure 10.7. Fourteen Steps to Useful Results.

Source: Inspired by Kaufman and Stone, 1982.

- *Thinking for a Living: Education and the Wealth of Nations* by Marshall and Tucker (1992)
- *Beyond Certainty: The Changing Worlds or Organisations* by Handy (1995–1996)
- *The Eden Conspiracy: Educating for Accomplished Citizenship* by Harless (1998)
- *A Systems View of Education: Concepts and Principles for Effective Practice* by Banathy (1992)
- *The Structure of Scientific Revolutions* by Kuhn (1970)

- *Victory Secrets of Attila the Hun* by Roberts (1993)
- *The Fifth Discipline: The Art and Practice of the Learning Organization* by Senge (1990)
- *A Performance Accomplishment Code of Professional Conduct* by Watkins, Kaufman, and Leigh (2000)

2. Define Partners and Stakeholders

No singular organization or individual is solely responsible for making improvements to the status quo. Each organization has many partners and stakeholders in the processes they implement every day . . . and the same is true in strategic planning and thinking. From providers of resources to external consultants, employees, community members, and internal partners, the implementation of strategic planning and Needs Assessment processes relies on the partners and stakeholders being involved and maintaining commitment to the accomplishment of useful results. The challenge at this stage is not to expand the participation to a point where there are "too many cooks in the kitchen," but to maintain adequate representation that implementation is possible. Groups of ten to fifteen are reasonable, although if larger groups are involved, facilitation tools (like nominal group techniques) are useful.

Useful resources for the implementation of step 2 include:

- *Mega Planning* by Kaufman (2000)
- *Stewardship* by Block (1993)
- *The Popcorn Report* by Popcorn (1991)
- *Useful Educational Results* by Kaufman, Watkins, and Leigh (2001)

3. Obtain Commitment

The partners and stakeholders of your organization must make a commitment to participation in the process. This is primarily a commitment of time and energy, and possibly other resources depending on their selected role in the achievement of high payoff results. If representatives of a particular stakeholder group are not able to participate, then an alternative representative with similar stakes in the process should be identified. Avoid isolating a group from the process that may later be essential in accomplishment of results.

Useful resources for the implementation of step 3 include:

- *Mega Planning* by Kaufman (2000)
- *Stewardship* by Block (1993)
- *Useful Educational Results* by Kaufman, Watkins, and Leigh (2001)

4. Commit to a Mega (Societal) Focus

When each of the partners and stakeholders has committed to participate, now it is time to commit to a planning framework and the achievement of high pay-off results. This will set the stage for all decisions that will follow and ensure that results are linked to Mega level Outcomes. By offering the OEM as a holistic framework for planning and assessment, the individual issues and agendas of each partner and stakeholder will be addressed as they relate to the overall focus on the achievement of useful results for society and external clients.

Useful resources for the implementation of step 4 include:

- *Mega Planning* by Kaufman (2000)
- *Post-Capitalist Society* by Drucker (1993)
- *Powershift: Knowledge, Wealth, and Violence at the Edge of the 21st Century* by Toffler (1990)
- *Stewardship* by Block (1993)
- *Strategic Planning Plus: An Organizational Guide* by Kaufman (1992)
- *Useful Educational Results* by Kaufman, Watkins, and Leigh (2001)

5. Identify Needs at Mega, Macro, and Micro

Needs (gaps in results) should be identified at the Mega, Macro, and Micro levels. At each level data will be collected to illustrate the What Should Be and What Is with regard to results. By examining any discrepancy between the What Should Be and What Is, gaps in results can be specified and justified.

Useful resources for the implementation of step 5 include:

- *General Systems Theory* by von Bertalanffy (1968)
- *Needs Assessment: A User's Guide* by Kaufman, Rojas, and Mayer (1993)
- *Strategic Planning Plus: An Organizational Guide* by Kaufman (1992)
- *Strategic Thinking* by Kaufman (1998)
- *Mega Planning* by Kaufman (2000)
- *Useful Educational Results* by Kaufman, Watkins, and Leigh (2001)

6. Prioritize and Select Needs

Here partners and stakeholders place the gaps in results in priority order for closure, starting with Mega level needs and then rolling down to include Macro and Micro level needs. This is commonly done first in small groups, and then in a larger group. The basis for making these difficult decisions is the relationship of "What is the cost to meet the need" versus "What is the cost to ignore the need?"

Useful resources for the implementation of step 6 include:

- *Needs Assessment: A User's Guide* by Kaufman, Rojas, and Mayer (1993)
- *Strategic Planning Plus: An Organizational Guide* by Kaufman (1992)
- *Useful Educational Results* by Kaufman, Watkins, and Leigh (2001)

7. Determine Change Requirements

Based on prioritized needs, change requirements can be determined. Change requirements specify the performance requirements in order for an identified need to be met. The addition of measurement criteria is usually necessary when moving from organizational goals to objectives.

Useful resources for the implementation of step 7 include:

- *Needs Assessment: A User's Guide* by Kaufman, Rojas, and Mayer (1993)
- *Strategic Planning Plus: An Organizational Guide* by Kaufman (1992)
- *Strategic Thinking* by Kaufman (1998)
- *Mega Planning* by Kaufman (2000)

8. Determine Likely Causes of Needs

Likely causes of gaps should be identified at each level of results. The information from this causal analysis will be essential in identifying and selecting among alternative solutions.

Useful resources for the implementation of step 8 include:

- *Figuring Things Out: A Trainer's Guide to Needs and Task Analysis* by Zemke and Kramlinger (1982)
- *Strategic Planning Plus: An Organizational Guide* by Kaufman (1992)
- *Mega Planning* by Kaufman (2000)
- *Useful Educational Results* by Kaufman, Watkins, and Leigh (2001)
- *Improving Performance: How to Manage the White Spaces on the Organization Chart* by Rummler and Brache (1995)

9. Identify Alternative Methods-Means

For each gap in results, multiple alternatives for closing the gap should be identified. These could include training interventions, motivational systems, electronic performance support tools, or a wide array of solutions. Solutions should be linked to gaps based on their ability to meet the performance requirements as well as their capability to address the likely causes of the need. It is often suggested that a minimum of three alternative solutions be identified for each gap in results, noting that some solutions will overlap with several gaps. *Note that for the first time we have now shifted our attention from "what" to "how."*

Useful resources for the implementation of step 9 include:

- *An Ounce of Analysis Is Worth a Pound of Cure* by Harless (1975)
- *Figuring Things Out: A Trainer's Guide to Needs and Task Analysis* by Zemke and Kramlinger (1982)
- *Strategic Planning Plus: An Organizational Guide* by Kaufman (1992)
- *Mega Planning* by Kaufman (2000)
- *Improving Performance: How to Manage the White Spaces on the Organization Chart* by Rummler and Brache (1995)

10. Select Appropriate Methods-Means

The most effective and efficient solutions are usually desirable, although unique situations often obscure what would otherwise be considered easy decisions. Constraints should be addressed, and previously collected data should be used to illustrate the likely success of a solution and the costs of needs that are not addressed.

Useful resources for the implementation of step 10 include:

- *An Ounce of Analysis Is Worth a Pound of Cure* by Harless (1975)
- *Figuring Things Out: A Trainer's Guide to Needs and Task Analysis* by Zemke and Kramlinger (1982)
- *Improving Performance: How to Manage the White Spaces on the Organization Chart* by Rummler and Brache (1995)
- *Human Competence: Engineering Worthy Performance* by Gilbert (1978)

11. Make, Buy, or Obtain Methods-Means

When a solution or intervention is selected as the most appropriate for the identified needs, required resources should be acquired for implementation. Depending on the nature of solution and the organization, these methods-means can be obtained, produced, or bought.

Useful resources for the implementation of step 11 include:

- *Systems Thinking and Systems Doing* by Brethower and Dams (1999)
- *Handbook of Procedures for the Design of Instruction* by Briggs and Wager (1982)
- *The Development of Authentic Educational Technologies* by Clark and Estes (1999)

- *A Proposal for the Collaborative Development of Authentic Performance Technology* by Clark and Estes (2000)

- *Essentials of Learning for Instruction* by Gagne and Driscoll (1988)

- *Human Competence: Engineering Worthy Performance* by Gilbert (1978)

- A series of books by Robert Mager, including:
  - *Making Instruction Work: Or Skillbloomers* (1988)
  - *What Every Manager Should Know About Training: Or "I've Got a Training Problem"* . . . *and Other Odd Ideas* (1992)
  - *CRI: Criterion Referenced Instruction* (with Pipe) (1983)
  - *Analyzing Performance Problems* (with Pipe) (2nd ed.) (1984)
  - *Preparing Instructional Objectives* (1997)

- *Improving Performance: How to Manage the White Space on the Organization Chart* by Rummler and Brache (1995)

- *Human Performance Technology: Research and Theory to Practice* by Stolovitch (2000)

- *Handbook of Human Performance Technology: A Comprehensive Guide for Analyzing and Solving Performance Problems in Organizations* edited by Stolovitch and Keeps (1992)

12. Implement and Manage

This is the time for action. Now all the pieces are in place for implementation of the plan that has been created. Throughout implementation, the strategic planning partners and stakeholders should be included in decisions that may be alterations from the plan. If alternative implementation processes are required, then adjustments to the strategic plan should be made, and consequences for the accomplishment of high payoff results identified.

Useful resources for the implementation of step 12 include:

- *Improving Performance: How to Manage the White Space on the Organization Chart* by Rummler and Brache (1995)

- *Management: Tasks, Responsibilities, Practices* by Drucker (1973)

- *Managing at the Speed of Change* by Conner (1992)

- *Out of the Crisis* by Deming (1986)

- *Principles of Instructional Design* by Gagne, Briggs, and Wager (1988)

- *The Systematic Design of Instruction* by Dick, Carey, and Carey (2000)

- *T&D Systems View* by Wallace (2001)

- *Fundamental of Performance Technology* by Van Tiem, Moseley, and Dessinger (2000)

13. Determine Effectiveness and Efficiency

During all phases of implementation, both effectiveness and efficiency should be assessed to determine whether the desired results are still in focus. Performance requirements at the Mega, Macro, and Micro levels are used as the measurement criteria, and objectives are compared with achieved results. Fine-tuning of organizational processes may be required to ensure the accomplishment of high payoff results.

Useful resources for the implementation of step 13 include:

- *Evaluating Training Programs: The Four Levels* by Kirkpatrick (1994)
- *Evaluation Without Fear* by Kaufman and Thomas (1980)
- *Out of the Crisis* by Deming (1986)

14. Revise and Improve as Required

As data from the assessment of effectiveness and efficiency is identified, planning partners and stakeholders should use that information to make decisions regarding the continuous improvement of the planning and assessment Processes. Like all Processes in an organization, the implementation of the Process described above will also require continuous improvement by the partners and stakeholders. Improvements could include consideration of alternative priorities in needs, differing measurement criteria for specific objectives, or even alternate solutions for accomplishing results. In addition, the Processes for making those decisions should also be reviewed for effectiveness and efficiency.

Useful resources for the implementation of step 14 include:

- *Mega Planning* by Kaufman (2000)
- *Strategic Planning Plus: An Organizational Guide* by Kaufman (1992)
- *Useful Educational Results* by Kaufman, Watkins, and Leigh (2001)
- *Improving Performance: How to Manage the White Spaces on the Organization Chart* by Rummler and Brache (1995)

In implementing each of the fourteen steps, the six-step problem solving process (Figure 10.3) can provide the necessary template for achieving high payoff results. The six-step problem solving model offers a systematic and rational process for making decisions related to any and all of the fourteen steps. By using the template, decision makers can identify the appropriate actions to be taken in achieving results that add value at the Micro, Macro, and Mega levels.

A GENERAL PROBLEM SOLVING PROCESS MODEL

Any time one wants to move from needs to high payoff results, the six-step problem solving process (discussed earlier) may be used. In an earlier chapter we noted that you could take two approaches to problem solving—one for simple problems and one for complex problems. Both approaches have the following in common:

Identify (or Verify) Problems Based on Needs (*Not Wants*). Here the data from the Needs Assessment allows one to identify the gaps in results, prioritize them, and identify the problems to be resolved. Note that a "need" is a gap in results and a "problem" is a need selected for closure or resolution, that is, no "need," no problem.[3] (For additional resources, refer to Kaufman, 2000; Kaufman, Watkins, & Leigh, 2001; Leigh, Watkins, Platt, & Kaufman, 2000.)

Determine Solution Requirements and Identify (*But Don't Select*) Solution Alternatives. Once the needs and associated problems are identified and selected, an analysis process identifies the detailed requirements at lower and lower levels of building block results.[4] Also, for each of the detailed requirements, possible methods and means (tactics and tools) for meeting the requirements may be identified but not selected (in order to keep from selecting a solution before the problem and its detailed requirements have been identified). Additional tools and concepts for this step can be found in Kaufman, 2000; Kaufman and Watkins, 1999; and Kaufman, Watkins, and Leigh, 2001.

Select Solutions from Among Alternatives. Based on the data from the last two steps, the effective and efficient interventions and methods are selected. Tools for this include costs-consequences analysis in Kaufman, 1998, 2000; Kaufman, Watkins, and Leigh, 2001; Kaufman, Watkins, and Sims, 1997; Watkins, Leigh, Foshay, and Kaufman, 1998.

Implement. Now one goes from planning to doing and delivering. Here an implementation is conducted based on the requirements and solutions selected. Project management/implementation tools and techniques may be found in Kaufman, 1992, 1998, and 2000.

Determine Effectiveness and Efficiency. This phase is where evaluation takes place—where we compare our results with our objectives. Sources for such evaluation may be found in Kaufman, 1998 and 2000.

Revise as (and Whenever) Required. Here one uses the data from comparing results with intentions and uses that data to revise as required and whenever required. Note that this step is shown as a dotted/revision line and that it can occur at any point in moving from the identification of needs to the evaluation step. You don't have to move in lock-step fashion through the five steps (or functions) before revising. This sixth step allows responsiveness, responsibility, and contemporaneous development.

Question: If one does not use this six-step process, what else makes sense?

AVOIDING SUCCESS

For change initiatives to accomplish high payoff results, all of us (trainers, learners, managers, executives, and all in society) must begin to think "out of the box" of conventional practices. These alternative approaches to "how we have always done it around here" will, however, often be met with some levels of resistance.

Some common resistive arguments include: "But *they* will never let this happen."

The infamous "they" are notorious for supporting the status quo and stifling required change. This self-defeating perspective of some administrators, politicians, bureaucrats, colleagues, and others will only keep organizations from achieving the required success of the future. Ideal results can be achieved, but only if we set out to achieve them. In accordance, we must be wary of the temptation to claim responsibility only for our successes, while blaming others for shortcomings. As we shall see, strategic thinking and planning provides a common direction for all within an institution. In this pursuit it is critical that we use data regarding our progress for learning, fixing, and rewarding—and never blaming.

But we did OK last year without doing this. Deriving an expanded definition of success does not imply previous achievements were not worthwhile; rather it is in response to a shift in the realities (paradigms) that guide our decision making. Just as corporations changed in response to the "information age" in the 1990s, in the future organizations must remain responsive, flexible, and fluid so that they can achieve success in this century and beyond.

This isn't for us, we just do our jobs and go home each day. Futurist and management guru alike, each recognizes that everyone in an institution is important and knowledge, skills, attitudes, and abilities differentiate successful institutions from those that fail (Kaufman, Watkins, & Leigh, 2001). We are all members in a system (society) and a subsystem (our institution) that depend on us to contribute to their success. Merely meeting the minimal standards and "surviving" will only contribute to long-term institutional failure (see Marshall & Tucker,

1992). Increasingly, organizations bear a "responsibility for the greater good" and must demonstrate their ability to serve as "stewards of society" (Block, 1993; Maynard & Mehrtens, 1993). *Sure, but there just are some "bad" people out there who will never change.* Even if this is true, why let them stop you from doing what is right, correct, useful, and ethical. If you don't step up and do it, then this small minority will get their way. Just move ahead with what you know is right.

The "*. . . but*" responses to institutional change should be replaced with a "*yes . . . and*" attitude toward change that focuses on the achievement of high payoff results for our institutions, our society, and ourselves.

Four common tactics for *avoiding* success when applying the strategic thinking and planning approach are:

1. *Apply Only Systems Thinking.* Focus only on those individual aspects of Mega (the environment, crime, hunger) that are of the greatest interest to you and your organization. This sub-optimization at the system level most assuredly leads to systemic failures. This often diversionary tactic misses the interrelated nature of system thinking and planning, as well as the requirements for interaction and integration.

2. *Set Only Limited Objectives.* Setting "realistic" or "practical" objectives has never led to great accomplishments. We cannot hope to achieve high payoff results if we limit ourselves to only those goals and objectives that are clearly achievable with little personal or organizational stretch. And while limiting ourselves only to those targets that have been declared "safe" by the pioneers of our profession may seem reasonable to many, it is the role of the leader to inspire his or her organization to accomplish useful results at the Micro, Macro, and Mega levels.

3. *Include Beliefs and Values.* The relationship of ends (Mega, Macro, and Micro results) and means (Processes and Inputs) is often blurred with good intentions. It is commonly a challenge for many of us not to include our beliefs and values when applying the OEM. Commonly, we want those accomplishments that we believe are of great importance (and we therefore value greatly) to be classified as Mega level Outcomes, even when they are not. It is important to remember that the levels of the OEM do not represent a relationship of importance; rather, they provide a framework for relating all that an organization uses, does, produces, and delivers with the contributions to external clients and society.

4. *"Go Native" and Do What Everyone Else Does.* It is tempting to allow the pressure of conventional paradigms and the habits of others to let one want to "go native" and do what others are doing rather than

swimming against the tide. Being popular instead of contributing is a personal and ethical choice. Just fitting in with everyone else is comforting at first, but now that you know what the right things to do are and how to do them, will you really find the comfort you seek? Fitting in is not professional. Keep your personal and professional integrity.

So, based on previous experiences we may highly value the process we undertake each day (for example, evaluating health care practitioners, developing educational software, and so forth) and firmly believe that it produces high payoff results. Only by honestly classifying it within the OEM as a Process can we effectively and objectively determine the complexities and relationships within our system. This objectivity is essential when we are asked to make difficult decisions or plan for a successful future.

Also, take a moment to review the common mistakes that were identified in Table 4.10.

SUMMARY

The successful implementation of strategic thinking and planning requires a continued focus on the high payoff results that link the Mega, Macro, and Micro levels. Through proactive change creation and management, any organization can accomplish long-term objectives for our shared society, while maintaining short-term objectives like profitability and increased market share. The achievement of these high payoff results will likely require a shift in paradigms and meaningful planning . . . yet the accomplishment of useful results is an accomplishment well worth the time.

Notes

1. We apologize for the constant reminder of "need" being a gap in results, but we do it because the conventional usage (need as a verb) is so firmly installed in our current everyday language. As professionals specializing in change, we suggest that this definition of "need" is one we can practice and model ourselves.

2. Systematic, systemic, systems approach, and system approach are related but not the same (Kaufman & Watkins, 2000). One can be systemic—affect the whole subsystem being considered—without being effective. We can be systematic without being useful.

3. It should be noted that sometimes there are no gaps in results—no needs—but one wants to assure that a gap in results does not happen. In this case, maintenance of the no need situation is achieved by design.

4. A process called "system analysis" (not systems analysis) can be used here. The tools and concepts for this analysis may be found in Kaufman, 1998 and 2000.

Paradigm Shift for Teaching/Learning

The following (Table A.1) is a summary of a paradigm shift in how to design instructional performance systems that produce measurable performance improvement. This comparison identifies changes to how one designs and delivers instruction based on Mega thinking and planning. The new teaching/learning paradigm is contrasted to the traditional "knowledge" based paradigm that is still practiced by many schools, universities, technical institutes, and HRD/training organizations. The new paradigm has evolved out of thirty plus years of research and application in a wide range of performance areas.

The comparison of the two teaching/learning paradigms shown in the table highlights the significant differences between them. Your judgment about which paradigm is more relevant to you will, of course, be influenced by what worked for you in the past. Paradigms have some upsides and downsides, as outlined below:

1. Those who are most successful under the traditional paradigm will be at most risk under the new paradigm, which is one of the reasons why the institutional leaders of education are most likely to continue the status quo that made them successful. To learn the new paradigm requires admitting that "flat earth" skills are insufficient for performing on the "round earth." When a new paradigm is introduced, everyone is back to zero on knowledge and skills.

Table A.1. Old vs. New Paradigm.

Old Paradigm (Traditional Knowledge Based Model)	New Paradigm (Performance Based Model)
1. Curriculum is derived from domains of knowledge. Content is "subjects," "topics" broken into lessons about the subject. The purpose is primarily acquisition of knowledge.	1. Curriculum is derived from an assessment and analysis of the performance requirements of the role, job, or occupation and the contributions these all make to external clients and society (Mega). Lessons are designed to provide practice and feedback on specific skills. The purpose is performance improvement in real life roles.
2. Interpretation of what content to include in the lesson is left to individual designer, subject-matter expert, instructor, professor, or tutor.	2. The content is driven by the end performance desired. Content is the means to provide learners with practice and feedback on the desired performance. Content is linked to adding value at the individual performance level, organizational contributions, and external and societal (Mega) contributions and value added.
3. Goals of instruction are often vague and stated in non-specific terms. Goals are derived from instructor's interpretation of the topic subject or knowledge of the "instructor."	3. Objectives of instruction are derived from observation and analysis of what successful performers do in a role, job, occupation, or life task. Objectives are specific and measurable. Objectives link value to be added at the individual, organizational, and external client and societal levels.

Table A.1. (*Continued*)

Old Paradigm (*Traditional Knowledge Based Model*)	New Paradigm (*Performance Based Model*)
4. Teaching tactics are based on tradition, intuition, the instructor's skills, or convenience. Little if any scientifically based logic to justify methods of teaching.	4. Instructional tactics are derived from research into how people learn to learn and perform. Tactics are matched to the category of learning, for example, mental, psychomotor, affective, or interpersonal skills. Empirical evidence of effectiveness determines the instructional tactic.
5. The exam (test) samples the content. Learners must often guess the exam content. Test items will often come as a surprise. Exam items are often open to wide interpretations on the desired result.	5. The tests are derived from desired performance and match the instructional objectives. Criteria (standards) are explicit and available to the learner at all times. Learners know what is expected of them. No surprises.
6. Objectives or goals of teaching are not always available to the learner, and testing criteria are often a secret. The exam is kept a secret and learners are expected to guess the content. The exam samples the content.	6. Objectives are written for the learners and specify in measurable terms the results expected in terms of what the learners will be able to do and perform. The objectives and test criteria are available to the learners. All critical instructional objectives are tested.
7. The desired performance or knowledge level is expected to vary along the normal curve of distribution. Not all learners are expected to achieve high levels on the test/exam (norm based testing).	7. Desired performance levels are derived from an analysis of what successful performers do in real world situations. The standards are clearly defined in measurable terms, and most if not all learners are expected to achieve them (criterion referenced testing).

(*Continued*)

Table A.1. Old vs. New Paradigm. (*Continued*)

Old Paradigm *(Traditional Knowledge Based Model)*	New Paradigm *(Performance Based Model)*
8. The instructor, professor, or tutor drives the learning process and learners are expected to conform to administrative requirements. The learner has a narrow range of choices about timing, materials, learning events, and pace of learning. The administration decides time of learning (formal lessons); resources; time of exams; and pace of learning.	8. The process is centered on the learner. The learner has a wide range of choices about pace of learning; feedback; learning events; learning materials; when to take the test; and amount of practice.
9. Evaluation of the learning usually blames the learner if the student fails the test or exam. No matter how many fail, the instructor keeps teaching the same way.	9. Evaluation is used to improve the instructional process and produce more successful performers who add value to internal and external clients. Measurement is used to improve materials, learning events, and feedback. The purpose is to help participants perform real tasks to the standards of a successful performer.
10. The teaching model is built on intuition, history, and accumulated practices of what the instructor should do to dispense knowledge. Professional practice is historical rather than scientific.	10. The instructional model is built on fifty plus years of behavioral and cognitive research into how learners learn to perform real life tasks. Practice is built on scientific findings that repeat successful performance.
11. Because the purpose is acquisition of knowledge, there is low emphasis on practice and feedback.	11. Performance based instruction defines levels and categories of skill from simple to complex. A high level of practice and frequent feedback is a distinguishing characteristic.

Table A.1. (*Continued*)

Old Paradigm (Traditional Knowledge Based Model)	New Paradigm (Performance Based Model)
12. Parts of the curriculum have little relevance to real life performance, and those parts are included because of instructor's biases and preferences.	12. All parts of the curriculum are selected to help people perform relevant tasks in real life roles. Context is derived from analysis of what successful performers do in real life roles.
13. There is no requirement to recognize prior learning. Everyone gets the same content irrespective of background and experience.	13. Prior learning is recognized. If learners can demonstrate knowledge and skill they can be credited with skill and are able to move on to a higher or more complex level of skill.
14. All participants are given the same amount of time to learn the same knowledge. Little allowance is made for different rates of learning or different learning styles. The exam is only offered once, usually with large time gaps before repeats. Repeat exams are determined by administrators. Failure means you must wait another time frame, for example, one year, before attempting the exam.	14. Within the restraints of resources, all learners can have as much practice as they require to master the skill. Varying learning styles are catered to. Learners can choose to take the test whenever they are ready and can also have repeat attempts after feedback on failing first attempts. Failure means you are not yet ready and that you require more practice and feedback before attempting the test again.
15. Much of the curriculum is delivered on the myth that knowledge equals performance. It is assumed that learners can discover how to perform a complex task by attending lectures and studying harder, rather than through guided practice and feedback. Performance is defined implicitly as knowing about rather than	15. Knowledge and skill can be classified by levels from simple knowledge recall through to complex non-repetitive operations. Knowledge alone is insufficient to guarantee performance. Performance is defined as relevant behavior plus a worthy result. Performance is developed through frequent relevant practice and timely specific feedback.

(*Continued*)

Table A.1. Old vs. New Paradigm. (*Continued*)

Old Paradigm (Traditional Knowledge Based Model)	New Paradigm (Performance Based Model)
knowing how to do. Classification of levels of knowledge is built on historical philosophy, for example, epistemology that has no evidence to support it as a method for helping adults to learn. It is implicitly assumed that learners will translate "knowledge about" into "how to do it." The institution acts as if learning can be dissociated from doing.	Writing essays on mountain biking or answering multiple choice questions will not develop high performing "bikers." You must have frequent practice and timely, specific feedback. Classification models for skill and knowledge have empirical merit, for example, Gagne's hierarchy of learning indicated a well-proven and documented sequence for learners to follow. Learning is directly related to practicing doing real life tasks.
16. Standards are variable. The instructors, tutors, and/or professors decide the standards from hour to hour, year to year. They can vary from vague, ambiguous intents to precisely defined standards such as in surgery. Standards are not usually for real life roles (obvious exceptions are medicine and engineering). Standards are sometimes explicit, but more often implicit such that the learner must guess or stumble on them by chance. The standards in many instances are hidden, secret, and controlled by the professors and can vary considerably in interpretation, leaving it to the learner to guess the right answer or interpretation. There is no underlying scientific model used to define the curriculum or exam standards The subject-matter experts decide, and they often disagree.	16. There exists an empirically researched model for analyzing and deriving standards through the observation and study of successful performers. Real life roles can be analyzed to identify the requisite knowledge and skills that successful performers use versus novices. The analytical process can be applied to any human role in any domain of knowledge from complex to simple roles. Standards are specific and measurable. Learners learn to perform through specific practice, not through generalizations. Standards are specified for specific performance areas rather than vague generalizations that require interpretations and further analysis to be of value to the learner.

Table A.1. (*Continued*)

Old Paradigm (Traditional Knowledge Based Model)	New Paradigm (Performance Based Model)
17. Learners learn to "know about" and pass exams. They seldom learn to perform real life tasks to "best performer" standards. Learners are expected to translate generalized knowledge into specific performance. It doesn't happen.	17. The learner practices to perform realistic tasks that are specific and relevant to a chosen role, occupation, job, or citizen task. The learners are able to do this as a result of instruction.
18. The learning environment may or may not be supportive of the learner. Inflexible administrative processes drive many universities and technical institutes.	18. The learning environment is highly supportive of the learner. Desired performance is recognized and reinforced. Practice is relevant, and feedback opportunities are timely and frequent.
19. In many instances the system produces knowledgeable yet incompetent graduates.	19. The purpose of this model is to produce knowledgeable and competent performers who demonstrate the standards of successful performers.
20. Low return on investment. Human capital produced is well below potential of what we know can be delivered through application of scientifically proven teaching and learning methods. The process falls short of delivering successful performers. In many instances the process subtracts value from society. Standards are mediocre and more of the same.	20. Human capital can be precisely calculated and the cost of incompetence calculated in terms of diminished results for society. Similarly, the value added of knowledgeable and competent people can be defined in measurable terms. The value of knowledge is shown through worthy performance. The process is driven to produce more successful performers. The standards are continuously improving.
21. Some content is taught because someone decides it is worth knowing, even if you never have anything to do with it. Knowledge for knowledge's sake is valued.	21. Time is spent analyzing and identifying what is worth knowing by connecting it to a relevant real life role or situation. What is worth knowing should add value to society.

(*Continued*)

Table A.1. Old vs. New Paradigm. (*Continued*)

Old Paradigm (Traditional Knowledge Based Model)	New Paradigm (Performance Based Model)
22. Studying is believed to be good for you. The harder you study the more you are assumed to improve. Long study hours cramming mountains of knowledge is one of the criteria to be labeled a good student.	22. Practice plus feedback is proven to be the most effective way to improve learning and performance. Study is a waste of time. Cramming knowledge is not practice; it doesn't improve real life performance. Using the knowledge on relevant situations to achieve worthy results is the primary standard for an effective learner.
23. The exams or tests have low validity and reliability for assessing performance. They are poor indicators of whether a person can actually perform a real life task to "best performer" level. A person's marks on an exam are assumed to be an indicator of intelligence, motivation to learn, and performance potential. The exam usually samples the content covered; learners have to guess the specific exam content. Traditional exams and tests do not measure performance. They are not valid measures of intelligence, or performance potential.	23. Intelligence and motivation are poor indicators of performance potential. If the desired results of learning are poorly defined and irrelevant to real life tasks and little if any practice and feedback are provided, no value is added to society and the learner fails to perform worthy tasks. Performance based learning links intelligence and motivation to a measurable, worthy performance. The tests are valid and reliable; they measure whether a person can perform to the standards of a "best performer." The tests match the desired learning and performance objectives.
24. Evaluation of the whole process of teaching is primitive. The process of teaching is left to the instructor to decide—academic freedom tolerates poor teaching practice. The exam results are used to evaluate the success or failure of the curriculum. Good exam results	24. Evaluation is at five levels and is concerned ultimately with impact on society. The levels are as follows: (1) affective impact (smile factor); (2) skill/knowledge acquisition; (3) process improvement—does the real life process perform better?;

Table A.1. (*Continued*)

Old Paradigm (Traditional Knowledge Based Model)	New Paradigm (Performance Based Model)
generate more funding, even if the exam is invalid, unreliable, and irrelevant to real life performance. The social impact of the teaching process is not rigorously measured; for example, producing X historians for a market that has no use for them is deemed OK. Social impact is seldom assessed.	(4) customer impact—does the learner add value to the customer as a result of what he or she can now do?; and (5) societal impact—does the performer add value to the community, to society? The performance paradigm at its best evaluates all five levels.
25. The language of the paradigm includes: • Domains of knowledge treated in isolation from each other. • Departments organized around subjects—history, philosophy, and engineering. The relationships between domains are formally ignored. • People are professors, instructors, tutors, deans, heads of department, learners. • Qualifications are diplomas, degrees, Ph.D.s. • Grading is based on levels of knowledge—grades can have multiple interpretations. • Curriculum design is built around knowledge structures. • People are classified and treated mechanistically, for example, "good" engineers only require engineering knowledge; emotional intelligence is ignored.	25. The language of this paradigm is evolving and sometimes confusing. However, some shared concepts and models are understood and applied: • Performance is treated as interrelated and interconnected. • Domains of performance are determined by real life roles and occupations. • People are learners, instructors, trainers, performance analysts, needs assessors, facilitators, managers of learning, coaches. • Grading is based on if one is competent or not, yet competent as defined by the standards of successful performers in a role. • Curriculum design is systematic using instructional system design (ISD) models that identify performance requirements and then design and develop practice events to achieve the performance requirements.

2. At times, two major paradigms will clash like the great plates of the earth's structure. The clash is seldom perceived as an opportunity for growth and renewal, but more as a threat to treasured beliefs and values. Some paradigms are trivial so the impacts of changes are trivial. Some paradigms are strategic; changes will affect tomorrow's citizens and us—now and in the future.

3. There is frequently more than one "right answer" or best solution. The traditional educational/training paradigm did some good things and produced some stunning results in all fields of human performance. We don't want to throw out the baby with the bath water. Those who claim absolute truth are playing god. By changing my paradigm, I make a choice to change my perception of the world. Paradigm shifts allow you more choices.

4. Innovation, design, and creativity can only occur with paradigm shifts. The certainty of one paradigm creates "paradigm paralysis."

5. Paradigm blindness occurs when your present paradigm is consistently failing to produce results in response to both old and new problems, but you stick to working harder at more of the same. Or you use new technology to do the same thing badly. This occurs frequently in education and health. More computers with old lesson plans make no difference to the quality of learning. More antibiotics subtracts from the capability of the immune system to cope with future viruses. In addition, the paradigm blind will ignore and screen out the advantages of the new paradigm.

6. Speaking across paradigms requires a high level of relating skills. The language of the clashing paradigms is different. The words mean specific perceptions to the paradigm holder. You can't assume the two clashing parties have the skills or willingness to explore each other's world view, rules, and individual mental models. Both parties must have active listening skills, patience, and the ability to hold a dialogue in which the paradigms are explored and judgment is initially suspended.

7. The best way to start challenging paradigms is to gather evidence about the gaps in worthwhile results achieved by the traditional paradigms. Education, health, and peace are all worldwide domains of performance that exhibit frequent failure to achieve worthy results using the traditional approaches. Gather the evidence about gaps in results, define the priority problems, challenge the methods that no longer work, and design new paradigms to create a better world. By understanding the nature of significant paradigm shifts, we are thinking strategically because the only way to create a better world is to break out of our present non-performing paradigm and design new rules and ways of acting to produce better societal results for ourselves and tomorrow's children.

A Glossary and Classification of Terms and Tools

To be successful in planning and in demonstrating value added, we must use words with rigor and precision. Language that is crisp, to the point, and focused on results (including societal payoffs) is essential for professional success. And then we must match our promises with deeds and payoffs that measurably add value.

To set the framework, let's define some basic terms, relate them, and then use them to put other vocabulary in context:

System Approach. Begins with the sum total of parts working independently and together to achieve a useful set of results at the societal level—that adds value for all internal and external partners. We best think of it as the large whole and we can show it like Figure B.1.

Systems Approach. Begins with the parts of a system—subsystems—that make up the "system." We can show it like Figure B.2.

It should be noted here that the "system" is made up of smaller elements or subsystems, shown as "bubbles" imbedded in the larger system. If we start at this smaller level, we will start with a part and not the whole. So when someone says he or she is using a "systems approach" that person is really focusing on one or more subsystems and is unfortunately focusing on the parts and not the whole. When planning and doing at this level, one can only assume that

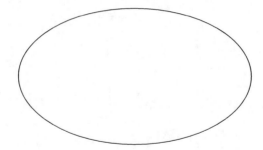

Figure B.1. System Approach.

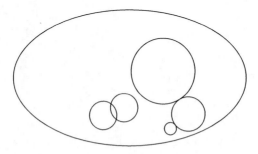

Figure B.2. Systems Approach.

the payoffs and consequences will add up to something useful to society and external clients, and this is usually a very big assumption.

Systematic Approach. An approach that does things in an orderly, predictable, and controlled manner. It is a reproducible process. Doing things, however, in a systematic manner does not assure the achievement of useful results.

Systemic Approach. An approach that affects everything in the system. The definition of "the system" is usually left up to the practitioner and may or may not include external clients and society. It does not necessarily mean that when something is systemic it is also useful.

Interestingly, these terms are often used interchangeably. Yet they are not the same. Notice that when the words are used interchangeably and/or when one starts at the systems level and not the system level, it will mean that we might not add value to external clients and society.

Semantic quibbling? We suggest just the opposite. If we talk about a "systems" approach and don't realize that we are focusing on splinters and not on the whole, we usually degrade what we use, do, produce, and deliver in terms of adding value inside and outside of the organization. When we take a "systems" approach, we risk losing a primary focus on societal survival, self-sufficiency, and quality of life. We risk staying narrow.

A primary focus on survival, health, and well-being—the Mega level—is really important. It really is, even though it is not yet the conventional focus. We must focus on societal payoffs—on a "system" approach for both survival and ethical reasons. What organizations that you personally do business with do you expect to really put client health, safety, and well-being at the top of the list of what they must deliver?

It is the rare individual who does not care whether or not the organizations that affect their lives have a primary focus and accountability for survival, health, welfare, and societal payoffs. Most people, regardless of culture, want safety, health, and well-being to be the top priority of everyone they deal with.

What we do and deliver must be the same as that which we demand of others. So if we want Mega—value added for society—to be at the top of the list for others (airlines, government, software manufactures), why don't we do unto others as we would have them do unto us? At best we give "lip service" to customer pleasure, profits, or satisfaction . . . and then go on to work on splinters of the whole. We work on training courses for individual jobs and tasks, and then we hope that the sum total of all of the training and trained people adds up to organizational success. We too often don't formally include external client survival and well-being in our performance plans, programs, and delivery. We rarely start our plans or programs with an "outside the organization" outcome[1] that is clearly and rigorously stated before selecting the organizational results and resources (Outputs, Products, Processes, and Inputs).

The words we use in our everyday work might get in the way of a societal added value focus. To keep our performance and value added focus, we should adjust our perspective when reviewing the literature and as we listen to speakers at meetings. Far too often we read and hear key terms used with altering (or case specific) definitions. There seem to be many words that sound familiar, and these words are often comfortable and identify us as professionals, so we neglect to question the meaning or appropriateness of their use within the context. And when we apply the words and concepts inconsistently, we find that their varying definitions can abridge success.

The words and phrases we communicate to ourselves and others are important since they operationally define our profession and communicate our objectives and processes to others. They are symbols and signs with meaning. When our words lead us away, by implication or convention, from designing and delivering useful results for both internal and external clients, then we must consider changing our perspectives and our definitions.

If we don't agree on definitions and communicate with common and useful understandings, then we will likely get a "leveling" of the concepts—and thus our resulting efforts and contributions—to the lowest common denominator.

Let's look as some frequently used words, define each, and see how a shift in focus to a more rigorous basis for our terms and definitions will help us add value to internal and external clients.

The following definitions[2] come from our review of the literature and other writings. Many of the references and related readings from a wide variety of sources are included elsewhere in this book. Italics provide some rationale for a possible perspective shift from conventional and comfortable to societal value added.[3] In addition, each definition identifies whether the word or phrase relates most to a system approach, systems approach, systematic approach, or systemic approach (or a combination). The level of approach (system, systems, and so on) provides the unit of analysis for the words and terms as they are defined here. Alternative definitions should also be analyzed. If we are going to apply system thinking (decision making that focuses on valued added at the individual, organizational, and societal levels), then definitions from that perspective should be applied in our literature, presentations, workshops, and products.

Here are the terms, definitions, and comments:

ADDIE Model (systems approach, systematic approach, systemic approach). A contraction of the conventional instructional systems steps of *A*nalysis, *D*esign, *D*evelopment, *I*mplementation, and *E*valuation. *It ignores or assumes a front determination through assessment of what to analyze, and it also assumes that the evaluation data will be used for continuous improvement.*

Change creation (system approach). A proactive approach to change that defines and justifies, proactively, new and justified destinations. If this is done before change management, acceptance is more likely. *This is a proactive orientation for change and differs from the more usual "change management" in that it identifies in advance where individuals and organizations are headed, rather than waiting for change to occur and be "managed."*

Change management (systems approach, systemic approach, systematic approach). Assuring that whatever change is selected will be accepted and implemented successfully by people in the organization. *Change management is reactive in that it waits until change requirements are either defined or imposed and then moves to have the change accepted and used.*

Comfort zones (system approach, systematic approach, systemic approach). The psychological areas, in business or in life, where one feels secure and safe (regardless of the reality of that feeling). *Change is usually painful for most people. When faced with change, many people will find reasons (usually not rational) for why not to make changes and modifications. This give rise to Tom Peter's (1997) observation that "It is easier to kill an organization that it is to change it."*

Costs-consequences analysis (system approach, systems approach). The process of estimating a return on investment analysis before an intervention is implemented. It asks two basic questions simultaneously: what do you expect to give and what do you expect to get back in terms of results? *Most formulations do not compute costs and consequences for society and external client (Mega) return on investment. Thus, even the calculations for standard approaches steer away from the vital considerations of self-sufficiency, health, and well-being (Kaufman, 1998, 2000; Kaufman & Keller, 1997; Kaufman, Keller, & Watkins, 1998).*

Criteria (system approach, systems approach, systematic approach, systemic approach). Precise and rigorous specifications that allow one to prove what has been or has to be accomplished. Many processes in place today do not use rigorous indicators for expected performance. If criteria are "loose" or unclear, there is no realistic basis for evaluation and continuous improvement. Loose criteria often meet the comfort test but don't allow for the humanistic approach to care enough about others to define, with stakeholders, where you are headed and how to tell when you have or have not arrived.

Deep change (system approach, systemic approach). Change that extends from Mega (societal value added) downward into the organization to define and shape Macro, Micro, Processes, and Inputs. It is termed "deep change" to note that it is not superficial or cosmetic, or even a splintered quick fix. *Most planning models do not include Mega results in the change process, and thus miss the opportunity to find out what impact their contributions and results have on external clients and society. The other approaches might be termed "superficial change" or "limited change" in that they only focus on an organization or a small part of an organization.*

Desired results. Ends (or results) identified through Needs Assessments that are derived from soft data relating to "perceived needs." *"Desired" indicates these are perceptual and personal in nature.*

Ends. Results, achievements, consequences, payoffs, and/or impacts. The more precise the results, the more likely that reasonable methods and means can be considered, implemented, and evaluated. Without rigor for results statements, confusion can take the place of successful performance.

Evaluation (systems approach, systematic approach). Compares current status (What Is) with intended status (what was intended) and is most commonly done only after an intervention is implemented. *Unfortunately, "evaluation" is used for blaming and not fixing or improving. When blame follows evaluation,* *people tend to avoid the means and criteria for evaluation or leave them so loose that any result can be explained away.*

External Needs Assessment (system approach). Determining and prioritizing gaps, then selecting problems to be resolved at the Mega level. *This level of Needs Assessment is most often missing from conventional approaches. Without the data from it, one cannot be assured that there will be strategic alignment from internal results to external value added.*

Hard data (system approach, systems approach, systematic approach). Performance data that is based on objectives and is independently verifiable. *This type of data is critical. It should be used along with "soft" or perception data.*

Ideal Vision (+). The measurable definition of the kind of world we, together with others, commit to help deliver for tomorrow's child. *An Ideal Vision defines the Mega level of planning. It allows an organization and all of its partners to define where they are headed and how to tell when they are getting there or getting closer. It provides the rationality and reasons for an organizational mission objective.*

Inputs (systems approach, systematic approach). The ingredients, raw materials, physical and human resources that an organization can use in its processes in order to deliver useful ends. *These ingredients and resources are often the only considerations made during planning, without determining the value they add internally and externally to the organization.*

Internal Needs Assessment (systems approach). Determining and prioritizing gaps, then selecting problems to be resolved at the Micro and Macro levels. *Most Needs Assessment processes are of this variety (Watkins, Leigh, Platt, & Kaufman, 1998.)*

Learning (systems approach). The demonstrated acquisition of a skill, knowledge, attitude, and/or ability.

Learning organization (systems approach, systematic approach). An organization that sets measurable performance standards and constantly compares its results and their consequences with what is required. Learning organizations use performance data related to an Ideal Vision and the primary mission objective to decide what to change and what to continue. They learn from their performance and contributions. Learning organizations may obtain the highest level of success by strategic thinking: focusing everything that is used, done, produced, and delivered on Mega results—societal value added. *Many conventional definitions do not link the "learning" to societal value added. If there is no external societal linking, than it could well guide one away from the new requirements.*

Macro level of planning (systems approach). Planning focused on the organization itself as the primary client and beneficiary of what is planned and delivered. *This is the conventional starting and stopping place for existing planning approaches.*

Means (systems approach, systematic approach). Processes, activities, resources, methods, or techniques used to deliver a result. Means are only useful to the extent that they deliver useful results at all three levels of planned results: Mega, Macro, and Micro.

Mega level of planning (system approach). Planning focused on external clients, including customers/citizens and the community and society that the organization serves. *This is usually the missing planning level in most formulations. It is the only one that will focus on societal value added: survival, self-sufficiency, and quality of life of all partners. Also termed "strategic planning plus," it is suggested that this type of planning is imperative for getting and proving useful results.*

Mega thinking (system approach). Thinking about every situation, problem, or opportunity in terms of what you use, do, produce, and deliver as having to add value to external clients and society. Same as Strategic Thinking.

Methods-means analysis (systems approach, systematic approach). Identifies possible tactics and tools for meeting the needs identified in a "system analysis." The methods-means analysis identifies the possible ways and means to meet the needs and achieve the detailed objectives that are identified in this Mega plan, but does not select them. *Interestingly, this is a comfortable place where some operational planning starts. Thus, it either assumes or ignores the requirement to measurably add value within and outside the organization.*

Micro level planning (systems approach). Planning focused on individuals or small groups (such as desired and required competencies of associates or supplier competencies). Planning for building block results. *This also is a comfortable place where some operational planning starts. Starting here usually assumes or ignores the requirement to measurably add value to the entire organization as well as to outside the organization.*

Mission analysis (systems approach). Analysis step that identifies: (1) what results and consequences are to be achieved; (2) what criteria (in interval and/or ratio scale terms) will be used to determine success; and (3) what are the building block results and the order of their completion (functions) required to move from the current results to the desired state of affairs. *Most mission objectives have not been formally linked to Mega results and consequences, and thus strategic alignment with "where the clients are" are usually missing (Kaufman, Stith, Triner, & Watkins 1998).*

Mission objective (systems approach). An exact, performance based statement of an organization's overall intended results that it can and should deliver to external clients and society. *A mission objective is measurable on an interval or ratio scale so states not only "where we are headed" but also adds "how we will know when we have arrived." A mission objective is best linked to Mega levels of planning and the Ideal Vision to assure societal value added.*

Mission statement (systems approach). An organization's Macro level "general purpose." A mission statement is only measurable on a nominal or ordinal scale of measurement and only states "where we are headed" and leaves off rigorous criteria for determining how one measures successful accomplishment.

Need (system approach, systems approach, systematic approach, systemic approach). The gap between current results and desired or required results. This is where a lot of planning "goes off the rails." By defining any gap as a "need," one fails to distinguish between means and ends and thus confuses what and how. If "need" is defined as a gap in results, then there is a triple bonus: (1) it states the objectives (What Should Be); (2) it contains the evaluation and continuous improvement criteria (What Should Be); and (3) it provides the basis for justifying any proposal by using both ends of a need (What Is and What Should Be in terms of results). Proof can be given for the costs to meet the need as well as the costs to ignore the need.

Needs analysis (systems approach). Taking the determined gaps between adjacent Organizational Elements and finding the causes of the inability for delivering required results. A needs analysis also identifies possible ways and means to close the gaps in results—needs—but does not select them. *Unfortunately, "needs analysis" is usually used interchangeable with "Needs Assessment." They are not the same. How does one "analyze" something (such as a need) before knowing what should be analyzed? First assess the need, and then analyze it.*

Needs Assessment (system approach, systems approach). A formal process that identifies and documents gaps between current and desired and/or required results; arranges them in order of priority on basis of the cost to meet the need as compared to the cost of ignoring it; and selects problems to be resolved. *By starting with a Needs Assessment, justifiable performance data and the gaps between What Is and What Should Be will provide the realistic and rational reason for both what to change as well as what to continue. When the Needs Assessment starts at the Mega level then the "+" is appropriate.*

Objectives (system approach, systems approach). Precise statement of purpose or destination or where we are headed and how will we be able to tell when we have arrived; the four parts to an objective are (1) what result is to be demonstrated; (2) who or what will demonstrate the result; (3) where the result will be observed; and (4) what interval or ratio scale criteria will be used. *Loose or process oriented objectives will confuse everyone (Mager, 1997). A Mega level result is best stated as an objective.*

Outcomes (system approach). Results and payoffs at the external client and societal level. Outcomes are results that add value to society, community, and external clients of the organization. These are results at the Mega level of planning.

Outputs (systems approach). The results and payoffs that an organization can or does deliver outside of itself to external clients and society. *These are results at the Macro level of planning, where the primary client and beneficiary is the organization itself. It does not formally link to Outcomes and societal well-being unless it is derived from Outcomes and the Ideal (Mega) Vision.*

Paradigm (system approach, systems approach, systematic approach, systemic approach). The framework and ground rules individuals use to filter reality and understand the world around them (Barker, 1992). *It is vital that people have common paradigms that guide them. That is one of the functions of the Mega level of planning and Outcomes so that everyone is headed to a common destination and may uniquely contribute to that journey.*

Performance (system approach, systems approach, systemic approach, systematic approach). A result or consequence of any intervention or activity, including individual, team, or organization. An end.

Performance accomplishment system (PAS) (system approach, systems approach, systemic approach). Any of a variety of interventions (such as "instructional systems design and development," quality management/continuous improvement, benchmarking, reengineering, and the like) that are results oriented and are intended to get positive results. These are usually focused at the Micro/Products level. *This is my preferred alternative to the rather sterile term "performance technology" that often steers people toward hardware and premature solutions (Kaufman, 1999, 2000).*

Processes (systems approach, systematic approach). The means, processes, activities, procedures, interventions, programs, and initiatives an organization can or does use in order to deliver useful ends. *While most planners start here, it is dangerous not to derive the Processes and Inputs from what an organization must deliver and the payoffs for external clients.*

Products (systems approach). The building block results and payoffs of individuals and small groups that form the basis of what an organization produces and delivers inside as well as outside of itself, and the payoffs for external clients and society. *Products are results at the Micro level of planning.*

Quasi-need (systems approach, systematic approach). A gap in a method, resource, or process. Many so-called Needs Assessments are really quasi-needs assessments since they tend to pay immediate attention to means (such as training) before defining and justifying the ends and consequences (Watkins, Leigh, Platt, & Kaufman, 1998).

Required results (system approach, systems approach, systematic approach, systemic approach). Ends identified through Needs Assessment that are derived from hard data relating to objective performance measures.

Results. Ends, Products, Outputs, Outcomes; accomplishments and consequences. *Usually misses the Outputs and Outcomes.*

SMARTER objective (system approach, systems approach, systematic approach, systemic approach). A new formulation of what an objective should contain and do, using the acronym of SMARTER: S = Specific performance area; M = Measurable in ratio or interval terms; A = Audacious; R = Results focused; T = Time bound; E = Encompassing; and R = Reviewed frequently.[4]

Soft data (system approach, systems approach). Personal perceptions of results. Soft data is not independently verifiable. While people's perceptions are reality for them, they are not to be relied on without relating to hard, independently verifiable data as well.

Strategic alignment (system approach).[5] The linking of Mega/Outcomes, Macro/Outputs, and Micro/Product level planning and results with each other and with Processes and Inputs. By formally deriving what the organization uses, does, produces, and delivers to Mega/external payoffs, strategic alignment is complete.

Strategic planning plus—Mega planning (system approach). Five steps or elements for defining and delivering a preferred future that include: (1) deriving the tactical and operational plans; (2) making/buying/obtaining resources; (3) implementation; and, simultaneously, (4) continuous improvement/formative evaluation; and then (5) determine effectiveness and efficiency. *While not strictly planning, this is the part that puts all of the previous planning to work to achieve positive results.*

Strategic thinking (system approach). Approaching any problem, program, project, activity, or effort—noting that everything that is used, done, produced, and delivered must add value for external clients and society. *Strategic thinking starts with Mega.*

System analysis (system approach). Identifies and justifies WHAT should be accomplished based on an Ideal/Mega Vision and is results focused. It is a series of analytic steps that include mission analysis, function analysis, and (if selected) task analysis. It also identifies possible methods and means (methods-means analysis) but does not select the methods-means. *This starts with rolling down (from outside to inside the organization) linkages to Mega.*

Systems analysis (systems approach). Identifies the most effective and efficient ways and means to achieve required results. Solutions and tactics focused. *This is an internal—inside the organization—process.*

Tactical planning (systems approach). Finding out what is available to get from What Is to What Should Be at the organizational/Macro level. Tactics are best identified after the overall mission has been selected based on its linkages and contributions to external clients and societal (Ideal Vision) results and consequences.

Wants (systems approach). Preferred methods and means assumed to be capable of meeting needs.

What Is. Current operational results and consequences; these could be for an individual, an organization, and/or for society.

What Should Be. Desired or required operational results and consequences; these could be for an individual, an organization, and/or society.

Wishes (−). Desires concerning means and ends. It is important not to confuse "wishes" with needs.

Making Sense of Definitions

What can we surmise by a close consideration of the above definitions and the consideration of the possible perspective (unit of analysis) differences between conventional use and what is suggested here? What is often taken for granted is not always true. What is often assumed to be true may not be reality based. Here are some often assumed equivalencies that might not be equivalent:

1. System approach ≠ systems approach ≠ systematic approach ≠ systemic approach.
2. Mega level planning ≠ Macro level planning ≠ Micro level planning.
3. System analysis ≠ systems analysis.
4. Client satisfaction ≠ useful results and consequences.
5. Hope ≠ reality.
6. Means ≠ ends.
7. Outcome ≠ Output ≠ Product ≠ Process ≠ Input,
8. There are three levels of planning: Mega, Macro, and Micro and three related types of results: Outcomes, Outputs, and Products.
9. Need is a gap in results, not a gap in Process or Input.
10. Needs Assessment ≠ needs analysis (nor front-end analysis, nor problem analysis).
11. Strategic planning ≠ tactical planning ≠ operational planning.
12. Change creation ≠ change management.

Nitpicking? No. Semantic quibbling? No again. In order to assure that we help bring about positive change, we have to design, develop, and deliver that change. And we have to prove our contributions. So the words and concepts we use are much too important to leave loose and open to confusion.

Notes

1. As we will note later, this word is used in a fuzzy way by most people for any kind of result. We reserve Outcome for only results at the Mega/societal level.

2. This section, at first, might sound a bit tedious. We feel it important to carefully consider each term, definition, and implications in order

to make a rational decision on whether or not to participate in a perspective adjustment.

3. These are in alphabetical order. At first, some of the definitions won't "follow," but please scan the list for words not yet defined.

4. This is a modification based on the original formulation of Oakley-Browne.

5. The so-called U.S. Government Performance and Results Act (GPRA) does exactly this and demands links to a strategic plan. Evolving in this initiative is the linking of strategic planning to societal return on investment (Watkins, Leigh, Foshay, & Kaufman, 1998).

A Suggested Code of Professional Conduct for Defining and Delivering High Payoff Results[1,2]

Much recent attention has been dedicated to standards of ethics and integrity for performance improvement specialists. The International Society for Performance Improvement in 2002 initiated professional certification for practitioners in the field, and the criteria used are similar, but not identical, to what is suggested here.

Based on the concepts, tools, and orientation of this book, we build on it and on past work to suggest a "code of professional conduct" by which to integrate responsible, practical, and pragmatic ethics into the day-to-day activities of both consultants and clients: to define, design, and deliver high payoff results.

By measuring success based on quantifiable demonstrations of value added for internal and external stakeholders, both consultants and their clients can better ensure that they are contributing toward the results required by internal associates, work teams, the organization itself, and externally by society. A commitment to such an approach to business is necessary if we as a profession are to be able to make defensible data-based decisions regarding the interventions, policies, and solutions we select, recommend, implement, and/or evaluate for organizations.

As it has been discovered throughout history, the behaviors that led to success in the past are likely to lead to failure in the future. We suggest that, like many of these business practices, the informal code of professional conduct we now apply in our daily activities will likely lead us to failure in the future. Thus, it is now time for those committed to achieving a measurable "better tomorrow" through the improvement of individual and organizational performance to define a holistic and inclusive professional code of conduct that defines our profession and guides our activities.

Based on the Standards on Ethics and Integrity established by the Academy of Human Resources Development (Dean, 1999) and related literature in management ethics and conduct (Dean, 1993, 1994; Deming, 1972; Drucker, 1999; Pava & Krausz, 1995; Westgaard, 1988), we use this Appendix to build on these general guidelines and common set of values to create functional and durable applications for the performance accomplishment professional.

This code of professional conduct is intended to open a dialogue regarding the scientific based role we as professionals can and should play within organizations and communities.

Personal Commitment

The objective of my work as a professional is (a) to provide organizations and/or individuals with the skills, knowledge, abilities, and/or attitude necessary to create opportunities for achieving desired and/or required individual, organizational, and societal results; (b) to assist in the generation of new and valid knowledge that will lead to the attainment of results meeting the performance criteria demanded by individuals, organizations, and society; (c) to acquire the knowledge through systematic research methods without jeopardizing the success of my client, my client's clients, or society; and (d) to produce the results required by my client.

I will not enter into any engagement (a) that violates one or more of the codes of conduct stated here or the profession's standards on ethics and integrity; (b) in which the pending results cannot be linked to or are not aligned with the organizational mission and positive contributions to society; or (c) that will not lead to the achievement of measurable contributions to the attainment of the Ideal Vision (creating a measurably better world for future generations).

An engagement with a client requires certain responsibilities for the consultant or employee, as well as for the client organization. I will state these responsibilities as well as my biases explicitly to provide all stakeholders with the necessary information and expectations prior to making a decision regarding the acceptance of position or engagement.

Missing data *is* data. Thus, when my efforts uncover performance issues for which the client currently has no measures, I will include these "missing cells" in my report and suggest means by which the client can develop measures of successful accomplishment of required performance.

The Obligations of the Professional

As a professional, I will:

1. Never knowingly mislead or lie to my client. I will be truthful and inform clients of all procedures, costs, and anticipated results prior to conducting activities for which they are paying me (this may include providing information that is not aligned with what the client currently states as their desire).

2. Inform the client of any implications of what is accomplished or not accomplished in terms of internal and external impact and consequences.[3]

3. Not conduct activities outside the boundaries of my professional competence based on my professional experiences, training, and education. In those rare instances when achieving results requires work in emerging areas where experiences, training, and/or education are not available yet, I will inform the client of the appropriate measures that should be taken to ensure the competence of my work.

4. Assist my client in doing all that is necessary to verify that the "true" problem is being addressed (high priority gaps in results) and not merely the symptoms.

5. Identify and report "alternate plausible hypotheses" that may have led to, or influenced, the research findings. I will also recognize that biases on the part of the consultant and/or client can operate as one such alternate plausible hypothesis.

6. Recognize that generalizing from research conducted with one client or project to other contexts carries risks. These risks include the potential fallacy of assuming that a particular treatment can be expected to yield similar results with other populations, interventions, measures, and settings.

7. Examine and report to the client on the alternative solutions as well as alternative approaches and even paradigms that meet performance requirements, even if these alternatives are not process or products that my organization offers.

8. Do the research required to have adequate knowledge of new technologies that may be beneficial to the client, including: (a) reading journals inside and outside of the fields of management, training, performance improvement, and educational research; (b) attending conferences and professional meetings; and (c) consulting with credible colleagues in the field.

9. Be responsible for the results of my work (this may not be in an "all or none" relationship; I will take responsibility and/or credit only for the portion of results that are clearly linked to my efforts).

10. Keep information confidential. I will not publish specific data obtained from engagement with the client or concepts that require the identification of the client without their consent and review.

11. Not advertise the attainment of results that cannot be clearly linked to my work.

12. Make clear that any correlational relationships between findings do not necessarily imply cause-and-effect relationships. Rather, such causal linkages are best determined through empirical research on the basis of sound theory of a program or intervention, and are manifested in the results my client achieves—not merely the processes it engages in.

13. Target the achievement of only those results that can be aligned with both the organization's mission objective and positive contributions to society.

14. If at any time I reach a point where I am no longer qualified to meet the requirements of the client, I will, if appropriate (a) make this known to the client; (b) assist in locating another specialist; and (c) work with this expert to resolve the problem.

15. Inform clients of any probable decreases in effectiveness and efficiency if my recommendations are scaled up or down by my clients in use.

16. At no time make the client dependent on my services. To lessen this risk, I will make information concerning my procedures available to the client upon request.

17. Understand the value of focusing on results and consequences of the results. To that end my performance will be measured on the results I achieve for the client and not on the procedures I perform for the client.

18. Take on engagements only if in my judgement there is good promise of achieving the desired results that are aligned with both the client's mission objective and positive contributions to society.

19. Not take on an advisory role unless there are specified responsibilities for which I am qualified to contribute.

20. Reserve the right to take positions or engagements with additional clients (unless prohibited in my contract or if doing so could impair my professional objectivity). My aim is not to focus on the benefit for a particular client, but rather to achieve positive results that benefit the client organization as well as society.

21. Cooperate fully with my clients' requests to partner with individuals or firms representing my own competition, so long as such practice does not violate any of the tenets in this code of professional conduct.

22. Anticipate and prepare for both process and accountability audits of my efforts. To this extent I will maintain records of my procedures, meetings, correspondences, travel, and expenditures, as well as evidence of the usefulness of both my activities and results.

23. Be willing to terminate my contract with the client if there are deviations from this code of professional conduct that the client cannot, or will not, remedy.

The Responsibilities of the Client

As the client, I will:

1. Provide adequate expert knowledge of my business. Any evidence of dishonest or inaccurate information will result in the termination of the engagement.

2. Arrange for the direct access to the information, people, and resources required for the professional to do the job as specified in the agreement.

3. Inform professionals of implementation and results thereof, generated by ideas from their work.

4. Make no changes to the procedures recommended without taking over the responsibility for results (this may not be an "all or none" relationship).

5. Have the final decision on the implementation.

6. Publish or print reports regarding the results of the professional's work in full, and not omit any parts without the professional's consent.

7. Not mention verbally, in correspondence, or in print, the names of the consultants without their approval.

8. Make explicit the turnaround time for my approval and/or negotiation of changes to the consultant's deliverables, and meet these deadlines. I understand that any aberration from this approval process will likely affect the remainder of the project's timeline, and for this the consultant will not be held at fault.

9. Not insist on any solution, process, intervention, or method when there are performance data to indicate that these will not measurably add value to what my organization uses, does, produces, and delivers to external clients and stakeholders.

10. Be willing to terminate my contract with the consultant if there are deviations from this code of conduct that the consultant cannot, or will not, remedy.

Professional Practices

We suggest the following tactics as practical steps each of us can take to apply a code of professional conduct to our activities:

Use the Code of Conduct as a Contract Discussion Check Sheet. The responsibilities of the professional as well as the client organization are offered in the code of professional conduct. These responsibilities can be used as a pragmatic checklist when coming to agreement with a potential client or employer. And although at first some of the statements in the code of professional conduct may seem extreme, impractical, or outside the current paradigm of your organization, we suggest that if either party is not willing to meet each of these elements, then the long-term success of the agreement is in jeopardy from the start.

Use an Ideal Vision as the Starting Place for All Decision Making. An Ideal Vision is a measurable statement of the world we are committed to creating for future generations (Kaufman, 1998, 2000). The elements of the Ideal Vision are based on the collective future to which people from around the world aspire (Kaufman, 1998, 2000; Meadows, 1999). By using this pragmatic approach to direction setting, individuals and organizations can pursue a common objective that is focused on all clients and stakeholders. As an individual or organization makes decisions, implements interventions, and/or evaluates its own success, it can use the Ideal Vision as a benchmark of success.

Client satisfaction and financial rewards are not enough to drive long-term success. If they were, we would all find jobs in drug trafficking. Rather, we each must define and contribute to the achievement of the future we want to create. And while this may seem idealistic, impractical, and not something you would dare bring to the discussion with a client, if you do not intend to contribute to an Ideal Vision, just what alternative results do you intend to achieve for your clients, their clients, and our shared communities?

Standardize Our Language. Unlike many professions, ours seems to be one that competes for definitions. Terms are defined and redefined by authors, practitioners use the same words interchangeably, phrases defined by other professions are used with alternative meaning—and in the end clients are left to merely guess as to what we are referring. A standardized language will assist us in communicating with clients and society the valuable information we have gained from thirty plus years of research and practice.

Ask Some Tough Questions. Ask both yourself and your clients some tough questions. Some places to start are given in Table C.1.

Table C.1. Basic Questions to Be Asked and Answered.

Basic Questions to Be Asked and Answered	Do You Commit?	
	Yes	No
Do you commit to deliver organizational contributions that add value for your external clients AND society?		
Do you commit to deliver organizational contributions that have the quality required by your external partners?		
Do you commit to produce internal results that have the quality required by your internal partners?		
Do you commit to have efficient internal products, programs, projects, and activities?		
Do you commit to create and ensure the quality and appropriateness of the human, capital, and physical resources available?		
Do you commit to deliver: a. Products, activities, methods, and procedures that have positive value and worth? b. The results and accomplishments defined by our objectives?		

Note: After Kaufman, 1998.

If either you or your client cannot reach agreement on these questions and the code of professional conduct, then we suggest the long-term success of the partnership is unlikely. Making (and documenting) measurable contributions both to the client and to society are the future of our profession. We can continue to use the tactics and tools that have led to our success in the past, or we can adapt what we use, do, produce, and deliver to fit the new demands of organizations.

Notes

1. Based in part on an article of the same name in the April 2000 issue of *Performance Improvement* by Ryan Watkins, Doug Leigh, and Roger Kaufman.

2. Many elements offered in this code of professional conduct are related to those Deming used to guide his work as a consultant of statistical studies (Deming, 1972) and are based on the Academy of Human Resources Development's Standards on Ethics and Integrity (Dean, 1999).

3. There is an analogy of this to medical "informed consent" that lets risks be known, especially those that might subtract value for shareholders, associates, and society.

REFERENCES

Ackoff, R. (1981). *Creating the corporate future.* Somerset, NJ: John Wiley & Sons.

Albrecht, K. (1994). *The northbound train.* Saranac Lake, NY: AMACOM.

Argyris, C. (1982). *Reasoning, learning & action.* San Francisco, CA: Jossey-Bass.

Argyris, C. (1990). *Overcoming organizational defenses.* Old Tappan, NJ: Allyn & Bacon.

Argyris, C., & Schon (1978). *Organizational learning: A theory in action perspective.* Old Tappan, NJ: Addison-Wesley Longman.

Banathy, B. H. (1992). *A systems view of education: Concepts and principles for effective practice.* Englewood Cliffs, NJ: Educational Technology Publications.

Barker, J. A. (1989). *The business of paradigms: Discovering the future.* Videotape. Burnsville, MN: ChartHouse Learning Corporation.

Barker, J. A. (1992). *Future edge: Discovering the new paradigms of success.* New York: William Morrow.

Bateson, G. (2000). *Steps to an ecology of mind.* Chicago, IL: University of Chicago Press.

Beals, R. L. (1968, December). Resistance and adaptation to technological change: Some anthropological views. *Human Factors.*

Belbin, M. (1993). *Team roles at work.* West Chadswood, Australia: Butterworth-Heinemann.

Beer, S. (1985). *Diagnosing the system for organizations.* Chichester, England: John Wiley & Sons.

Block, P. (1993). *Stewardship.* San Francisco, CA: Berrett-Koehler.

Block, P. (2000). *Flawless consulting* (2nd ed.). San Francisco, CA: Jossey-Bass/Pfeiffer.

Braksick, L. (1999). *Unlock behavior, unleash profits.* New York: McGraw-Hill.

Brethower, D. M., & Dams, P-C. (1999, January). Systems thinking (and systems doing). *Performance Improvement, 38*(1), 37–52.

Bridges, W. (1991). *Managing transitions.* Reading, MA: Addison-Wesley.

Briggs, L. J., & Wager, W. W. (1982). *Handbook of procedures for the design of instruction* (2nd ed.). Englewood Cliffs, NJ: Educational Technology Publications.

Brodie, R. (1996). *Virus of the mind.* Marina del Rey, CA: Integral Press.

Bunker, B., & Alban, B. (1997). *Large group interventions.* San Francisco, CA: Jossey-Bass.

Burke, W. W., & Litwin, G. H. (1989). A causal model of organizational performance. In J.W. Pfieffer (Ed.), *The 1989 annual: Developing human resources.* San Francisco, CA: Jossey-Bass/Pfeiffer.

Carelton, J. R., & Lineberry, C. (2003). *Cultural due diligence: A manager's guide to increasing the success of mergers and acquisitions.* San Francisco, CA: Jossey-Bass/Pfeiffer.

Checkland, P., & Scholes, J. (1990). *Soft system methodology in action.* New York: John Wiley & Sons.

Churchman, C. W. (1971). *The design of inquiring.* New York: Basic Books.

Clark, R. E., & Estes, F. (1999, March/April). The development of authentic educational technologies. *Educational Technology, 38*(5), 5–11.

Clark, R. E., & Estes, F. (2000, April). A proposal for the collaborative development of authentic performance technology. *Performance Improvement, 38*(4), 48–53.

Conner, D. (1992). *Managing at the speed of change.* New York: Villard Books, Division of Random House.

Conner, D. (1998). *Building nimble organizations.* New York: John Wiley & Sons.

Csikszentmihalyi, M. (1990). *Flow.* Audiocassette. Niles, IL: Nightingale-Conant.

Daniels, A. (1989). *Performance management.* Tucker, GA: Performance Management Publications.

Daniels, A. (1994). *Bringing out the best in people.* New York: McGraw-Hill.

Dean, P. (1993). A selected review of the underpinnings of ethics for human performance technology professionals—Part one: key ethical theories and research. *Performance Improvement Quarterly, 6*(4), 3–32.

Dean, P. (1994). Some basics on ethics. *Performance and Improvement, 33*(10), 42–45.

Dean, P. (1999). Standards on ethics and integrity for the professors and professionals in the field of learning and performance improvement and for the practice of HRD/HPT. *Performance Improvement Quarterly, 12*(3), 3–30.

Deming, W. E. (1972). Code of professional conduct. *International Statistics Review, 40*(2), 215–219.

Deming, W. E. (1986). *Out of the crisis.* Cambridge, MA: MIT Center for Advanced Engineering Technology.

Deming, W. E. (1990, May 10). *A system of profound knowledge.* Personal memo.

Dick, W., Carey, L., & Carey, J. (2000). *The systematic design of instruction* (5th ed.). Boston, MA: Addison-Wesley.

Drucker, P. F. (1973). *Management: Tasks, responsibilities, practices.* New York: Harper & Row.

Drucker, P. (1993). *Post-capitalist society.* New York: HarperBusiness.

Drucker, P. F. (1994, November). The age of social transformation. *The Atlantic Monthly,* pp. 53–80.

Drucker, P. F. (1999). Management's new paradigms. *Forbes.* www.forbes.com/forbes/98/1005/6207152a.htm.

Drucker, P. F. (2001, November). The next society: A survey of the near future. *The Economist,* pp. 3–20.

Fairhurst, G., & Sarr, R. (1996). *The art of framing.* San Francisco, CA: Jossey-Bass.

Forbes, R. (1998, August). The two bottom lines: Let's start to measure. *The Quality Magazine, 7*(4), 17–21.

Gagne, R. M, Briggs, L. J., & Wager, W. W. (1988). *Principles of instructional design* (3rd ed.). New York: Holt, Rinehart and Winston.

Gagne, R., & Driscoll, M. P. (1988). *Essentials of learning for instruction* (2nd ed.). Upper Saddle River, NJ: Prentice Hall.

Garratt, B. (1994). *The learning organization.* London: HarperCollins.

Gilbert, T. F. (1978). *Human competence: Engineering worthy performance.* New York: McGraw-Hill.

Goethe, J. (2001). *Faust.* Gordonsville, VA: Farrar, Straus & Giroux.

Goleman, D. (1998). *Working with emotional intelligence.* Westminster, MA: Bantam Books.

Greenleaf, R. (1977). *The power of servant leadership.* San Francisco, CA: Berrett-Koehler.

Greenwald, H. (1973). *Direct decision therapy.* New York: Peter Wyden.

Gruender, C. D. (1996, May/June). Constructivism and learning: A philosophical appraisal. *Educational Technology, 36*(3), 21–29.

Haeckel, S. (1999). *The adaptive enterprise.* Boston, MA: Harvard Business School Press.

Hamel, G., & Prahalad, C. (1990). *Competing for the future.* Boston, MA: Harvard Business School Press.

Hames, R. (1999). *Burying the twentieth century.* Warriewood, N.S.W., Australia: Woodslane Pty.

Handy, C. (1995–1996). *Beyond certainty: The changing worlds or organisations.* Boston, MA: Harvard Business School Press.

Handy, C. (1997). *The hungry spirit.* New York: Broadway Books.

Harless, J. H. (1975). *An ounce of analysis is worth a pound of cure.* Newnan, GA: Harless Performance Guild.

Harless, J. (1998). *The Eden conspiracy: Educating for accomplished citizenship.* Wheaton, IL: Guild V Publications.

Hesselbein F. (2002). *Hesselbein on leadership.* San Francisco, CA: Jossey-Bass/Pfeiffer.

Jacobs, R. (1997). *Time strategic change.* San Francisco, CA: Berrett-Koehler.

Jaques, E. (1989). *Requisite organization.* Rockville, MA: Cason Hall & Co.

Jennings, M., & Entine, J. (1999). Business with a soul: A reexamination of what counts in business ethics. *Journal of Public Law and Policy, 20.*

Kaplan, R. S., & Norton, D. P. (1992, Jan–Feb). The balanced scorecard: Measures that drive performance. *Harvard Business Review,* pp. 71–79.

Kaplan, R. S., & Norton, D. P. (1996a, Jan–Feb). Using the balanced scorecard as a strategic management system. *Harvard Business Review,* pp. 75–85.

Kaplan, R. S., & Norton, D. P. (1996b, Fall). Linking the balanced scorecard to strategy. *California Management Review,* pp. 53–79.

Kaplan, R., & Norton, D. (2000). *The strategy-focused organization.* Boston, MA: Harvard Business School Press.

Kaufman, R. A. (1972). *Educational system planning.* Upper Saddle River, NJ: Prentice Hall.

Kaufman, R. (1987, May). On ethics. *Educational Technology.*

Kaufman, R. (1992). *Strategic planning plus: An organizational guide* (rev ed.). Thousand Oaks, CA: Sage.

Kaufman, R. (1994, February). Auditing your needs assessment. *Training & Development.*

Kaufman, R. (1996, July). Why hire a consultant if you already know what's best? *Performance and Instruction.*

Kaufman, R. (1997, May/June). Avoiding the "dumbing down" of human performance improvement. *Performance Improvement.*

Kaufman, R. (1997, October). A new reality for organizational success: Two bottom lines. *Performance Improvement, 36*(8).

Kaufman, R. (1998). *Strategic thinking: A guide to identifying and solving problems* (rev. ed.). Arlington, VA: American Society for Training & Development and Washington, DC: International Society for Performance Improvement.

Kaufman, R. (1999, July). Research, practice, comfort, and our future. *Performance Improvement.*

Kaufman, R. (1999). From how to what to why: The handbook of performance technology as the gateway to the future. In H. Stolovitch & E. Keeps, *The handbook of performance technology* (2nd ed.). San Francisco, CA: Jossey-Bass.

Kaufman, R. (2000). *Mega planning.* Thousand Oaks, CA: Sage.

Kaufman, R. (2001, Summer). Strategic thinking and planning for our ever-changing world. *Performance in Practice,* pp. 10–11.

Kaufman, R. (2001, Winter). We now know we have to expand our horizons for performance improvement. *ISPI News & Notes.* (A modified version, "What performance improvement specialists can learn from tragedy: Lesson learned from September 11, 2001" is published on the ISPI website at www.ispi.wego.net/)

Kaufman, R., & English, F. W. (1979). *Needs assessment.* Englewood Cliffs, NJ: Educational Technology Press.

Kaufman, R., & Forbes, R. (2002). Does your organization contribute to society? *Instruments: 2002 team and organization development sourcebook.* New York: McGraw-Hill.

Kaufman, R., & Guerra, I. (2002, March). A perspective adjustment to add value to external clients. *Human Resource Development Quarterly, 13*(1), 109–115.

Kaufman, R., & Keller, J. (1994, Winter). Levels of evaluation: Beyond Kirkpatrick. *Human Resources Quarterly, 5*(4), 371–380.

Kaufman, R., Keller, J., & Watkins, R. (1995). What works and what doesn't: Evaluation beyond Kirkpatrick. *Performance and Instruction, 35*(2), 8–12.

Kaufman, R., & Lick, D. (2000). Mega-level strategic planning: Beyond conventional wisdom. In J. Boettcher, M. Doyle, & R. Jensen (2000), *Technology-driven planning: Principles to practice.* Ann Arbor, MI: Society for College and University Planning.

Kaufman, R., & Lick, D. (2000/2001, Winter). Change creation and change management: Partners in human performance improvement. *Performance in Practice,* pp. 8–9.

Kaufman, R., Rojas, A. M., & Mayer, H. (1993). *Needs assessment: A user's guide.* Upper Saddle River, NJ: Educational Technology.

Kaufman, R., Stith, M., & Kaufman, J. D. (1992, February). Extending performance technology to improve strategic market planning. *Performance & Instruction.*

Kaufman, R., & Swart, W. (1995, May/June). Beyond conventional benchmarking: Integrating ideal visions, strategic planning, reengineering, and quality management. *Educational Technology,* pp. 11–14.

Kaufman, R., Thiagarajan, S., & MacGillis, P. (Eds.). (1997). *The guidebook for performance improvement: Working with individuals and organizations.* San Francisco, CA: Jossey-Bass/Pfeiffer.

Kaufman, R., & Thomas, S. (1980). *Evaluation without fear.* New York: Franklin Watts.

Kaufman, R., & Watkins, R. (1996, Spring). Costs-consequences analysis. *HRD Quarterly, 7,* pp. 87–100.

Kaufman, R., & Watkins, R. (2000). Getting serious about results and payoffs: We are what we say, do, and deliver. *Performance Improvement, 39*(4), 23–32.

Kaufman, R., & Watkins, R. (2000). Assuring the future of distance learning. *The Quarterly Review of Distance Education, 1*(1), 59–67.

Kaufman, R., Watkins, R., & Leigh, D. (2001). *Useful educational results: Defining, prioritizing, and achieving.* Lancaster, PA: Proactive Publishing.

Kaufman, R., Watkins, R., & Sims, L. (1997). Cost-consequences analysis: A case study. *Performance Improvement Quarterly, 10*(2).

Kaufman, R., Watkins, R., Triner, D., & Stith, M. (1998). The changing corporate mind: Organizations, visions, mission, purposes, and indicators on the move toward societal payoff. *Performance Improvement Quarterly, 11*(3), 32–44.

Kaufman, R., & Zahn, D. (1993). *Quality management plus: The continuous improvement of education.* Newbury Park, CA: Corwin Press.

Kirkpatrick, D. L. (1994). *Evaluating training programs: The four levels.* San Francisco, CA: Berrett-Koehler.

Kondratieff, N. D. (1935). The long waves in economic life. *Review of Economic Statistics, 17*(6).

Kuhn, T. (1970). *The structure of scientific revolutions.* Chicago, IL: University of Chicago Press.

LaFeur, D., & Brethower, D. (1998). *The transformation: Business strategies for the 21st century.* Grand Rapids, MI: IMPACTGROUPworks.

Langdon, D., Whiteside, K., McKenna, M. (1999). *Intervention resource guide: 50 performance improvement tools.* San Francisco, CA: Jossey-Bass/Pfeiffer.

Leigh, D., Watkins, R., Platt, W., & Kaufman, R. (2000). Alternative models of needs assessment: Selecting the right one for your organization. *Human Resources and Development Quarterly, 11*(1), 87–93.

Lewin, K. (1936). *Principles of technological psychology.* New York: McGraw-Hill.

Lick, D., & Kaufman, R. (2000–2001, Winter). Change creation: The rest of the planning story. *Planning for Higher Education, 29*(2), 24–36.

Lineberry, C., & Carelton, J. R. (2003). *Cultural due diligence: A manager's guide to increasing the success of mergers and acquisitions.* San Francisco, CA: Jossey-Bass/Pfeiffer.

Mager, R. F. (1988). *Making instruction work: Or skillbloomers.* Belmont, CA: David S. Lake.

Mager, R. F. (1992). *What every manager should know about training: Or "I've got a training problem" . . . and other odd ideas.* Belmont, CA: Lake Publishing Co.

Mager, R. (1997). *Preparing instructional objectives.* Atlanta, GA: Center for Effective Performance.

Mager, R. F., & Beach, K. M., Jr. (1967). *Developing vocational instruction.* Palo Alto, CA: Fearon.

Mager, R. F., & Pipe, P. (1983). *CRI: Criterion referenced instruction* (2nd ed.). Carefree, AZ: Mager Associates.

Mager, R. F., & Pipe, P. (1984). *Analyzing performance problems* (2nd ed.). Belmont, CA: Pitman.

Mager, R. F., & Pipe, P. (1997). *Analyzing performance problems* (3rd ed.). Atlanta, GA: CEP Press.

Manganelli, R. (1993, November/December). It's not a silver bullet. *Journal of Business Strategy,* p. 45.

Martin, J. (1995). *The great transition.* Saranac Lake, NY: AMACOM.

Marshall, R., & Tucker, M. (1992). *Thinking for a living: Education and the wealth of nations.* New York: Basic Books.

Matathia, I., & Salzman, M. (1999). *Next.* New York: Overlook Press.

Maynard, H. B., & Mehrtens, S. E. (1993). *The fourth wave: Business in the 21st century.* San Francisco, CA: Berrett-Koehler.

McClelland, D. (1989). *Human motivation.* Cambridge, UK: Cambridge University Press.

Meadows, D. (1999, Sept. 27). Don't we all want the same thing? *Brattleborro Reformer.*

Meredith, J. R. (1995). Project management: A managerial approach, 3rd Ed. New York: John Wiley & Sons, Inc.

Mintzberg, H. (1995). Strategic thinking as "seeing." In B. Garratt (Ed.), *Developing strategic thought: Rediscovering the art of direction-giving.* London: McGraw-Hill.

Mitroff, I. (1998). *Smart thinking for crazy times.* San Francisco, CA: Berrett-Koehler.

Morrison, I., & Schmid, G. (1984). *Future tense.* New York: William Morrow and Co.

Muir, M., Watkins, R., Kaufman, R., & Leigh, D. (1998, April). Costs-consequences analysis: A primer. *Performance Improvement, 37*(4), 8–17, 48.

Naisbitt, J. (1982). *Megatrends.* New York: Warner Books.

Naisbitt, J., & Aburdene, P. (1990). *Megatrends 2000: Ten new directions for the 1990s.* New York: William Morrow.

Nanus, B. (1992). *Visionary leadership.* San Francisco, CA: Jossey-Bass.

Nirenberg, J. (1997). *Power tools.* Riverside, NJ: Simon & Schuster.

Noer, D. (1993). *Healing the wounds.* San Francisco, CA: Jossey-Bass.

Pascale, R. (1990). *Managing on the edge.* Riverside, NJ: Simon & Schuster.

Pava, M., & Krausz, J. (1995). *Corporate responsibility and financial performance: The paradox of social cost.* Westport, CT: Quorum Books.

Peters, T. (1987). *Thriving on chaos: Handbook for a management revolution.* New York: Alfred A. Knopf.

Peters, T. (1997). *The circle of innovation: You can't shrink your way to greatness.* New York: Alfred A. Knopf.

Popcorn, F. (1991). *The Popcorn report.* New York: Doubleday.

Robbins, A. (1991). *Awaken the giant within*. New York: Simon & Schuster.

Roberts, W. (1993). *Victory secrets of Attila the Hun*. New York: Doubleday.

Rummler, G. A., & Brache, A. P. (1995). *Improving performance: How to manage the white space on the organization chart* (2nd ed.). San Francisco, CA: Jossey-Bass.

Salzman, M., & Matathia, I. (2000). *Next: Trends for the near future*. New York: Overlook Press.

Senge, P. M. (1990). *The fifth discipline: The art and practice of the learning organization*. New York: Doubleday-Currency.

Smith, P., & Kearney, L. (1994). *Creating workplaces where people can think*. San Francisco, CA: Jossey-Bass.

Sowell, T. (1987). *A conflict in visions*. New York: William Morrow & Co.

Spencer, L., & Spencer, S. (1993). *Competence at work*. Somerset, NJ: John Wiley & Sons.

Stacey, R. (1994). *Strategic management and organizational dynamics* (2nd ed.). London: Pitman.

Stolovitch, H. D. (2000, April). Human performance technology: Research and theory to practice. *Performance Improvement, 39*(4), 7–16.

Stolovitch, H. D., & Keeps, E. J. (1992). *Handbook of human performance technology: A comprehensive guide for analyzing and solving performance problems in organizations*. San Francisco, CA: Jossey-Bass/Washington, DC: National Society for Performance & Instruction.

Thomas, C., & Clegg, S. (1998). *Changing paradigms*. New York: HarperCollins.

Tichy, N. (2001). *Control your destiny or someone else will*. New York: HarperInformation.

Triner, D., Greenberry, A., & Watkins, R. (1996). Training needs assessment: A contradiction in terms. *Educational Technology Magazine, 36*(6), 51–55.

Toffler, A. (1970). *Future Shock*. New York: Random House.

Toffler, A. (1990). *Powershift: Knowledge, wealth, and violence at the edge of the 21st century*. New York: Bantam Books.

Van Gundy, A. (1988). *Techniques of structured problem solving*. Somerset, NJ: John Wiley & Sons.

Van Tiem, D. M., Moseley, J. L., & Dessinger, J. C. (2000). *Fundamentals of performance technology: A guide to improving people, process, and performance*. Silver Spring, MD: International Society for Performance Improvement.

von Bertalanffy, L. (1968). *General systems theory*. New York: George Braziller.

Wallace, G. W. (2001). *T&D systems view: Learning by design versus learning by chance*. Naperville, IL: CADDI, Inc.

Watkins, R., & Kaufman, R. (1996, November). An update on relating needs assessment and needs analysis. *Performance Improvement, 35*(10), 10–13.

Watkins, R., Kaufman, R., & Leigh, D. (2000, April). A performance accomplishment code of professional conduct. *Performance Improvement, 35*(4), 17–22.

Watkins, R., Leigh, D., Foshay, R., & Kaufman, R. (1998). Kirkpatrick plus: Evaluation with a community focus. *Educational Technology Research and Development Journal, 46*(4), 90–96.

Watkins, R., Leigh, D., Platt, W., & Kaufman, R. (1998). Needs assessment: A digest, review, and comparison of needs assessment literature. *Performance Improvement, 37*(7), 40–53.

Watkins, R., Triner, D., & Kaufman, R. (1996, July). The death and resurrection of strategic planning: A review of Mintzberg's the rise and fall of strategic planning. *International Journal of Educational Reform.*

Westgaard, O. (1988). *A credo for performance technologists.* Western Springs, IL: International Board of Standards for Training, Performance and Instruction.

Wheatley, M. (1992). *Leadership and the new science.* San Francisco, CA: Berrett-Koehler.

Zemke, R., & Kramlinger, T. (1982). *Figuring things out: A trainer's guide to needs and task analysis.* Reading, MA: Addison-Wesley.

INDEX

ABOUT THE AUTHORS

Roger Kaufman, Ph.D., is a professor and director of the Office for Needs Assessment and Planning at Florida State University. In addition, he is director of Roger Kaufman & Associates. He has previously held professorships at Old Dominion University, the University of Central Florida, United States International University (now Alliant International University), and Chapman University. He has also taught courses in strategic planning, needs assessment, and evaluation at the University of Southern California and Pepperdine University. His Ph.D. in communications is from New York University. He pursued his undergraduate work in psychology, statistics, sociology, and industrial engineering at Purdue and George Washington universities.

Before entering higher education, Dr. Kaufman was assistant to the vice president for engineering as well as assistant to the vice president for research at Douglas Aircraft Company. Prior to that, he was director of training system analysis at U.S. Industries; head of training systems for the New York office of Bolt, Beranek & Newman; head of human factors engineering at Martin Baltimore; and a human factors specialist at Boeing. He has served two terms on the U.S. Secretary of the Navy's Advisory Board on Education and Training.

His work is in the areas of strategic planning, change management-change creation, quality management, needs assessment, evaluation, distance learning, and organizational improvement for clients worldwide.

He is a Fellow of the American Psychological Association, a Fellow of the American Academy of School Psychology, and a Diplomate of the American

Board of Professional Psychology. He has received the highest honor of the International Society for Performance Improvement, an organization for which he also served as president, by being named a "Member for Life." He has been awarded the Thomas F. Gilbert Professional Achievement Award by that same organization.

Dr. Kaufman has published thirty-five books, including *Mega Planning, Strategic Planning Plus,* and *Strategic Thinking (Revised),* and co-authored *Useful Educational Results: Defining, Prioritizing, and Accomplishing* and *Practical Strategic Planning: Designing and Delivering High Impact Results* as well as more than 240 articles on strategic planning, performance improvement, distance learning, quality management and continuous improvement, needs assessment, management, and evaluation.

Hugh Oakley-Browne is managing director of Hugh Oakley-Browne Associates of New Zealand. He also is curently an executive responsible for performance improvement with BHP Steel in Wollongong, Australia.

Ryan Watkins, Ph.D., is an assistant professor at George Washington University. He received his doctoral degree from Florida State University in instructional systems design. He has additional formal training in both change management and program evaluation. Dr. Watkins has designed and taught courses (both online and in the classroom) in instructional design and development, needs assessment, and system analysis and design, as well as technology management. Previously, he was an assistant professor of instructional technology and distance education at Nova Southeastern University.

Dr. Watkins has also been a member of the research faculty in the Office for Needs Assessment and Planning at the Learning Systems Institute at Florida State University. There he led and managed efforts on several research agendas, including the development of a costs-consequences analysis for Florida's workforce development programs, a quality management self-assessment for Florida's Department of Corrections, a return-on-investment study of the policy advice of Florida TaxWatch, and a needs and assets assessment for human services in Leon County, Florida. Additional projects included the development of performance evaluation system for leadership training in the U.S. Navy, as well as the assessment, design, and development of technology-based facilitator training.

Dr. Watkins has published more than thirty articles on the topics of return-on-investment analysis, evaluation, needs assessment, and strategic planning. He is a co-author of *Useful Educational Results: Defining, Prioritizing, and Achieving* (2001) with Roger Kaufman and Doug Leigh. He is an active member of the International Society for Performance Improvement (ISPI) and has served as vice president of the Inter-American Distance Education Consortium (CREAD).

Doug Leigh, Ph.D., is an assistant professor with Pepperdine University's Graduate School of Education, where he teaches courses in change theory, research methods, and program planning, development, and evaluation. His work experience ranges from the private sector to the public in settings such as K12 education (Florida Department of Education), higher education (Florida State University's Learning Systems Institute and Office for Needs Assessment & Planning), corporate training (Arthur Andersen), and nonprofit (Florida TaxWatch), the military (U.S. Navy), and government (U.S. Veterans Benefits Administration, State of Ohio Workforce Development). Dr. Leigh is a frequent author, lecturer, and consultant concerning needs assessment, evaluation, accountability, societal responsibility, change creation, and strategic planning. His ongoing research and publication interests are in these and related topics. He is the chair of the American Evaluation Association's Topic Interest Group in Needs Assessment and co-author of *Useful Educational Results: Defining, Prioritizing, and Accomplishing* (2001; ProActive Publications). His Ph.D. was earned in instructional systems from Florida State University, where he received the Gagne-Briggs award for "Outstanding Doctoral Student of the Year." He may be contacted at doug@dougleigh.com or on the web at http://www.dougleigh.com.

International Society for Performance Improvement

The **International Society for Performance Improvement (ISPI)** *is dedicated to improving individual, organizational and societal performance.* Founded in 1962, ISPI is the leading international association dedicated to improving productivity and performance in the workplace. ISPI represents more than 10,000 international and chapter members throughout the United States, Canada, and 40 other countries.

ISPI's mission is to develop and recognize the proficiency of our members and advocate the use of Human Performance Technology. This systematic approach to improving productivity and competence uses a set of methods and procedures—and a strategy for solving problems—for realizing opportunities related to the performance of people. It is a systematic combination of performance analysis, cause analysis, intervention selection, change management, and evaluation that can be applied to individuals, small groups, and large organizations.

Website: **www.ispi.org**

Mail: International Society for Performance Improvement
1400 Spring Street, Suite 260
Silver Spring, Maryland 20910 USA

Call: 1.301.587.8570

Fax: 1.301.587.8573

E-mail: info@ispi.org

For short, current articles on performance improvement,
visit ISPI's www.PerformanceXpress.org.

HOW TO USE THE CD-ROM

SYSTEM REQUIREMENTS

Windows PC

- 486 or Pentium processor-based personal computer
- Microsoft Windows 95 or Windows NT 3.51 or later
- Minimum RAM: 8 MB for Windows 95 and NT
- Available space on hard disk: 8 MB Windows 95 and NT
- 2X speed CD-ROM drive or faster
- Netscape 3.0 or higher browser or MS Internet Explorer 3.0 or higher

Macintosh

- Macintosh with a 68020 or higher processor or Power Macintosh
- Apple OS version 7.0 or later
- Minimum RAM: 12 MB for Macintosh
- Available space on hard disk: 6 MB Macintosh
- 2X speed CD-ROM drive or faster
- Netscape 3.0 or higher browser or MS Internet Explorer 3.0 or higher

NOTE: This CD requires Netscape 3.0 or MS Internet Explorer 3.0 or higher. You can download these products using the links on the CD-ROM Help Page.

GETTING STARTED

Insert the CD-ROM into your drive. The CD-ROM will usually launch automatically. If it does not, click on the CD-ROM drive on your computer to launch. You will see an opening page. You can click on this page or wait for it to fade to the Copyright Page. After you click to agree to the terms of the Copyright Page, the Home Page will appear.

MOVING AROUND

Use the buttons at the left of each screen or the underlined text at the bottom of each screen to move among the menu pages. To view a document listed on one of the menu pages, simply click on the name of the document. To quit a document at any time, click the box at the upper right-hand corner of the screen.

Use the scrollbar at the right of the screen to scroll up and down each page.

To quit the CD-ROM, you can click the Quit option at the bottom of each menu page, hit Control-Q, or click the box at the upper right-hand corner of the screen.

TO DOWNLOAD DOCUMENTS

Open the document you wish to download. Under the File pulldown menu, choose Save As. Save the document onto your hard drive with a different name. It is important to use a different name, otherwise the document may remain a read-only file.

You can also click on your CD drive in Windows Explorer and select a document to copy it to your hard drive and rename it.

IN CASE OF TROUBLE

If you experience difficulty using this CD-ROM, please follow these steps:

1. Make sure your hardware and systems configurations conform to the systems requirements noted under "Systems Requirements" above.

2. Review the installation procedure for your type of hardware and operating system. It is possible to reinstall the software if necessary.

3. You may call Jossey-Bass/Pfeiffer Customer Care at (800) 956-7739 between the hours of 8 A.M. and 5 P.M. Eastern Standard Time, and ask for Jossey-Bass/Pfeiffer Technical Support. It is also possible to contact Technical Support by e-mail at *techsupport@JosseyBass.com.*

Please have the following information available:

- Type of computer and operating system
- Version of Windows being used
- Any error messages displayed
- Complete description of the problem.

(It is best if you are sitting at your computer when making the call.)